THE SALT-WATER
FISHERMAN'S BIBLE

THE SALT-WATER FISHERMAN'S BIBLE

ERWIN A. BAUER

DOUBLEDAY & COMPANY, INC.
GARDEN CITY, NEW YORK,

ISBN: 0-385-02337-5
Library of Congress Catalog Card Number 62–14182
15   14

Contents

THE SALT-WATER
FISHERMAN'S BIBLE

Chapter One

THE WILDEST ONES
TARPON, LADYFISH

TARPON

Enrique Thimms would seem to live on the edge of paradise—if you happen to be a tarpon fisherman. His home, a neat bungalow he shares with a wife and enough kids to make a football team, is at the point where the Río Parismina enters the Caribbean on the east side of Costa Rica. Almost at his back door is one of the most incredible concentrations of big tarpon it's the good fortune of any fisherman to find.

All this is extremely handy because Thimms is a tarpon guide. When we landed on the black sand beach at Boca Parismina, the mouth of the Parismina, he was waiting nearby with a vintage outboard attached to a *canoa* he had gouged from a single *cedro* log.

This cluster of huts at the *boca* isn't on any main highway. You reach it by charter-flying in from Limón and landing on the beach. Or you go by boat and this takes three days of winding through jungle lagoons and bayous almost without end. Flying is the best bet by far, but landing is risky on the "airstrip," which is always cluttered with cattle, goats and *muchachos*. Tom McNally, Jorge Yankelewitz and I flew because we wanted to cover as much of Costa Rica's fishing as is possible during a three-week junket.

Jorge was our host. He knew the Parismina River better than any outsider. It was he who, a few years before, caught the first tarpon on light tackle there. But Thimms had been catching tarpon all his life along Costa Rica's Caribbean coast and perhaps has accounted for more tarpon than anyone else in Central America. But until he began to guide for Jorge, all of them were taken with spear or harpoon—to feed his family.

We had our tackle loaded in Thimms's *canoa* even before the pilot took off again for Limón. The rusty old outboard stuttered and coughed but finally "caught" and we buzzed quickly up the murky river. The guide knew nothing about streamlining or modern boat design but his thin, homemade craft could skim along very neatly with only three horses pushing from behind.

For a Midwesterner, this trip up the Parismina River is an extraordinary adventure. On both sides is unbroken jungle as dense as any in the world. Water vegetation is green and lush in the shallow edges. There was a constant flushing of water birds ahead of the craft: herons, egrets, gallinules and others we couldn't identify. Thimms had to dodge in and out among hyacinth "islands," and in places the river passed completely beneath tunnels of vegetation. Then Thimms turned into a vast, roily lagoon. He cut the motor and we drifted into the kind of completely primitive scene that far too few fishermen ever see.

"*Sábalos*," he whispered. "*Mire sábalos*. See the tarpon."

The lagoon was working alive with fish. In

Tarpon are among the greatest jumpers of all fish, fresh or salt. (*Photo by Florida State News Bureau*)

fact, it seemed to be boiling in the tropic sun. Everywhere we looked were schools of tarpon rolling and cavorting on the surface. And these were no baby tarpon.

We were sitting in the middle of hundreds of 100-pounders. Perhaps some were even bigger than that. It made the bristles stand on the back of my neck. Somehow Tom's hands stopped shaking enough to make the first cast with his fly rod.

My companion needed several false casts to get out 40 feet of line and then he dropped a yellow hackle streamer in front of several cruising tarpon. For a minute . . . nothing. But suddenly the rod was almost torn from his hands as line evaporated from the reel. A hundred feet away a big tarpon catapulted out of the water, shaking, and then fell back into a patch of hyacinths. Tom reeled in a broken leader. The whole contest was finished just like that—in one split second or so.

To describe our fishing that morning would simply be to describe that incident over and over again. We hooked tarpon and we lost them wholesale. We couldn't hold those critters any better than we could a runaway rhinoceros. When a thunderstorm broke late in the after-

noon, we still hadn't boated the first one. I suppose we saw more than one hundred magnificent jumps and that alone is worth traveling halfway around the world to see.

"*Mañana*," Jorge promised us, "the fish will be striking better and we'll do better, too."

I had to laugh. If the fish struck any better than that, I'd wind up with a pair of broken arms. And a permanently damaged ego.

Just what kind of critter is this fish that breaks rods and is said to frighten fishermen? Scientifically the tarpon is called *Tarpon atlanticus*. Elsewhere he is known as the silver king or savanilla or—in Louisiana—grande ecaille. He is also called silverfish and in Latin America, where tarpon are often most plentiful, he's known as *sábalo*. The Seminoles call him *show-a-wee*, but by any name the tarpon is a member of an international family that includes the herring and two other illustrious members, the bonefish and the ladyfish.

The tarpon is built like an enormous herring with a deep and compressed body that is shining silver almost from head to the tip of the tail. Some specimens have a slight pinkish tint on the sides and others have a faint olive tinge. The females have larger girth measurements than the males. In some areas they are believed to be more agile and more lively in action, but most guides who have taken many tarpon of both sexes can see no difference in the type of contest they wage after being hooked. The truth is that both sexes are excellent, uninhibited, shoot-the-works battlers.

The agile body of a tarpon is entirely covered with large, almost circular scales that range in diameter from 1 to 3½ inches. Each scale is composed of thin transparent layers of a parchmentlike substance and is, in effect, almost an armor plating.

It is customary after a fisherman captures a tarpon to remove one scale or two and then to release the fish. The scale becomes a permanent souvenir on which is written the name, the date, the fish's weight and the place of capture.

Far too little is known about the life history of a tarpon and what makes it tick. Virtually nothing is known of the critter's spawning habits or of his spawning areas, but it's assumed—from scale studies—that at the end of one year a tarpon will be between 12 and 24 inches long. At the end of the second year it may be from 24 to 36 inches long, and after three years a tarpon should measure a formidable 4 to 5 feet. Of course, these figures are only approximate. In some regions, tarpon grow far faster than

that; in other regions the growth may be much slower.

An average adult tarpon encountered by anglers will range in size from 25 to 75 or 80 pounds. There are many exceptions to the following, but generally the smaller tarpon inhabit estuaries, creeks, canals and similar places a few miles back from the coastline. Often these places will be in brackish water or even in completely fresh water. Larger specimens up to 100 or more pounds are normally found in deep holes at entrance passes to oceanic and open Gulf of Mexico waters. Tidal channels are excellent places to find the larger fish, but again it must be emphasized that large tarpon may also be found in shallow inshore waters as in the Parismina River in Costa Rica.

The tarpon grows to a length of more than 8 feet but few that size have ever been seen, dead or alive. The largest specimen ever recorded was taken with a net by commercial fishermen on August 6, 1912, near Hillsboro Inlet on the Florida east coast. It measured 8 feet 2 inches long and its estimated weight was 352 pounds. The world's record for rod and reel was a 247-pounder that measured 90 inches in length, 46 inches in girth, and was caught by H. W. Sedgwick in the Pánuco River of Mexico. The average tarpon today might run between 30 and 40

Wybert Ebanks about to gaff a jumping tarpon for George Laycock at Isle of Pines, Cuba.

Fred Bear (left) and Captain Dick Rode wrestle a big tarpon aboard near Bahia Honda bridge, Florida Keys.

pounds but 100-pounders are not especially rare.

Too often when an average fisherman thinks about tarpon fishing he also thinks about sleek cabin cruisers, heavy tackle, deep waters and a big dent in the budget. Although large tarpon, or even small ones, *can* be taken on all this heavy gear, it's still a light-tackle fish that can be taken on almost the same tackle used in freshwater fishing. The truth of the matter is: I consider the tarpon the greatest light-tackle fish on the face of the earth.

Tarpon are a top-notch game species because they're any man's fish. You can catch them from a skiff or an outboard runabout at least as well and probably better than in an expensive charter boat because the fastest tarpon fishing of all occurs in relatively shallow, sheltered places within easy reach of land. You can't even take a big cruiser into some of these areas.

Depending on their size, tarpon can be taken on virtually any sort of tackle and more and more sportsmen simply fish just for the kicks and the crazy jumps. If they lose the fish, they don't care. Nothing is lost. They only try to hook another one.

An ideal outfit for medium to heavy tarpon is a boat rod or heavy two-handed casting rod with 6-ounce tip and a star drag reel full of 20- to 40-pound test line. Tarpon can be killed quicker on heavier line, of course, but this also takes some of the aerial tactics out of them, too.

The best bait, bar none, is a live mullet or needlefish from 8 to 12 inches long. They'll hit other small fish, such as small jacks and catfish, but the mullet is the one they cannot resist.

Anglers who cast artificials rather than bait for tarpon generally stick to two specific types: the saltwater jigs, or bucktails, and the darting topwater or just-under-the-surface plugs. It's impossible to say which is most effective because each works best for a specific time or circumstance. But there are few more dramatic moments in all the outdoors than the instant a heavy tarpon savagely attacks a plug retrieved on the surface. On some occasions they will bat the plug high into the air and slash at it several times before actually grabbing it. And when they eventually feel the hook, they go completely berserk.

But tarpon are more than pure aerialists. They're extremely powerful fish and a 50-pounder, for example, can make any angler sweat plenty before he gets the fish close to the boat.

Since World War II, spinning for tarpon has become both a popular and widespread practice. Armed only with medium or fairly heavy saltwater spinning outfits, anglers now travel widely to fish in tarpon country, where they find sport that they didn't believe possible only a decade before.

There are many productive spinning techniques, but perhaps the most common is to travel or cruise across shallow bays, in the mouths of rivers, among mangrove islands, until a school of tarpon is sighted. Quite often it is possible to find them as they roll and travel close to the surface, a maneuver visible from far away. The object then is to cast a lure ahead of them and then to retrieve it with sharp jerks of the rod tip. Some days a fast retrieve is best; more often a slow to medium speed is most successful. If all goes off as intended, a tarpon will strike, and if the hook is solidly set, a wild battle is on.

Another most effective way to fish for tarpon,

particularly when they are not in evidence on the surface, is to cast blindly in channels and in other similar areas washed by the tide. Generally it is best on a rising or falling tide, rather than a slack tide, but in either case the idea is to cast a jig or a strip of live bait, to allow it to settle to the bottom, and then to retrieve it in short, steady, sharp jerks back along the bottom. Some days the technique is absolutely deadly. On other days it's only good exercise. If it doesn't work, try slowing down to a very slow, creeping retrieve.

In recent years the fly rod has become an important weapon for tarpon just as it has in other saltwater fishing. And it isn't really difficult to catch tarpon on the fly rod. It can sometimes be a frustrating experience for beginners, but it's never lacking in excitement and thrills, simply because tarpon are such splendid tackle busters on any gear.

Fly casting was made for the small tarpon, which are often called baby tarpon, in the 1- to 10-pound class, but which probably average about 5 pounds. These compact editions are extremely vulnerable to artificial flies—and to tiny spinning lures as well—because of their preference for small items of food. The heavier lures can't begin to imitate the small grass shrimp, the fingerling mullet, the other minnows and strange aquatic insects which make up most of a baby tarpon's diet. And strangely enough, on occasion, even big tarpon seem to prefer the very small items of food. Quite often an angler using a fly rod or spinning gear in an area full of baby tarpon will suddenly hook an old grandpa that makes him wonder if fishing is a safe sport after all.

Tarpon are not as selective as trout when rising to flies. They do seem to prefer streamer-type or bucktail flies. In general, saddle-hackle streamers tied either in flat-winged style or with hackles back-to-back to give an effect of a scissortail are extremely good. Any of these streamer flies should be tied on 3X or 4X long-shanked hooks.

One of the special thrills in fly-rod fishing is to use the popping or wounded-minnow-type bass bugs. There are days when this type of bug—moved more rapidly across the surface than would be best technique for freshwater-bass fishing—is strong medicine for tarpon found loitering in mangrove channels, and perhaps lying far back underneath the overhanging mangroves. There is one difficulty to using these small surface lures. Tarpon, because of their underslung bony mouths, are hard to hook in the first place. If you manage to hook—permanently—one out of every ten or twelve strikes on a surface bass bug, you are having excellent luck. Or maybe you're just plain skillful.

There are almost as many different opinions on a tarpon's favorite color as there are tarpon fishermen. Probably most experienced fishermen would favor either yellow or white, whether the lures be streamer flies or bucktail jigs. Still others prefer brown and combinations of yellow and brown and yellow and red. Nowadays, many of the casting plugs are designed in completely authentic mullet finishes. These are good. So are the blue-tinted plugs. These are also especially good in the nearly transparent, silvery surface plugs, which seem to be pure murder on some days. Recently a natural needlefish finish has proven effective.

The greatest and best tarpon fishing of all exists at night. There's no doubt about it, because these jumbo herring are largely nocturnal. A few fishermen have pioneered in this chilling after-dark sport; still not too much is known about it. But this much is certain: to radically increase the odds of tying into a record-book fish, plus thrills no one can describe, there is no better time to try for tarpon than a warm, sultry, summer night.

So far we haven't said anything about trolling, which actually was the first sporting method used to take tarpon and which is still very popular today. Year after year the largest tarpon are taken by trolling and this is only natural because heavier tackle, which can handle the larger fish, is used. But like plug casting or spinning or fly casting, catching tarpon successfully by trolling is largely a matter of knowing which waters to fish. Once that is determined, it is only a matter of tossing a whole mullet, a strip of mullet, a needlefish, a balao, a large plug or a large bucktail jig overboard and drawing it behind the boat.

Trolling is also a good way to explore and to probe new waters because the bait is working for you all the time. Often while fishing the Gulf Coast between Port Isabel, Texas, and southward toward Tampico, Mexico, we located new waters simply by trolling until we found action.

Then we would stop to cast in that general area to see if we had found only a single tarpon or if others were in the vicinity. Usually there were others. It's a good practice and it will pay off. It's even possible to use the same tackle that's used for casting when trolling in waters that are likely to contain tarpon weighing less than 40 pounds apiece.

Just as any other sport, tarpon fishing has its champion. He happens to be a New Jersey Irishman, Gerald Coughlan, who would rather fish for the silver jumpers than do almost anything else. For the past twelve years Coughlan has won top tarpon honors in the Metropolitan Miami Fishing Tournament. This is all the more outstanding when you realize that tens of thousands in America's top anglers migrate to Florida each winter to compete in this unique fishing competition and that the odds against winning a victory in any one year are fantastic.

What makes Coughlan's feat even more startling is the fact that he lands these big fish with a simple bass-fishing outfit such as he might use at home in a farm pond. He never uses line larger than 15-pound test because the maximum permissible line strength in the Tournament's plug casting division is 18 pounds. This light line is carried on a conventional, freshwater, Pflueger Supreme Reel which does not have a star drag of any kind and which is mounted on a standard 6-foot plug-casting rod. With this outfit, Coughlan, who only weighs 140 pounds himself, has taken tarpon up to 160½ pounds.

Recently, Coughlan has taken to hunting for and catching record tarpon on a fly rod and his best effort to date is a 110½-pounder, which would seem to be an impossible catch.

Probably the biggest tarpon ever taken on a fly rod was the 148½-pounder taken by Joe Brooks near Little Torch Key, Florida. His guide was Stu Apte, who was knocked in the water when the big fish jumped over the boat during a two-hour struggle. Brooks used a 9½-foot rod, GAF line, a leader tapered to 12-pound tippet, to which had been added 10 inches of 80-pound monofilament to avoid fraying on the tarpon's cheeks and lips.

But Coughlan is always aiming at even bigger stuff than Brooks's record, and he has many definite ideas on tarpon and how best to catch the brutes. Obviously it's a wise angler who keeps these points in mind.

"First," Coughlan will tell you, "a tarpon fisherman should always keep his hooks needle-sharp. There's no overemphasizing that. It's tough enough to hook a tarpon solidly with sharp hooks and it's almost impossible with dull ones."

In addition, Coughlan frowns upon the careless, but familiar, practice of using old line and unreliable equipment. He changes lines frequently and always tests them before fishing to make sure that there are never any weak points or frayed places.

Other Coughlan advice to prospective anglers is quite simple: "A quiet day is preferable, especially if there is a very gentle ripple so that wary tarpon will not see the boat too easily.

"Even a shadow from a line passing overhead will sometimes spook a wary tarpon, and always wear polaroid glasses so the fish are more easily visible in the water.

"Never make unnecessary noise. Try not to clatter objects against the sides or on the floor of

World champion tarpon fisherman, Jerry Coughlan of New Jersey, with a 110½-pounder taken on a fly rod near Islamorada in the Florida Keys.

the boat. Never operate a motor near any places you intend to fish. This is poison. [Author's note: This may not necessarily be true, because tarpon have been taken on plugs trolled right behind the motor and directly in the wake of an outboard.] Even a carelessly handled push-pole striking hard against the bottom can flush tarpon from shallow flat areas. And once tarpon are moving nervously, they are extremely hard to tease into striking.

"I found it best to use a three-quarter-ounce, yellow top-water plug with a red head or a red throat. Beginners, however, may do better with underwater plugs, since most of them have built-in action. I fish my own plug with a slow retrieve, casting it close to the fish as soon as I spot him. But the cast shouldn't be made too close, say about four to six feet ahead of the tarpon to intercept his route of travel. I do not like to cast on top of a fish.

"After the fish strikes, set the hook and keep the line tight except when he jumps. Then give him slack so he can't fall back on your taut line and break it. But as soon as the tarpon hits the water again, apply all the pressure you can and maintain it until you have him whipped. As he weakens, he'll come to the surface more often.

"About fly fishing," Coughlan explains, "I've known, or rather I've suspected all along, that tarpon will take a fly in preference to a plug. Also, the longer rod has an advantage in that you can cast better to a tarpon. There is no large splash to scare off a spooky fish—no heavy hunk of wood or plastic to strike the water. In fact, the fly rod enables you to pick up the fly quickly and sometimes to present it as many as five or six times to the same fish.

"Of course, fly casting has its disadvantages, too. For one thing, even a ten- or fifteen- or twenty-mile-an-hour wind can complicate your casting. And you can't put as much strain on a fly rod as in a plug rod, but the pressure from a fly rod *is* more persistent. And sometimes I believe it will wear down the fish much faster."

But although all the best precautions and all the best advice is followed, tarpon have made chumps out of more fishermen than any other species of fish. They're not as hard to fool, really, as are brown trout or even the bonefish, the tarpon's own cousin. But once a big silver is hooked, he goes wild . . . wild . . . completely wild. He somersaults, spins, swaps ends, shakes vio-

lently in the air, wallows and is even said to climb trees.

Tarpon come and go, appear and disappear mysteriously. No one has been able to plot their travels and migrations with complete accuracy, but their natural range includes all the fringe waters of the Gulf of Mexico plus the coastal waters of such islands as Cuba and Puerto Rico.

Beginning at Key West or thereabouts, tarpon follow the U.S. east coast northward in springtime and early summer, going about as far as North Carolina, at which point they're often seen and caught from July to early September. Also starting from Key West, they follow the west coast of Florida northward, probing into all the rivers and bays all the way to Panama City and Pensacola, where the fishing is best in August. It's the same month when tarpon appear in numbers all along the Texas coast, especially from Corpus Christi to Brownsville and beyond.

Any list of outstanding tarpon waters would have to include the following places: the Pánuco and Tampico rivers in Mexico, the area around Carmen and Campeche in Mexico, the San Juan River in Nicaragua, all the rivers that drain into the Atlantic Ocean in Costa Rica, the entire Gulf of Mexico coast of Panama, as well as the Canal Zone waters, which are extremely good. One of the best places of all to catch a record fish is Surinam (or Dutch Guiana). Such jungle rivers as the Coesiwijne and Tibiti are teeming with them.

LADYFISH

When you find a school of actively feeding ladies, you can figure on keeping busy for a long, long time. It's a grand experience. The lightning-like strikes will come so rapidly that fishermen always find them hard to believe when they encounter ladies for the first time. These tiny cousins of the tarpon are superlative performers *anytime*, but when they're on a feeding spree, they're even wilder and faster than usual.

The minute a lady feels the hook, she goes into a series of unbelievably violent catapults into the air, and these continue sometimes until exhaustion. It's the only fish I know which can run while jumping and jump while running. For fast concentrated action, there's no fishing on earth exactly like ladyfishing.

Ladyfish are also called chiros and tenpounders, but that last is certainly a strange name because it's doubtful if any ladyfish ever reached 10 pounds. A 3-pounder or 4-pounder is an extremely good one. But if ladies *did* grow as big as tarpon, it would be virtually impossible to land them on any tackle. Their scientific name is *Elops sauris.*

Throughout the years the ladyfish has been confused with the bonefish or banana fish (*Albula vulpes*), but except for the silver color and the fact that both belong to the same family as the herring, there is little resemblance between the two. The bonefish never jumps and the ladyfish never stops jumping. And rarely does a ladyfish venture out onto the shallow flats in the same manner as does a bonefish.

There's evidence that ladies range as far north as Maine, but they're seldom caught north of Florida and only rarely as far north as the Carolinas. In Florida waters they might be found anywhere except in the open sea. They even move occasionally into brackish water and have been taken in the southeast corner of Florida in water almost completely fresh. They're most numerous in Gulf of Mexico waters from Tampa Bay southward.

I have seen tremendous concentrations of ladyfish in a number of areas and have enjoyed every encounter with them. It would be impossible to forget the morning that Vern Walsh and I—Vern in a brand-new pair of patent-leather cowboy boots—waded out into the shallow sand flats where the Rio Grande enters the Gulf of Mexico. Acres and acres of water were in a constant boil and turmoil because ladyfish that weighed from 1 to 2 pounds apiece were gorging on a school of tiny baitfish.

We didn't have any trouble hooking these ladies on any bait at all. I started by using a light spinning outfit with a ⅛-ounce jig, but that was too easy. Soon I waded to shore and assembled a light, 7-foot, panfish fly rod. With this tiny wand, and using small bluegill floating bugs,

Casting for ladyfish at the mouth of the Rio Grande on the Texas-Mexico border. Gulls reveal the presence of fish in large numbers.

Here I'm landing a ladyfish, the tarpon's crazy wild-jumping cousin.

I had ladies climbing all over each other to get at the bugs. It was a wild and woolly session and it ended only because I was too tired to cast anymore.

I suppose that not many people fish especially for ladyfish, probably because they are so completely inedible. But on light spinning tackle or or fly-casting tackle there isn't a more lively fish to catch, and that point is certainly worth repeating. Some of the better lures are the yellow-and-white streamer flies or bucktail jigs in ⅛- and ¼-ounce sizes. Fly-rod poppers are also excellent because of the action they can stir up on the surface. Perhaps the most effective bait of all, however, is a tiny silver spoon or a silver spinner in ¼-ounce size. Ladyfish simply go crazy over these.

It isn't difficult at all to catch ladyfish once you've found a school of them or once you've found a location where many of them are concentrated. There is just one important bit of advice to give and that is to retrieve the lure as rapidly as possible in short sharp jerks. Completely unwary, and never shy or temperamental, ladyfish can be taken by anybody who can cast well enough to hit the water once in a while. They like to feed in inlets and passes and along the beaches and bayous of the Gulf Coast. They seem to move in these places on a strong incoming tide, but the truth is that they're busy nearly all the time and you can catch them in good numbers on an ebb tide.

If it isn't already the greatest game fish in the world, the ladyfish lacks only one quality—big size. Big ladyfish could be downright dangerous.

Chapter Two

SNOOK, PIKE OF THE SEA

Bob Whitaker is one of the best and most serious fishermen in Florida. We'd met on a winter fishing trip the year before. That was when he told me that, for his money, no sport in the state measures up to the annual spring run of snook around Marco Island. "If you can come back during the spring tide—when the royal poinciana begins to bloom in the yard around the Marco Island Inn—I guarantee you will agree with me."

"But how will I know when your tree begins to bloom?" I asked.

"I'll call you," he promised.

It wasn't until the tag end of May that Bob finally called. Several days later I caught a plane in Columbus, Ohio, where I live, for the 5-hour trip to Miami. Then in a rented car I hurried along the Tamiami Trail to Marco, a lonely bit of real estate halfway between Everglades City and Naples.

I checked in at the famous and handsome old Marco Island Inn, which Whitaker manages in his spare time. He considers fishing as his main occupation. The Inn is the best-known landmark in the region, having been built by an old fur and plume buyer in 1883 when the area was a trackless wilderness. Then it was almost the only habitation between Key West and Punta Gorda, but now it's a busy sportsmen's headquarters.

Early that evening we hung our rods in brackets on the gunwales of Doyle Doxsee's boat and opened the throttle wide. The sea had a good

Aerial view of Florida's Shark River country, a great snook hot spot. *(Photo by Florida State News Bureau)*

chop, but Doyle's boat, which he'd built himself, negotiated it smoothly. It's a fine all-around boat for bay and channel fishing such as that at Marco. It's roomy and maneuverable and the design is certainly worth a more detailed mention here because it can be adapted to so many other situations a saltwater angler is likely to encounter.

The boat is a 22-footer and is 8 feet wide. The motor housing and steering wheel are mounted in the center, leaving room for casting and playing big fish completely around the deck. A cooler and an ice chest are located in the stern. Brackets for rods and stringers for lures

Anglers playing snook off the south coast of Cuba.
(Photo by Mercury Outboard Motors)

are located inside the gunwales and on the back of the motor housing. Power is supplied by a Ford automobile engine. Doyle figured that he has less than $1500 invested in the boat.

The sheltered bay just inside Big Marco Pass that evening turned out to be a popular spot. After we made the three-quarter-mile run from the Inn, we found a fleet of about twenty-five boats already on the scene and trolling in a giant circle. We simply joined them.

It was the closest approach to merry-go-round fishing I have ever seen. Since the area of greatest snook concentration is generally small, I learned, only a few boats would be able to troll this area unless some orderly pattern was followed. By trolling in a circle, many boats can participate, and as more and more boats join the ring, the space between them shortens until sometimes it seems that each boat is trolling its plugs directly beneath the bow of the boat behind.

But snook aren't nearly as cooperative as these anglers were. The minute a good fish strikes, it's pure bedlam. Two fishermen who had just come over from Fort Lauderdale to catch the run and who were trolling nearby, had a solid strike. Their snook didn't understand the rules about staying in the circle and before it was hauled aboard it had caused half a dozen boats to veer out of

formation and several lines had to be cut. Then quickly the boats were back in formation again, but not for long.

I felt my plug thump the bottom twice and I thought it had snagged a weed when all at once the rod was almost torn from my hands. About a hundred feet away a snook bounced out of the water and then fell back hard again. The fish didn't like the looks of things in Big Marco Pass and therefore didn't create as much confusion as the first fish hooked there. Instead, he headed for the heart of the Everglades, away from the crowd, and I watched too much line melt from my reel. There was little else to do.

This snook wasn't much of an aerialist. Except for a brief wallowing on the surface it kept going down and down until I thought my rod would have a permanent set. But the pressure was too much and eventually Doyle swung the fish aboard. It was a 14-pounder. Before the evening was over, I boated two more of 13 and 14 pounds apiece and lost another. But still Doyle wasn't happy.

"Snook weren't hitting well tonight," he said on the trip back. "One of these evenings they're going to bust that pass wide open."

This annual run of snook is a big event on Florida's outdoor calendar. The jumbos, the biggest snook of all, pour in great numbers through such passes as Caxambas, Big and Little Marco, presumably to spawn. For several weeks, usually sometime between mid-May and mid-

Snook action shot made near Caxambas Pass, Florida. That's guide Doyle Doxsee.

July, they stay in the same vicinity and at regular intervals go on a feeding rampage which is a rare sight to see. It's a great experience because the species must be rated with the best game fishes in our saltwaters. They're strong, fairly fast, lively jumpers and terrific on the table.

Snook fishing in the Marco area has an interesting though brief background. Until twenty-five or thirty years ago, anglers came to the Marco region only to fish for tarpon and until that time a major expedition and plenty of time was required just to reach the place. But in the years before World War II, both commercial and sport fishermen "discovered" the snook run and began to make extraordinary catches.

Doyle Doxee and his father and brother, Dwight, were among the busiest commercial fishermen around Marco. Using stout cane poles and live bait, they would catch 1000 pounds of snook in one night during the peak of the run. Occasionally they caught very large fish—40- and 45-pounders—which would have crowded the present world's record: a 50½-pounder taken at Gatun Spillway, Canal Zone, in 1944. Doyle figures they may have hooked many snook bigger than that because he remembers when time and again their cane poles would suddenly be snapped like toothpicks.

Eventually commercial fishing took too heavy a toll and the regular runs of snook fell off to almost nothing. But several seasons ago commercial fishing for snook was banned in Florida and these grand game fish are in the middle of a dramatic comeback. It isn't likely that any new world's records are lurking around now because in recent years 30-pounders have been absolutely tops. Still, the area offers a fisherman just about the best bet anywhere for catching the snook of his lifetime.

Quite a few trophy snook are released around Marco every year and Bob Whitaker is responsible for it. He's a serious conservationist and he hopes to see the time when the snook runs will reach their former size again. Every year Bob is a contender and often a winner in the Metropolitan Miami Fishing Tournament for the most fish released. His attitude has rubbed off on many of the sportsmen who fish the Marco area.

As a snook fisherman, Bob is almost uncanny. He prefers light spinning tackle because it gives more action per fish and he feels that the finer line and smaller lure will fool more snook. He

Guide Doyle Doxsee (left) and Bob Whitaker with snook near Caxambas Pass, Florida.

has even developed a cardboard lure that is sensational for night-fishing around docks, piers and pilings where small- and medium-size snook often congregate. He'll bet anyone that on any night of the year he can catch a snook near his dock within five minutes. In five years he's missed only once when using the cardboard lure.

The lure is extremely simple to make. Bob cuts out a fish-shaped piece of thin cardboard about 3 inches long and attaches it like a strip of pork rind to a ¼-ounce, yellow Upperman bucktail. When retrieved quickly near the surface the wet cardboard has a fluttering action that snook can't resist.

Bob gets a lot of friendly kidding over his theory that snook fishing begins when the royal poinciana tree in his yard begins to bloom. Most years it really does happen that way. Bob has been accused of watering and fertilizing the tree to encourage blossoming long before the usual blossoming day late in May, just to make better fishing.

It has been said that snook are big for their size and that's a most fitting description for a great game fish. There really is something about a snook, especially a big one, which causes even veteran fishermen to forget all they know about fishing. They may freeze on the reel and apply too much pressure, or they may forget to apply any pressure at all. It doesn't matter because the fish usually escapes anyway.

A snook is a relatively slender and handsome fish shaped somewhat like a freshwater walleye. Its head is certainly pikelike, long and flattened with the lower jaw protruding. Its color is silvery according to the color of the water from which it comes, and sometimes it has a lemon-yellow tint. The lateral line is always a solid black.

Somehow the game fishes of America always manage to have quite a number of popular local names and the snook is no exception. In Florida, snook is pronounced snuke as the Doxsees pronounced it. Elsewhere it's called robalo, snooker, sergeant fish, sea pike, brochet de mer, and ravallia. Scientifically it's a member of the genus *Centropomus*.

There are three kinds of snook in Florida waters, another in the West Indies and others in the Pacific off the Central American coast. Of the three Florida snooks, one is a small critter that rarely grows more than a foot long. It's

Jean Crooks with what is probably the largest snook ever taken on fly-casting tackle. It weighed 28 pounds. Catch was made near Miami in a canal. (*Photo by Miami News Bureau*)

quite uncommon and of little interest to fishermen.

A second Florida snook is fairly numerous on the lower east coast and it only reaches a top weight of about 3 pounds. But the one that is of most value to fishermen is *Centropomus undecimalis*, which averages from 3 to 5 pounds and probably grows to 60 pounds. In Florida, 10-pounders are fairly common and every year a number of snook are taken over 30 pounds.

The snook ranges from Venezuela northward along the Gulf coast of Central America to Texas and then eastward to Florida, including the entire Florida coastline except the northern half of the east coast. It also occurs around some of the Caribbean islands, such as Puerto Rico, but it is unaccountably absent around many others where there is extremely good snook environment. The snook could be classified as an inshore tropical and subtropical species because it never ventures very far into the sea. At least it's never caught far from land. It concentrates along beaches and in channels and tidal rivers, which comprise much of our southern coastline.

Dr. Luis R. Rivas of the University of Miami's Marine Laboratory is probably the world's top authority on snook and he states that any snook will spend as much as half his lifetime in freshwater. He points out that snook frequently ascend creeks and rivers into freshwater and in these places shows many of the tendencies of freshwater fishes.

Snook are very much like largemouth bass in certain of their characteristics. When the food supply is good enough, some snook probably never leave the freshwater creeks or canals in which they are born. Others travel widely and move to saltwater. There is much room for biological research here. Intensive tagging studies would reveal much about the habits and migrations of snook.

Snook have been taken in the Caloosahatchee River and the St. Lucie Canal, which combine with Lake Okeechobee to form the cross-Florida waterway. Perhaps they even use this waterway to travel from the Atlantic Ocean to the Gulf of Mexico. While fishing for bass, I have seen snook in the Moonshine Bay area of Lake Okeechobee but I have never been able to hook one there.

In many ways the snook is a plug caster's dream come true because on occasion it can be ridiculously easy to fool. Other days it is a little more difficult, but generally speaking it's just hard enough to catch to be interesting. This is also a fish that doesn't require any digging of live bait. It's a good bet that more snook are taken on jigs and plugs than any other saltwater fish.

Either feather or bucktail or nylon jigs are especially effective in inlets and passes, in the surf and in any water that is deeper, say, than 5 or 6 feet. They're especially deadly when snook seem to be lying on the bottom. It's effective to cast a jig up into the tide and to retrieve it in short sharp jerks right along the bottom, kicking up clouds of mud or sand as it is retrieved.

There are days when a wooden or plastic plug will do as well or perhaps better than a jig and this is particularly true when snook are in shallow water or lying up tight under the mangroves.

A surface plug is the most exciting of all to use because of those occasions when snook will practically try to chew it to pieces. Any angler who has had experience casting surface plugs for bass will have great success with snook because the fishing is almost exactly the same. The main difference is that the surface plug must be retrieved in faster, sharper jerks and it must be given more action.

An important word about using plugs: On the surface, the best plugs are those that have no built-in action and which the angler must manipulate with the clever use of his rod tip; but snook will take some of the plugs with built-in action when they are fished just under water. A good example is the Pflueger Pal-O-Mine, which has the typical "wiggle" that snook seem to like. I've had great luck with it with medium-size snook of 5 to 10 pounds. This is standard size in the canals of southern Florida. And the Pal-O-Mine

was great when cast in the tidal rivers and mangrove channels off British Honduras.

The best color in artificial lures is a highly debatable matter, but probably more than half of all of the best snook fishermen prefer yellow, with red or red-and-white, or orange following closely.

It's hard to match the fly rod and fly-casting tackle for getting the most action out of snook. Both streamer flies and large-size, sturdy, bass popping bugs are murder on snook of small to medium size. But there is one drawback to fly fishing: snook are terribly tough on the tackle.

If you are fishing in fairly open water, as in a bay or lagoon, where there is enough room for a fish to run and cavort freely, OK, fine. But if you're fishing in mangrove country, you'll be snagged and hung up a good part of the time. If you don't mind that, stick to the fly fishing and have the time of your life, but remember that it's expensive.

Fly casting is especially deadly in most of the canals of southern Florida, especially the canals close to the Tamiami Trail, which are heavily fished by natives and tourists. A surface plug will often spook some of the more gun-shy snooks. It's in these waters that streamers and bass popping bugs will catch as many as five to ten times as many snook as casting lures. The best-size streamer or bucktail fly is about 3 inches long tied in size 2 to 1/0. As in plugs and jigs, yellow seems to be the most popular color.

No angler should go forth for snook without using a wire leader between his line and lure. Snook have razor-sharp, sawtooth spurs on their gill covers and with these they can neatly cut any fishing lines. But a light, braided, stainless steel leader from 12 to 18 inches long will take care of that.

Chapter Three

THE GLADIATORS
SAILFISH, SWORDFISH, MARLIN

Cruising and wandering across the tropical ocean currents is a magnificent family of fishes known as *Istiophoridae*. All are pelagic, which means they roam and live on the open seas. All are distinguished for their spearlike noses.

This clan of billfishes—or gladiators—includes the sailfish (which are the smallest of the family); swordfish or broadbill swordfish; white, striped, black and blue marlin. It's possible that the blue marlin is only a color phase of the black or vice versa. At any rate, many marine biologists classify the two of them together.

But no matter what the classification, all are incomparable game fishes and unlike most other fishes described in this *Bible*, special tackle, special techniques and boats, plus other considerations are necessary to catch them.

SAILFISH

Actually there are two sailfish in American waters. The Atlantic sailfish ranges throughout the tropical Atlantic and occurs from Massachusetts to Brazil. The Pacific sailfish occurs throughout the tropical Pacific and Indian oceans. In the American Pacific, it occurs from Baja California to northern Peru.

Today in Florida alone, sailfishing is a multi-million-dollar industry with hundreds of charter boats and private cruisers plying the blue Gulf Stream in search of these splendid fighters. The same is true elsewhere. In Mexico, such Pacific coast and Gulf of California cities as Acapulco, Mazatlán and La Paz have grown many times

The billfishing fleet as it leaves Miami, Florida, almost every morning of the year. (*Photo by Miami News Bureau*)

their original size in recent years, all because of the excellent sailfishing that occurs offshore.

Scientists call the Atlantic sailfish *Istiophorus americanus*, while the Pacific sailfish is known as *Istiophorus greyi*. The word *Istiophorus* means sail-bearer and refers to the fish's high dorsal fin, which folds into a groove along the back except when the fish surfaces or becomes extremely excited.

The sailfish is a beautiful, metallic, dark blue along the back, and this blends into silvery

Lifting sailfish aboard a charter boat off Miami Beach, Florida. (*Photo by Miami News Bureau*)

sides and a white belly. The sail is exquisite—a mixture of purple and blue with vertical rows of small black dots.

But it isn't until a sailfish is startled, excited or injured that it becomes really vivid. During those times, whole waves of color flash through the entire body of the sailfish. It is quite common to see this occur when a fish is hooked near the boat.

There is a shocking lack of knowledge about the life histories of most saltwater game fishes, but thanks to the work of biologist Gilbert L. Voss, quite a bit more is known about the Atlantic or Florida sailfish than any of the billfishes. It's known to spawn, for example, in late spring and early summer in certain shallow waters along the Florida sands. At this particular period the females, heavy with roe, are sluggish fighters, and no wonder, because a single female may carry as many as 4,675,000 eggs. Talk about being prolific!

The number of sailfish in our oceans, or even in the Gulf Stream, would be fantastic if all these eggs hatched and the larvae survived. But of course countless predators feed on the eggs and young. Only a very small percentage reach maturity.

The baby sailfish, which bear no resemblance to their parents for quite a period after they hatch, gorge themselves on tiny shrimplike copepods. Then as they grow they gradually turn from a diet of mollusks to gobbling down small fish. Once researcher Voss found a greedy young specimen no more than three quarters of an inch

long—including the bill—which had a viperfish nearly as long as itself folded up inside its stomach.

As they grow in size, sailfish become more and more able to fend for themselves and sometimes they move inshore in numbers. Juveniles from 5 to 8 inches long have been found along the Carolina coast in summertime. But cold weather and northerly winds seem to drive them south. Within a year after birth they may have reached 5 or 6 feet in length and that's of suitable size to please most sport fishermen. Three or four years seems to be the normal life-span for Florida sails.

Sailfish travel alone, occasionally in pairs or in small groups, and infrequently in small "packs." It is always an extremely exciting thing to see several at once. On one memorable occasion, while fishing out of Marathon, Florida, I was lucky enough to see between twenty and thirty of them in one group. They appeared to have a school of small fish, probably blue runners, all balled up in one spot. It made me think of timber wolves on the Alaskan tundra.

Occasionally a sailfish would dash into the smaller fish, slashing at them with his bill, while the others circled and jumped wildly into the air in a strange and frenzied manner. It was a savage, primeval spectacle and a good example of the law of the sea, which has large fish eating small fish and small fish eating smaller fish to survive.

When striking a bait, sailfish sometimes behave in a similar manner. Some of them will strike the instant they sight the bait, and this is one of fishing's most thrilling moments. They lash out with their bills, sometimes over and over again before grabbing the bait. But a few sails will seize the bait in their mouths immediately. Still others will follow it for five minutes . . . or ten minutes . . . or even longer, stalking closely behind it as a hyena follows a stricken antelope. Maybe they're merely curious, but when they act this way the mounting suspense is almost impossible to stand.

Unfortunately these following sailfish seldom strike, even when certain tactics are used to tantalize the fish such as cutting the motor and permitting the trolled bait to sink slowly. Occasionally, but only occasionally, the fish will grab it at once. Then the fun begins.

Practically all sailfish are taken by two techniques: on live bait and/or by trolling. The most preferable live baits are blue runners from 8 to 10 inches long—small enough for a sail to swallow easily. Many charter-boat captains consider live mullet as more effective, in fact, the best bait of all. But more often than not they settle for sand perch or grunts because these are easier to obtain than mullet. It's only a simple matter to troll a small spoon or jig across a reef to catch enough grunts or sand perch for a whole day's fishing.

Live bait is normally fished from outriggers on each side of the fishing boat. The baits are allowed to swim along from 6 to 10 feet beneath the surface of the water. It's always possible to tell when a sailfish, or some other large game fish, approaches because the baitfish dash and dart frantically about, trying to escape. That's enough to start your adrenalin pumping and it's just another reason why billfishing is the popular and exciting sport it is.

Any fishermen can be worked into a fever pitch while a sailfish decides whether or not to strike a freely swimming baitfish. If he doesn't strike immediately, it's often a good idea to yank the clothespin from the outrigger, thereby freeing more line and allowing the baitfish to swim farther and more freely from the boat.

Equally as popular for sailfishing as the use of live bait is the use of a whole fish—a mullet or a balao—trolled behind the boat. So that they appear as alive and as natural as possible, the entire backbone of the baitfish is removed so that it becomes limp and can give a genuine, live performance as it bounces across the surface of the sea. A skipping-type motion is achieved by speeding up the boat until the bait skips along the surface, leaping from wave to wave.

There are many different opinions on this, but no matter what bait is selected, a consensus of experienced sailfishermen would reveal that 5 or 6 miles an hour is the best trolling speed. Usually the outrigger baits are trolled from 40 to 60 feet behind the boat. And in addition, one or two teaser or fooler baits are sometimes trolled much closer to the boat.

Anyone, with or without skill at fishing, can catch a sailfish. The captain of almost any charter boat, no matter whether he is in Florida or in Acapulco, will take care of the job. In Florida, for example, you charter a boat from Palm Beach or Miami or Stuart or Marathon or any of the other communities near the Gulf Stream. The boat captain will hurry you out to the Gulf Stream, checking by radio to learn where the fish are hitting on that particular day. Meanwhile, the first mate will rig up the tackle, prepare the bait, place it on the hook, and all you have to do is sit back in your deck chair, holding the rod if you like or simply soaking up sunshine and marveling at the extraordinary blue of the water.

If you stay at this business of trolling long enough, a sail will eventually rap at your skipping bait. Ordinarily this is the signal to throw off the free-spool lever of the reel, to count ten as the bait falls back, to throw the free spool lever in gear again and to strike as hard as you can. This is the orthodox procedure and normally it works.

Every year sails are being taken on lighter and lighter tackle and for the most part this is all for the better. When given a chance a sailfish is a spectacular battler. He leaps and greyhounds across the ocean's surface time and again. But if you would choose to take sailfish on the lightest possible tackle, it is best to carry your own gear wherever you go. In too many cases the charter boat will supply you with "regulation" gear designed to handle marlin or tuna and it's just a bit too heavy for the most fun with sailfish.

The best rod for sailfish has a light 6-ounce tip, a 6/o reel and a hook size according to the test of line used. Recently, especially with the lighter glass rods, fishermen are using 4- and 5-

ounce tips. A 4/0 hook is matched to 12-pound line; 5/0 hook to a 20-pound line, 6/0 hook to 30-pound line and a 7/0 hook to 50-pound line.

But the larger the hook the heavier is the barb and the hardest part of the sail's mouth is the upper beak. It takes a good strong strike to set a big barbed hook deep enough into the beak to hold. A smaller barb does the better job of hooking, but if it is used on lighter line, the strike must be lighter in order not to break the line.

Although many sailfish have been taken on spinning tackle and even on fly-casting tackle, this is not always recommended as the best practice. With this kind of tackle the fish must be played so lightly that it is either dead or almost dead by the time it's brought to the boat. At best it may be so tired that even if released alive, the sharks will get it immediately.

Today the consensus among charter-boat skippers in the Florida Keys is that any line under 20-pound test is too light for sailfishing, especially if the angler is not experienced. It's figured that with a 20-pound test line an average sail—say from 35 to 40 pounds—can be landed in twenty to thirty minutes, after which the fish, when released, will still have enough energy left to fend for itself among its natural enemies.

Since sailfish have no commercial value and are not especially tasty on the table, nearly all except trophy fish should be released. In this case trophy fish are often the smallest rather than the largest fish. A 2- or 3- or 4- or even a 5-pound sailfish, for example, makes a handsome mount.

The average size of sailfish caught in the Atlantic is 35 or 40 pounds. Anything smaller than 25 pounds is a rarity. Anything larger than 60 pounds is an extremely fine, bragging-size fish.

The largest sail reported from the Atlantic by the International Game Fish Association measured 8 feet 5 inches and weighed 141 pounds, 1 ounce. It was caught in 1961 off the Ivory Coast, Africa. The largest Pacific sailfish, by contrast, measured 10 feet 9 inches long and weighed 221 pounds. This catch was made by C. W. Stewart in the Galápagos Islands. It isn't unlikely that a 300-pounder will be caught some day, possibly in the same Galápagos archipelago or near Cocos Island off Costa Rica.

Sailfishing does strange things to otherwise normal people and Horace Witherspoon of Corona del Mar, California, is another splendid example. He was fishing in an annual tournament off Acapulco with Frank Givens of Los Angeles and William Kortenhaus from Newark, New Jersey, when all hell broke loose.

Givens had a strike while trolling which gave him control of the boat. Accordingly the other anglers started to reel in their lines, but that's when a sailfish suddenly inhaled Witherspoon's bait and was hooked. Right away the sail started circling the boat as Witherspoon stood on the bow to keep the two lines from becoming tangled. Then Witherspoon fell overboard, lost his glasses and hat, but held on to his rod and reel!

Givens and Kortenhaus wanted to take over his rod and reel while he climbed back into the boat, but Witherspoon refused because under tournament rules a catch is disqualified if anyone else touches an angler's tackle.

Witherspoon managed to pull himself up enough to plant the rod in a porthole, loosening the reel drag so that his line wouldn't break. Then he climbed aboard, grabbed his gear and boated the fish twenty minutes later—unaided. Here is a serious sailfisherman, no matter how you view him.

Anglers from all over the western United States have been experiencing this fast and frantic fishing in the Pacific for many years now. There is good airline service daily between such

Sailfish is hooked by charter boat off Stuart, Florida. (Photo by Florida State News Bureau)

major cities as Los Angeles, San Diego and San Antonio with the various busy sport-fishing centers along the Gulf of California and also along the Pacific coast of Baja California.

But the excellent fishing for Pacific sailfish doesn't end at the Mexican border. Almost the year round, sails of unusual size and in great numbers exist all the way down the coast, past Costa Rica to Panama and even to northern Peru. Not much fishing for them has been done in most of this area so there is still much to be learned by the first pioneering parties.

SWORDFISH

About a generation ago, in his *Tales of Swordfish and Tuna*, Zane Grey wrote that "swordfishing takes more time, patience, endurance, study, skill, nerve and strength, not to mention money, than any game known to me through experience or reading." And to tell the truth the old writer of the purple sage really had something there. Fishing for swordfish is one sport that clearly marks the difference between the serious, dedicated fisherman and the casual angler.

Catching a broadbill swordfish is an outstanding angling feat that relatively few sportsmen have been able to do. In almost a half century of big game fishing since 1913, less than 800 broadbills have been taken by perhaps 200 or 300 fishermen. (This does not include fish taken commercially in any manner.) Best known among them was Zane Grey, who caught just 6 swordfish in a lifetime devoted to fishing which ended in 1939.

Once, for instance, Grey spent ninety days fishing off Santa Catalina. All together he sighted no less than 87 broadbills. The bait was presented to 75 of them and an even dozen were hooked and fought. But only one swordfish of 418 pounds was landed during that three months!

It isn't that broadbills are scarce. They exist in countless numbers off our North Atlantic coast and in temperate waters elsewhere around the world. Many of them are harpooned or caught on handlines by commercial fishermen. But the real trick to catching a swordfish is finding one that will take a trolled bait on the surface—much as a brown trout inhales a dry fly.

Even though a fisherman might spot as many as 5 or 6 fish on the surface in a day's exploration, it's very doubtful if even one can be teased into striking. Broadbills feed in deep water and

Fine broadbill swordfish taken off Wedgeport, Nova Scotia. (*Photo by Nova Scotia Information Service*)

when they are seen on the surface, the odds are long that they are only resting or sunbathing and therefore not interested in feeding. Most swords taken on the surface are found to have full stomachs, so the real problem is to excite their interest in a trolled bait without driving them down into deep water again.

Many methods to lure broadbills on the surface have been tested. But probably the best is to skip a bait—a bonito, a flying fish, a mackerel, or a herring—from an outrigger so that it will pass directly before the fish, maybe even touching its sword if the fish seems to be asleep. Sometimes this presentation arouses the fish enough to slash blindly, impulsively, at the bait in a fit of temper. Frequently this sudden slashing will cause the fish to foul-hook itself in the sword or the gill covers.

When a broadbill seems to be moving on the surface, rather than resting motionless, the most frequent tactic is to circle ahead and draw the bait just in front of the fish, crossing his line of travel until he either slashes at it or vanishes into deeper water.

When a swordfish taps the bait, the same procedure is followed as with all other billfish. The drag on the reel is released so that the bait falls back, allowing the fish to take it. Some experienced guides advise to count ten before throwing in the drag lever once more. Others may allow as much as 100 yards of line to drift out from behind the boat, without regard to time. In any event, it's wise to allow the fish to get a good firm bite on the bait.

There isn't any way to accurately predict what a broadbill will do after he is (miraculously) hooked. More often than not he will sound deep on a first, strong, headlong rush. After that he is likely to return to the surface and, at least for a short period, fight furiously on the top. In this case he will be exhausted much sooner than if he decides to wage a deep fight.

The deep fight is far more bewildering and painful to the fisherman because it is necessary to pump the fish to the surface only a few inches at a time. Also, a contest like this can last for a long, long time. Many 10- to 12-hour struggles with broadbills have been recorded. One 450-pounder required 19 hours and 50 minutes to gaff. And even then, at the last minute, a broadbill is likely to escape.

But no matter how you look at it, catching a broadbill swordfish is a terribly difficult proposition. Here's the way angling-author Kip Farrington, who has taken 12 swordfish in his lifetime and therefore rates among the most successful, rates an average fisherman's chances of scoring:

"Ten to one the day is not right for swordfish to surface. Ten to one that if the day *is* right, you will not see a fish. Fifteen to one that if you see a fish, it will not strike and it may even dissolve into the depths before you can present a bait. Three to one that, if it does strike, it will not pick up the bait. Five to one that if it takes the bait you won't hook it. Eight to one you will lose the fish if you hook it."

In spite of these staggering statistics, a fisherman who desperately wants a broadbill for his trophy room can do so at quite a number of widely scattered places. On the east coast there are a number of charter-boat captains who really understand swordfish and swordfishing in the Long Island and Martha's Vineyard areas. For furnishing everything from the necessary heavy tackle to cold beer in the cooler, the charter costs about $100 a day and upward. A man can reasonably figure to see a broadbill in a week of concentrated fishing.

Of course there will be weeks when he sees nothing. But invariably there will be times when swordfish will be spotted after the first hour out on the water. A swordfisherman must have something of Captain Ahab in his character because the swordfish is a Moby Dick among big game fishes. To engage him in combat, it's necessary to spend long days and long hours on a bright sea, searching with tired and burning red eyes for two dark symbols—a matched dorsal fin and tail—before a swordfish becomes a reality. Often it's a disheartening and exhausting business and the only reward is hours and hours of punishing battle in the fighting chair.

Although the swordfish is about 60,000,000 years old and although it lives in temperate waters almost completely around the earth, its spawning grounds, its habits and its migrations remain pretty much a personal secret. Only one spawning area in the New World has been located and that one exists on the north coast of Cuba. There, during late spring, a female swordfish may swim close enough to shore where the water is pale green and broadcast her eggs at random. When this is finished, she swims away.

Each egg is no larger than the head of a pin. The eggs simply drift with wind and tide and, of course, most of them are destroyed or eaten by other aquatic creatures. Enough survive, however, and eventually hatch into larval swordfish. Each one is less than ⅛-inch long. A few of these manage to reach maturity.

Only a few really small broadbills have ever been located, and those are certainly far from the handsome, streamlined adults that anglers are proud to catch. The skin is blotchy and covered with strange glassy scales. The dorsal fin flops along the back like a ribbon. Instead of a stout sword, the young fish has a thin, syringe-like beak that bristles with teeth. But it is voracious, strong, fast and probably has a ravenous appetite. When it reaches about a yard in length, or a little more, it begins to change. Soon the young broadbill becomes the near-perfect example of an extraordinary saltwater game fish.

Suddenly the scales are gone, the skin becomes blue black with silvery flanks, the dorsal fin has grown high and stiff, and the lower jaw has receded. All the teeth have vanished from the upper jaw and this has sprouted outward into a flat stubby sword—flat rather than round, as are the bills of sailfish and marlin.

The full-grown broadbill is a most efficient marine mechanism. He's probably the fastest fish in the world, although this is not an easy thing to judge. How can anyone accurately compare its top speed with such other will-of-the-wisp fishes as the wahoo and false albacore. The swordfish's backbone is short and strong. His sword and skull are neatly fitted together and there is a porous, foil-filled ethmoid bone in the forepart of the skull which acts as a sort of shock absorber when the broadbill is using his sword.

It's evident from his structure and also from commercial fishing catches that a broadbill can withstand the pressures of great depth. Its abnormally large eyes can gather in the faintest rays of light. It is extremely formidable and it's no wonder that blood-chilling newspaper stories appear from time to time of swordfish attacking small boats and generally causing havoc in the sea.

Even though swordfish are widely distributed, as we pointed out before, and even though they are really quite plentiful, broadbills are never commonplace and perhaps never will be on the weighing scaffolds around marinas and sport-fishing docks. Perhaps the best reason is that sport-fishing methods to date are too inflexible and too unimaginative.

It's known that commercial fishermen are able to hook and to catch swordfish in extremely deep water and this might be a good lead for sportsmen to follow. In Portugal, for example, anglers have learned that they can hook broadbill while drifting bait in water as deep as 50 fathoms. And off the Cuban coast, hundreds of broadbills are taken every season using deep handlines or Japanese "long" lines. From a sportsman's standpoint, however, the best broadbill waters in the world are those off Chile and Peru. The best known spot is at Cabo Blanco, Peru, which is now within easy reach by jet airliner from New York City or Miami. Here there is a year-round swordfish season and this is also the place where Alfred C. Glassell of Houston has landed most of the 19 broadbills to his credit. His record is second only to that of Michael Lerner of the Marine Laboratory at Bimini, Bahamas, who has taken 23 swordfish.

Except for that first 355-pounder taken by pioneer William Boschen in 1913, the greatest swordfish catch ever made was one boated by Lou Marron, a New Jersey oil company executive, who landed a 1182-pounder at Iquique, Chile, in May 1953. The fish required three hours to land and during that time Marron brought it to the boat ten times but was unable to hold it there long enough to sink a gaff. Finally on the eleventh pass, with Marron almost completely exhausted and his back worn raw from being bounced about in the fighting chair, the 14-foot 11½-inch fish was brought aboard. It was and still remains the largest swordfish ever taken on rod and reel.

It's interesting to note that the largest swordfish ever taken by a woman was the 772-pounder taken by Marron's wife, Eugenie, about a year later in the same area along the Chilean coast.

But for single-minded men, preferably with plenty of time and money to spare, plus new ideas in saltwater fishing techniques, there is much pioneering to be done. There's little doubt that 2000-pound swordfish—and even bigger ones—still remain in the sea.

There's room for much experimentation in swordfishing. And perhaps the avenue with the best prospects would be with wire or braided metal lines in an effort to catch big billfish at their normal feeding depth by deep trolling. A few fish have been taken this way but there still is much room for further development and only time will have the answer.

MARLIN

Many fishermen consider marlin the most spectacular big game fishes in the world, and they have good reason to do so. Marlin have all the qualities of a great game species. They're strong, they're fast and they leap repeatedly when hooked, sometimes tail-walking like a sailfish. And they can cross almost 100 feet of the surface in one tail-walking spree.

Often marlin and sailfish and swordfish are confused and a common mistake is to call all of them marlin swordfish. Of course, this is a misnomer because the bill or spear of a marlin is similar to that of a sailfish. It's round in cross section and therefore does not resemble the flat, bladelike weapon of the broadbill. Both are used for the same purpose, however, and that is to cripple or kill smaller fish when the billfish is feeding.

Three general species of marlin inhabit the deep blue waters and the ocean currents of the world. These are the white, the black and the striped marlin. The blue marlin, which is common in Atlantic waters from Venezuela northward, is probably a subspecies of the black marlin or vice versa. In addition, there are many other local names for unusually colored marlin found in tropical waters—the so-called silver marlin is an example—but these are only color phases of the black and or blue marlin. At least that's the current consensus of icthyologists.

Many outstanding new marlin waters have been discovered since World War II, and the development of new tackle has made it possible to catch the fish in difficult waters. The newest promised land for these biggest of billfish is off the coast of Peru, where the present world's record black marlin was taken.

Fishing for all the gladiators, for marlin as well as sailfish and swordfish, is pretty much the same. The common method is to troll, using outriggers so that the bait can be skipped across the surface. The most popular marlin baits are about the same as those used for broadbills—mackerel, bonito, herring, flying fish or whatever fish of these types are most abundant locally.

But marlin, especially the larger ones, have an unusual and disconcerting habit of their own. Frequently a huge, dark form will be spotted following the skipping bait for a quarter mile or more before the marlin decides to charge the bait, *if* it decides to charge the bait at all. Unlike sailfish and smaller marlin, the jumbos seldom grab the bait on their first rush. Instead they may rap it savagely several times with their bills.

There are two ways to handle a reluctant marlin. One method is the drop-back routine in which the reel is flipped onto free spool and the bait is allowed to drift freely far behind in the wake of the boat. The other way is to keep skipping the bait and perhaps even to gather in more line to make it bounce more lightly across the surface of the water. What occasionally happens in this case is the wildest, most chilling kind of strike at a bait which is half flying, that any angler can imagine.

A few sailfish and marlin charter-boat captains in the Florida Keys use still another trick to tease billfish. An inflated balloon or a kite is "trolled" in the air behind the boat. The balloon or kite then performs as an outrigger and from

it a strip of bait is lowered into the water where it skips only occasionally, sometimes bouncing from wave to wave, in imitation of a flying fish. Some days this technique is completely unsuccessful, but there are other occasions when it creates spectacular strikes.

Any fish with the great physical potential of a marlin can give a fisherman all the action he can handle. Occasionally it goes even further than that. Several years ago off Cuba, one Vincente Alcoriza was fishing for marlin with a handline. He successfully hooked his fish and then began to pull it in hand-over-hand as fast as he could. Unaccountably the fish came in willingly—until in a moment of stark terror Alcoriza found out why. When the marlin reached the surface, it didn't stop. It simply rammed head-on into the boat, spearing the fisherman with its bill on the way through. Alcoriza spent the next several months in a hospital and was lucky to escape with his life.

On another occasion Dr. Harry Minton of the Canal Zone was fishing in the Pearl Islands just off Panama. Early in the morning he hooked a good fish on 36-thread line. But by one o'clock he was still engaged with the fish. Somehow he was able to fight it down to a belly-up position right alongside the boat.

One of Minton's companions grabbed a gaff, reached over the side and sent the gaff home. That was like spashing turpentine on a tiger because at that instant the marlin came to life and jumped on board the ship. Then in a blinding display of gymnastics the marlin smashed just about everything on board, slashed out at the gaffer and jumped back into the sea.

Two hours and forty minutes later, Minton was finally able to bring the marlin to gaff a second time. That was quite a performance for a fish which weighed only 240 pounds.

The white marlin, *Makaira albida*, which is the smallest of the marlins, ranges in the Atlantic Ocean from Venezuela northward through the West Indies to Massachusetts. The rod-and-reel record for white marlin is a 161-pounder taken in the Gulf Stream off Miami Beach in 1938. Other good white-marlin waters would include Ocean City, Maryland; Rehoboth, Delaware; the Cape Hatteras region, North Carolina; off Montauk, Long Island; and about 35 miles off Virginia Beach, Virginia. All of these are especially good as the whites migrate up and down the coast each summer, appearing in numbers at first one place and then another in order.

Earlier in the spring, Walker Cay and the Biminis in the Bahamas are hot spots. Another outstanding white marlin fishing hole—from March through October—is off the north Venezuelan coast. Vast schools of marlin gather here to feed on concentrations of baitfish that congregate in these waters.

The striped marlin is found only in the Pacific from the Chilean coast northward to Baja California and it rarely reaches a weight in excess of 400 pounds. The world's record striped marlin is a 692-pounder taken off Balboa, California, thirty years ago, but some observers insist this was a black rather than a striped marlin. Of all the marlin, perhaps the striper is the one most inclined to make repeated, spectacular leaps out of the water. The white marlin ordinarily is the one that jumps least often.

Striped marlin, named for the conspicuous stripes along the sides of their bodies after death, a feature not typical of the other marlins, are caught only seasonally off Baja California. The summer and fall months are the best. They have been captured around Hawaii, Fiji, Korea, Japan, the Philippines, New Zealand, Formosa, Tahiti and several other Pacific localities.

Striped-marlin eggs have never been recognized, and to date very young striped marlin have not been positively identified. Adult stripers in spawning condition have been encountered only in the South China Sea and in the central Pacific Ocean. Most spawning in these waters apparently takes place during April, May and June. Once they have hatched, marlin probably grow quite rapidly and it is believed that they can attain a weight of 100 pounds in about three years.

The food of the striped marlin is predominantly fish, squid, crabs and shrimp. The last three make up lesser proportions of diet than do fish, however.

The best fishing locality in southern California waters is that belt which ranges from the east end of Santa Catalina Island to about San Clemente Island, and south in the direction of Los Coronados to the Mexican boundary.

It's interesting to note that a 200½-pound, 9-foot 6½-inch striped marlin was caught in 1953 by R. N. Anderson on only 12-pound test line. The catch was made near Las Cruces, Mexico, and remains a most outstanding angling achievement.

The Pacific black marlin, which is the largest of the billfish clan, is pretty much confined to the coasts of Chile, Peru and Ecuador. The most fabulous fishing of all for blacks occurs at Cabo Blanco, Peru, and this is the result of the confluence of two great and fertile ocean currents.

Surging up from the south, the cold Peru or Humboldt Current, a stream of water 150 miles wide, swings offshore to join the southward sweep of the Equatorial Current, which has already been united with the North Equatorial Current farther to the north. The junction of

Here we're landing my 86-pound white marlin taken off Cayo Mono, Cuba. Many anglers consider white the strongest of the marlins for their size.

these two ocean "rivers" creates an ichthyological traffic jam for Pacific game fish off northern Peru. The whole area contains an almost unprecedented abundance and variety of big fish, small fish, baitfish, squid and octopuses unlike any other place in the world. Almost every species of fish of any consequence caught in the Pacific Ocean can be found off Cabo Blanco, with the possible exception of the wahoo and the Allison tuna.

Black marlin have been taken in every month of the year off Cabo Blanco and so incidentally have swordfish. As this is being written, a total of 39 black marlin weighing more than 1000 pounds each have been boated near this one Peruvian port, where a modern fishing camp has been established. Thousand-pounders have been hooked within one mile of shore and it's a strange circumstance that none have been seen or caught more than 10 miles south of Cabo Blanco or 25 miles north of the place.

The largest black marlin of all was a 1560-pounder landed by Alfred C. Glassell, Jr., on August 4, 1953. About a year later Kimberly Wiss claimed the women's record black marlin with a 1025-pounder. These catches can be compared with the former world's record from New Zealand, a 976-pounder captured in 1926.

Although it may be a subspecies of the black marlin as we have mentioned before, the blue marlin (or Atlantic blue marlin or Cuban marlin), *Makaira nigricans ampla*, ranges throughout the West Indies and the Bahamas and appears in numbers along the East coast of the United States as far north as New Jersey. The largest game fish in Gulf Stream waters, it has never been encountered on the Florida west coast. It has, however, been taken off Texas—near Port Isabel—and around Cuba and Puerto Rico. Blue marlin fishing reaches a peak around Havana in July and many big ones have been landed just outside the city's harbor. That's also true at San Juan, Puerto Rico.

The greatest concentration of blue marlin occurs off Bimini, Bahamas, where the first individual was caught in 1933. Although they are present throughout the year, here is a pronounced run of the fish late each June. The peak concentration occurs from early July to about the first of August.

While the blue marlin is known to feed deep, it also feeds near the surface on occasion. Gulf Stream blues average out between 200 and 300 pounds, but there is an actual record of a blue marlin taken by nonsporting means which weighed about 1200 pounds.

A 742-pounder was taken off Bimini in 1949 by Aksel Wichfield of Palm Beach. According to International Game Fish Association records, that's the biggest marlin ever taken in the Atlantic.

Besides being the dazzling jumper that all marlin are, the blue of the Atlantic is also an extremely dogged battler. Fishermen have hung onto big ones in excess of 15 hours and the longer the battle continues, the greater the odds are stacked in favor of the fish. It's extremely good advice, therefore, for the prospective marlin fisherman—or swordfisherman or tuna angler—to get into good physical shape before he tackles these big gladiators.

It's extremely wise to exercise arm and shoulder muscles and even to develop one's wind. Handball and swimming are especially good training, but the best idea is to see a professional trainer or a doctor who specializes in muscles and muscle development. Either of these men can prescribe a set of training rules and a series of exercises which will not only strengthen the muscles but which will make fishing for any of the billfishes a more pleasant and productive experience.

Chapter Four

THE WONDERFUL BARRACUDA

Nearly every angler has preconceived ideas about barracudas long before he ever catches one. These are bloodthirsty killers, he'd heard, the wolves of the sea that run in packs. They're not game fish, is the conclusion, and they're not good to eat. They're simply dangerous brutes and warm saltwaters everywhere would be better off without them. These are typical opinions, and they couldn't be further from actual fact.

The truth is that the barracuda is one of the finest game fishes in the world. Of course it's a killer, but so is every other fish that swims. A barracuda is only more efficient, and what's more, he does not hunt in packs. With bridgework as sharp and deadly as a hundred scalpels, it can neatly cut a fish almost its own size in half, but that doesn't keep it from being a thrilling jumper and a strong, durable fighter. But best of all it's an abundant fish and it's widely distributed in warm saltwaters everywhere. No special, expensive gear is necessary to catch it. It's any man's game fish which can be taken from rowboats or from bridges as well as from expensive charter boats. You can find cudas in mangrove channels or on open weedy flats, while cruising over coral reefs or on the edge of ocean currents. This fish surely gets around.

There are many ways to catch barracudas, but day in and day out the trolled or skipped mullet fillet is the best of all. It's wise to remember one important point, though. Small cudas, up to 30 inches, say, are the most willing of strikers anytime you find them. The bait can be alive or artificial, floating or sinking; they'll usually wallop it as soon as they see it. But once a barracuda becomes an adult, it's a different story. He looks mighty carefully at artificials and then seldom likes what he sees. Most trophy specimens are taken on live or cut bait.

For small cudas, the best baits are ¼-ounce bucktail jigs in white or yellow fished on a light spinning outfit. The only differences from standard bass or trout fishing techniques must be a faster retrieve and a braided-wire leader. A leader is always essential, no matter what the tackle. A freshwater fisherman trying this for the first time should be certain his reel will not be damaged by use in the salt.

Several times in recent years I've fished with Captain Eric Jacques out of Tar-Bone-Cuda, his unique "botel" on Cudjoe Key. That's a little over halfway from Marathon to Key West. Eric likes comfort and plenty of room to stretch for both himself and his customers while fishing—and so he uses houseboats. You can fish on them and then stay out overnight in some remote Keys area to be ready to fish early the next day. The houseboats have all the modern plumbing and comforts of home. They also permit a wonderfully effective way of catching barracudas.

Eric's method is to anchor the houseboat on the edge of a reef or a tidal current somewhere and then to fish the bottom leisurely with cut bait. Usually it's a simple matter to catch a

Albert Whittaker with cuda showing lethal bridgework.

whole live box full of yellowtails, grunts, gag groupers or mutton snappers. Often enough a big red grouper or a jewfish is hooked to make it interesting. Anyway, the yellowtails and snappers are used whole and alive as bait. They're hooked through the dorsal fin, rigged several feet below a large cork float and then allowed to drift about 100 feet down-tide of the boat. If all goes well, barracudas will spot them quickly and a fisherman will have his hands full.

If action doesn't develop soon, the grunts (which are numerous enough to pave the bottom in places) are cut up and used as chum. Chumming, incidentally, is another technique to attract barracudas to any given spot.

Eric and I were anchored off Tarponbelly Key one morning when a school of cero mackerel suddenly appeared around us. We caught several on white bucktails, including a fine 12-pounder, when another cero hit close to the boat. In almost the same instant, a tremendous barracuda boiled up from behind and . . . then neatly clipped off the rear two thirds of the mackerel. I reeled in the head and noticed that the barracuda followed it in. Without removing the hook, I simply tossed the head back in again and the cuda grabbed it.

I let the fish run off with 30 feet of line, waited while it paused, and in the next instant set the hook hard into immediate, lightning resistance. I was using only 6-pound line on a reel that held about 200 yards of it—and I had visions of some sort of light-tackle record when that fish exploded out of the water. Maybe I

didn't have a chance, but for twenty minutes or more I was still in the game. I just held on and nothing more. The fish peeled off too much line, though, and after making a wide circle around the boat, a knot failed. But so it goes.

The barracuda is a formidable-looking, elongated, silvery fish with a weird grin. But perhaps its most important characteristic, at least to fishermen, is its unusual curiosity. Skin divers have long known and have been apprehensive about a cuda's habit of swimming close to them and of staying close by—watching everything that goes on. I don't recommend to my friends that they push this curiosity too far. There's no need to get reckless with such natural mayhem equipment as a barracuda's jaws.

But experienced anglers in the Florida Keys use this curiosity to considerable advantage. The motor of a boat seems to attract cudas as surely as chumming. Invariably they'll investigate the wake of a passing boat and sometimes follow it for a considerable distance. Divers have often seen them do this. The lesson here is to troll or to cast close in the wake of a moving boat rather than ahead of it or off to the sides.

Almost any sort of tackle is suitable for this trolling if you can afford to replace any broken items. Of course, extra-heavy tackle can take much of the wallop from the sport, but very light tackle is just as bad. There isn't much fun in the long and drawn-out kind of contest that can follow with too-light tackle. A good outfit is a salt-water spinning or casting outfit with 12- or 15-pound line. For the big cudas around outer reefs, which run 40 pounds or better, a 6/9 out-fit is fine. That means a 6-ounce rod tip and 9-thread (27-pound test) line.

Ordinarily the fly rod doesn't have too much place in barracuda fishing, but I remember one time when it did. We were fishing a mangrove bay in the West Bay section of Grand Cayman, a lonely tropical island with better than ordinary fishing, about 300 miles southeast of Havana. We had tarpon and snook in mind. Instead, we found the area alive with 2- to 3-foot cudas. They would hit nearly anything we tossed at them, but just for the novelty I rigged a fly rod and tied a large bass popping bug to the finest wire leader I could find. No bass ever hit the bug as hard or as often as these miniature cudas.

There are some monster cudas roaming our American coasts, but none are likely to exceed the existing world record, a 103¼-pounder caught in the Bahamas thirty years ago. It's conceivable, though, that the record for 12-pound line could be broken. This was a 42-pounder taken off the coast of Nigeria—where many over 50 pounds are taken on heavier gear—in 1951. The 20-pound-line record is a Florida fish that weighed 58 pounds. The women's world record is a 59½-pounder from near Key Largo.

An important characteristic of the barracuda is that it can be found in many different kinds of waters. We've mentioned how they congregate around bonefish flats and occasionally it's possible to take them there on regular bonefish tackle and bonefish lures. In many ways a barracuda is a much more exciting fish to catch in such shallow water because he will jump repeatedly, and this is something a bonefish will not do.

It has also been mentioned that cudas thrive over coral reefs and cruise offshore. But I've also found that extremely large ones like to linger around mangrove channels and small mangrove islands. An especially likely place is where a narrow channel widens into or joins a deep hole or depression. Such places are numerous from Florida to Panama.

While fishing in British Honduras recently with John Moxley, we spent many hours casting the fringes of mangrove "fingers" and islands for snook and tarpon. But wherever we found a pocket or deep hole in the mangroves, we would surely find barracuda lurking in each place. Usually it was a single big cuda rather than several small ones. Sometimes they would strike and sometimes they wouldn't, but their presence was always exciting.

The great barracuda is really an extraordinary mechanism. Besides his formidable bridgework which has been mentioned before, it has other physical characteristics in his favor. Even in the clear water it's often difficult to spot a barracuda because of a camouflage which enables it to be blended into coral heads, into grasses, into the shadows of mangroves and wharves and especially in the skeletons of old shipwrecks.

Out of the water a cuda is a shiny silver in color, but its dark green or bluish black and the darker bars and blotches on the sides tend to make it inconspicuous no matter where it happens to be. And the colors on a cuda's back and flanks become more dim or more dark according to the surroundings.

Some of the best waters for the great or Atlantic barracuda are those in the Bahama Islands and perhaps those in the more remote Florida Keys from Marathon to the Dry Tortu-

George Laycock casts and hooks big cuda near Isle of Pines, Cuba.

Barracuda lunges out of water near the Dry Tortugas. (Photo by Florida State News Bureau)

gas. A good outfit for a fisherman who is particularly interested in barracuda is a fairly stiff action, two-handed spinning rod about 7 feet long and weighing about 5 or 6 ounces. The reel, which should have a good line capacity and a smooth drag, should contain at least 200 yards of 10- or 12-pound line. But regardless of the tackle or the line, no bait should be presented without at least an 18- to 20-inch length of wire leader. Number 2 wire is suitable.

CALIFORNIA BARRACUDA

The California barracuda, *Sphyraena argentea*, is the only member of its family known to inhabit the Pacific coastal waters of the United States. Three smaller species are found in temperate and tropical waters south of California and about 22 kinds of barracudas have been identified from all the oceans of the world.

Even though the California cuda is the largest of 4 species found along the Pacific coasts of North and South America, it never approaches in size some of the giant barracuda of the tropical Atlantic or those taken far out in mid-Pacific.

Atlantic barracuda have attained weights in excess of 100 pounds whereas the largest California record seems to be a 17½-pound fish caught in 1958. Females grow bigger than males and almost all barracudas taken off California which are larger than 10 pounds are females.

California barracudas have been caught at various times all the way from near Wrangell,

Alaska, south to Magdalena Bay, Baja California. But in recent times they have seldom been taken or even observed very far north of Point Conception or San Francisco. Perhaps more than any of their cousins they are a schooling species and appear to prefer staying close to offshore islands and to the mainland.

A number of biological studies have been made on California cudas. These reveal, for example, that a six-year-old female which weighs under 7 pounds contained 484,000 mature eggs. About 75 percent of all California barracudas will spawn when they are two years old, and the spawning season usually extends from April through September, with the greatest activity in May or June. It's possible that a single cuda spawns more than once each season and the young ones up to 6 inches in length are quite often found in shallow waters close to shore. The smaller editions from 6 inches to a foot in length are excellent baitfish for other species.

The fact that barracudas are extremely voracious and that they feed on a large variety of small pelagic fishes is of a special value to fishermen who catch them in a number of different ways. Perhaps the greatest number are taken on live bait presented near the surface. Almost an equal number are taken on trolled artificial lures, some of the most effective of which are bone jigs, silver jigs, spoons and red and white feathers. Of course, strips of cut bait or whole fish can also be trolled.

Since the California barracudas are most often taken accidentally—on heavy tackle which is meant for other fishes—they do not give the impression of being extremely game. But taking them on spinning tackle or very light trolling tackle is an entirely different matter. A wise fisherman will always carry a light outfit on board in the event that he runs into a whole school of California barracudas.

The writer would like to make one point completely clear. In some regions, cudas are considered worthless as game fish. I've known boat captains who despised them enough to slit the belly of every one they caught and then throw it overboard while still alive.

I've also had cudas cut my best bonefish in half, eat a trophy cero mackerel as I was about to land it and in general become a nuisance. But still it's a truly great game fish. In my book it's among the greatest of all.

Chapter Five

THE WANDERERS

DOLPHIN, WAHOO, KING MACKEREL, SPANISH MACKEREL, CERO MACKEREL, BONITO, COBIA

DOLPHIN

There is something primitive and strangely beautiful about finding a school of dolphins far out on the open ocean. First you spot a piece of driftwood or a palm log, perhaps with a pair of albatrosses perched upon it. Then when you drift closer you spot a fluid, darting shadow just beneath. If you troll or cast a lure, almost any lure, close enough to the shadow . . . lightning strikes at once. And you can feel the sudden shock of it from the tip of your rod to the tips of your toes.

Maybe it seems impossible to have affection or perhaps admiration for a fish, but I make no apologies about my admiration for the dolphin, *Coryphaena hippurus*. I'd rate the fish among the three or four most game and exciting species in the world. It's extremely fast. And no other fish is more beautiful or more delicious on the table.

The dolphin is completely a wanderer of the warm, open seas entirely around the earth. Its movements and life history are secrets that neither fishermen nor biologists know. Its colors, which blend into blue or green or gold, seem to change with the mood of the fish. The color of an excited or injured fish can change while you watch. But gaff the fish and swing it aboard a boat, the vivid shades soon change with death to dull and lifeless brown.

With just one quick glance it's possible to tell the difference between a male and a female

False albacore, a great open-water species, taken by Bill Backus off Bermuda.

dolphin. The male has a blunt, high head, and the female, because she is more streamlined, has more pleasing lines. Her forehead is fashioned in a graceful curve from the mouth to the front of the blue or purple dorsal fin.

In North American waters, the dolphins range north along the Atlantic coast as far as Virginia, and occasionally they are caught still farther north. They are rather numerous in the Gulf Stream along the Florida coast. In the Pacific, dolphins range from San Diego to Panama and beyond, and perhaps they reach even greater numbers in the Pacific than in the Atlantic.

Large dolphins usually swim in pairs or at least in very small schools. Smaller ones school in vast numbers. And generally speaking, it can be said that the smaller the size the more dolphins will be together in one school. All of them, however, can be found in the open sea lurking underneath bits of grass, along weed lines, beneath jetsam, driftwood and any floating objects. In early summer, schools of small dolphins that weigh only a pound or maybe less, often appear in such great numbers that they cover areas several miles in extent. And a few large dolphins stay in the shade beneath them!

The average size of a dolphin taken on the Florida east coast would be about 7 or 8 pounds, but the species attains a length of nearly 6 feet and the largest fish on record taken by rod and reel is a 76-pounder caught near Acapulco, Mexico, by R. G. Stotsbery in 1957.

The largest North American record is a 67½-pounder from Waianae in the Hawaiian Islands which measured 5 feet 8½ inches in length. Fifty-pounders are rare along the Florida coast, but there is a record of a 61-pounder taken near Fort Lauderdale in 1935. However, in 1954 I saw a remarkable catch of four dolphins taken near Parguera, Puerto Rico, which weighed 210 pounds altogether. One of the four was a 60-pound bull.

Most dolphins are caught when trolling with strip baits, block-tin squid, spoons, jigs, or feathers. And a large percentage of them are hooked when the charter boat is fishing for larger fish and therefore with tackle too heavy for the dolphin to give its best fight. Ordinarily 6-thread line is highly satisfactory and 9-thread is enough to catch the largest dolphin in the Gulf Stream.

As it happened in the Pacific off Costa Rica, once a school of dolphins is hooked off the Florida coast, the balance of the school can be held within reach by tying the first one close to the stern of the boat after it is landed. The other dolphins will continue to strike as long as the fishermen are interested in such steady action. When found in schools, dolphins will strike at almost anything—surface or deep-running plugs, streamer flies, live bait, spoons, spinners. They're the most obliging of fishes.

Enough cannot be said about the game qualities of this rainbow-colored fish, especially on light tackle or spinning tackle. Although they are extremely strong swimmers, they do not fight with the sheer force of tunas and amberjack, but rely instead on their blinding speed and maneuverability. They seldom go very deep to sulk for long periods of time, as do some other ocean fishes, and ordinarily they do not run great distances in one direction. Rather they feint and spar, jump and go greyhounding across the ocean, sometimes in leaps from 10 to 20 feet which display their beautiful iridescent colors in the tropical sun. Few fish can approach them in jumping ability, in straightaway speed or in sudden change of pace.

Some confusion has resulted over the dolphin's name and perhaps it should be cleared up here. In ancient times, the Greeks used dolphin to identify a mammal of the porpoise family and porpoises of the Mediterranean are still called dolphin. So are they occasionally in waters along the Florida Keys. It's interesting to note that in early heraldry, the form or figure of the dolphin was used as a symbol of diligence, love and swiftness.

WAHOO

Another of the mysterious wanderers of the open sea is the jagged-tooth wahoo, *Acanthocybium solandri*, which looks very much like an assassin. It's also called peto, guarapucu, queen mackerel, queen or queenfish.

Actually it is a sleek, slim, handsome fish. Its dark-green or steel-blue sides with yellowish bars have a burnished silver finish which rubs off on a fisherman's fingers. The long low dorsal fin has around 25 spines and is followed by a series of finlets. It also has large irregular teeth and a beaklike upper jaw. It is only because this species is occasionally confused with the kingfish that these physical characteristics are given in detail here. Any other resemblance to the kingfish or a king mackerel is superficial.

In North American waters the wahoo roams farther at sea than most fishermen ever penetrate, and this is unfortunate. However, it is caught as far north as Cape Hatteras and southward to South America. It also exists in numbers in the Pacific, but only far out of sight of the Pacific coast, and in the Indian Ocean.

Some of the best wahoo fishing occurs around islands far from major coastlines. Bermuda is a good spot, and many large specimens are taken here. Another good example is the Cayman group in the Caribbean. Around both Bermuda and the Cayman Islands, the fish sometimes come in close enough to shore to be caught occasionally over the outer reefs. They seem to be most abundant or at least the most willing to strike in winter and early spring.

Except in areas where they are known to be abundant, little fishing is done specifically for wahoo. Mostly they are taken by anglers who are trolling for other larger fishes. They will strike spoons, feather jigs, large plugs or strip baits and the last is probably best of all.

Since the average weight of a wahoo is likely to be between 15 and 20 pounds, 6/9 tackle with 18-thread line is heavy enough for the best of them. And the best is a 139-pounder taken off Marathon, Florida.

In my book the wahoo is one of the most underrated game fishes in the sea. Its strike is extremely hard, thrilling, and when made on the surface close to a boat, is apt to give any fisherman something to talk about for a long time. And once he's hooked, the wahoo becomes a genuine striptease artist in that he can strip line off a reel faster than almost any other fish. The first run is usually long and fast. But if the fisherman can get that first run stopped in time, he has a fairly good chance of landing his fish. But no matter where or when the contact is made, there are no dull moments for the fisherman who is lucky enough to hook a wahoo.

KING MACKEREL
More often called kingfish or king in Florida waters, the king mackerel follows a migratory pattern which makes it very seasonal in its appearances as far as sport fishermen are concerned. Schools of kings follow a seasonal migratory route which goes south in the fall and north in the spring. The runs on Florida's east and west coasts coincide both in times and numbers. And both follow the same cycle, ranging from years of great abundance to other years when the fish are quite scarce.

Fine king mackerel landed by George Robey off Florida's Gulf Coast, where kingfishing is great.

Vast schools of kings winter in southern Florida waters from Fort Pierce or Stuart southward to the Dry Tortugas. However, they are not always available to fishermen since they spend a good part of this time in extremely deep water. It's interesting to note that the larger fish are sometimes found in the green waters closer inshore than the smaller kingfish which are caught on the edge of the Gulf Stream. Of course, this situation isn't always true.

The strike of a kingfish is sudden and shocking. Although it doesn't compare with a dolphin as an aerialist, occasionally it will make a remarkable jump above the surface of the water. One charter-boat captain told me that he had a kingfish jump completely over his boat and that meant it had to jump at least 6 feet out of the water for a lateral distance of more than 12 feet.

The average size of a Florida kingfish is about 8 pounds, but quite a number are caught each year from 40 to 50 pounds. It attains a length of about 6 feet and a maximum weight of 76½ pounds. That's the record taken in 1952 by Bob Maytag in Bimini, Bahama.

King mackerel are among the species of salt-water fish which can be chummed to the surface with live shrimp. Shrimp is also an effective bait to catch them. But no matter what the bait or no matter what the tackle, an average king-fish is a mighty sporty proposition when the tackle is on the light side. The 6/9 tackle is ample for trolling with block-tin squid, spoons, large feathers, balao and mullet strips. It's best to troll rather slowly and to get the bait down very deep, and this can be accomplished by using a wire line or by running the boat in tight circles or figure eights. Leaders should be as long as 20 or 30 feet when the fish are very deep.

SPANISH MACKEREL

Members of the mackerel family are found all over the world in tropical and temperate oceans and in many seas which adjoin them. They are extremely prolific. Although they are prey to many other fishes, and although they furnish an important part of the diet for some of these, they still remain abundant and supply a vast percentage of the world's fish markets. Of course they are widely caught and held in high esteem by sport fishermen.

In Florida waters where the species follows a migratory pattern almost identical to that of the king mackerel, the Spanish mackerel is the second most important fish commercially. Only the mullet has greater value to Florida commercial fishermen.

If you are fishing offshore in Florida and see an excited cloud of gulls and terns, the odds are good it will be a school of Spanish mackerel—or maybe cero mackerel—leaping from the surface as they work their way through a ball of baitfish. These mackerel seem to have an endless appetite for mullet, menhaden, silversides or any small fish found in numbers in their vicinity.

Often called the spotted mackerel because of the bronze or golden spots on its blue-green sides, the Spanish mackerel is quite a handsome fish with an iridescent silver belly and black and yellow pectoral fins. Although they may wander as far north as Cape Ann, Massachusetts, they are extremely rare north of New Jersey and exist there only in midsummer. They are most abundant around the Florida Keys.

The Spanish mackerel often wanders offshore in large schools, appearing a little closer inshore during midsummer, when it seems to be spawning. It feeds mainly near the surface on small fish and occasionally on squid. It reaches a length of 6 feet and a weight of 20 pounds, but the average Spanish mackerel would run only about 2 pounds. There is one record of a 25-pounder taken in commercial nets.

A wide variety of fishing techniques can be used to catch Spanish mackerel, but trolling and spinning with bucktails are the most common fishing methods. Many mackerel are taken by fishermen trolling for larger fishes. Feather jigs, small metal squids and spoons will always account for plenty of action when they are passed near a school of feeding fish. A mackerel strike is swift and its sizzling first run is really spectacular for the size of the fish.

Casting toward the edge of a school of feeding mackerel will provide a spincaster or fly-caster with all the excitement he can handle. These light-tackle methods are becoming increasingly popular along the Texas coast where Spanish mackerel gather each spring.

It's very important to use a fast retrieve or a fairly rapid trolling speed when after Spanish mackerel. Even feeding fish will often ignore a bait that is not retrieved fast enough. A 3-foot wire leader and plenty of backing line for a long run are always necessary. All mackerel, especially the Spanish, are delicious eating. But the fish must be cooled immediately to preserve its fine, delicate flavor.

CERO MACKEREL

The cero, third member of the mackerel family which inhabits North American Atlantic waters, is frequently confused with both the Spanish and king mackerel. In size it ranges somewhere between them. Its average weight is about 4 pounds but it attains a length of nearly 5 feet and more than 25 pounds. It tends more to live in tropical waters and is less migratory than the other mackerels.

Seldom found north of Miami Beach and most abundant in the Florida Keys, it is caught throughout the summer while fishing for other fishes. The tackle, bait and lures which are effective on Spanish mackerel are also effective on Ceros. Its flesh is not so oily as the other mackerels but it is the most delicious of them all.

COMMON BONITO

There is really nothing common about the common bonito because his speed and great fighting qualities make him a special kind of game fish. As streamlined as any fish in the sea, he is as fast a swimmer as any of the ocean fishes except for the dolphin, wahoo and swordfish.

Bonitos occur from Cape Cod southward to Florida and into the Gulf of Mexico. They usually roam the offshore waters along the edge of the Gulf Stream and swim in large, compact schools, staying fairly deep except to rise to the surface wherever they find schools of menhaden, alewives, and similar small fishes. Occasionally schools of 1- to 2-pound bonitos are encountered in inshore waters.

A 4/6 outfit is sufficient for any bonito fishing, but of course there are areas where a fisherman might also run into other larger fish and therefore it's wise to be rigged for heavier game. A wire leader is a necessity because of the bonito's small but extremely sharp teeth. Spoons, squid, and feather jigs are the most common artificial lures used. But small baitfish, crabs, clams or a strip bait behind a spinner are extremely effective when bonitos are busily feeding.

Since the bonito itself is an extremely fine bait for larger fish, charter skippers often troll weighted lines close behind the boat, using blocktin squids on feather lures for bait. On these short lines there is often quite a bit of action from bonito which, when landed, are converted into excellent strip baits for sailfishing. Of course many bonitos are caught on lures and on heavy tackle being trolled for sailfish, marlin and tuna.

But when hooked on light tackle, large bonito are extremely difficult to stop. The strike is hard and the first run is deep, fast and boring. They never seem to give up and even a 5-pounder is enough to make a fisherman feel that he has done a full day's work.

He's a wise flycaster or spin-fisherman who takes the opportunity, when he finds bonito feeding on the surface, to make a few casts into the center of the school. Ordinarily he'll need only one cast because no matter what the lure, a bonito will take it and from that point on it's a long hard tug-of-war which the fisherman will always remember.

Although the average common bonito, *Sarda sarda,* will only weigh about 2 pounds, it does attain a maximum weight of 20 pounds and a length of 30 inches.

OCEANIC BONITO

The oceanic bonito or skipjack tuna, *Katsuwonus pelamis,* mistakenly called arctic, is really a fish of tropical waters and is a closer relative of the tuna than of the bonito. In some regions it's called albacore and false albacore.

This sleek and heavy-bodied wanderer of the open ocean will average about 3 or 4 pounds but it attains a weight of 20 pounds. In 1952 a specimen weighing 39 pounds 15 ounces was taken off Walker Cay, Bahamas. And that is the largest known record for the species.

The appearance of oceanic bonito is very erratic off the United States coast. It never shows up in appreciable numbers, but when it does, it's generally in spring or summer. Often the species is found mixed up in schools of common bonitos, and of course the same type tackle will take either one of them.

I've encountered some schools of oceanic bonito feeding on the surface offshore from Bermuda. It was always a most thrilling experience whenever a school would approach our boat because they would strike readily at our spinning jigs and then make long powerful runs across the surface of the ocean. No matter whether we were trolling for wahoos in deep blue water or anchored over a reef far from land, someone on board would always keep a wary eye for feeding bonitos. That's a grand recommendation.

COBIA

In many, many years of saltwater fishing, I've only caught one cobia of respectable size, but I've had my share of experiences with them.

While fishing Key West waters, for example, with Captain Lefty Reagan, I hooked three cobia on three casts right underneath the lighthouse on Smith Shoal. Any one of these three cobia would have been worth a first prize in the Annual Metropolitan Miami Fishing Tournament, but all three of them wrapped my line around the barnacle-encrusted legs of the lighthouse and that was the end of that. One of these cobia, I should add, jumped repeatedly like a tarpon and this, Reagan assured me, isn't something that happens every day. But it did happen at a most unfortunate time for me.

The cobia, *Rachycentron canadus,* is a cocoa-brown fish with a single longitudinal stripe. From some angles it resembles a freshwater channel catfish, without the whiskers, or a saltwater shark. Also called ling, lemonfish and crabeater, its natural habitat is around floating logs, buoys, light towers, offshore wrecks, oil rigs or in the center of riptides. Most of its food consists of such bottom forms as flounders and crabs. And although the fish gives the impression of power and deliberate movement, it is swift enough to put on a sudden burst of speed which has surprised many a smaller baitfish as well as many an angler. In many respects, the old crabeater is as rakish in action as in appearance.

Ordinarily the cobia travels alone or in small groups of two or three. It is not particularly common along our south Atlantic seaboard and is seldom found north of Chesapeake Bay, but it does reach some abundance in the Florida Keys and along our Gulf Coast from Florida to Mexico.

From mid-March to mid-May are by far the best times to fish for lemonfish along the Gulf Coast. Usually they're caught by trolling with a spoon or by still-fishing with shrimp, croakers or similar live baits. Heavy tackle is advisable when fishing around oil rigs or sunken wrecks because the minute a cobia feels the hook it will dive beneath the nearest underwater obstruction and thereby try to slice the line.

One common technique which has been developed recently is to troll very close to any kind of offshore structures with heavy metal line. In this way the fish can be horsed to safety immediately after it strikes. Mostly a good fast troll of from 5 to 6 miles an hour is most effective.

Even though cobia will average as much as 20 pounds and attain a length of 6 feet and 100 pounds, I always think of the species as a medium- or light-tackle fish. I never pass a buoy, lighthouse or channel marker without making several

Big cobia hooked on feather jig near Panama City, Florida. (*Photo by Florida State News Bureau*)

These Pensacola fishermen display their catch of ling (cobia) that weighed (left to right) 41 pounds, 46 pounds, and 62 pounds. (*Photo by Florida State News Bureau*)

casts nearby, and it doesn't make too much difference which lures are cast because a cobia will take strip baits, eel skins, deep-running plugs and almost any artificial with a darting type action. Its strike is heavy and its runs are quick and unpredictable. A cobia is just as apt to run toward the boat as away from it. But no matter which way it moves, its extremely powerful and its fight is dogged and jarring. For trolling, 6/9 tackle is usually adequate.

One of the greatest concentrations of cobias occurs late each spring along the northwest Florida coast. There it's possible for a fisherman to catch quite a number of large specimens in a single day. Around Panama City the cobia is often found traveling in company with large mantas. Many fisherman deliberately search for these mantas and then troll and cast all around them. Perhaps the reason for this strange association is that the mantas uncover many items of food which a cobia would ordinarily miss.

The world's record cobia is a 102-pounder taken near Cape Charles, Virginia, in 1938. In 1952, Mary Black set the women's record with a 97-pounder taken near Oregon Inlet, North Carolina. Another outstanding catch is the 41½-pounder taken near Cape Florida, Florida, in 1951 on 12-pound test line.

Chapter Six

THE HORSE MACKERELS
BLUEFIN, YELLOWFIN, BLACKFIN TUNA

Men have been seeking tuna ever since they have been able to travel and to navigate on open seas. Pliny, in the first century after Christ, relates that the multitude of tuna which met the fleet of Alexander the Great on one occasion was so vast that only by advancing in battle formation, as on an enemy, were the ships able to cut their way through the school. Evidently exaggeration about fish isn't an invention of modern writers.

But even before Pliny, the regular appearances of vast schools of tuna were known throughout the Mediterranean. In ancient Rome the capture of the first tuna of the season signaled the beginning of a great festival called Thunnaeum. This was a pageant during which a fish was sacrificed to Neptune, God of the Sea. Today fishermen still search for tuna in the Mediterranean, and in the New World as well, and they still celebrate the first catch. But in two thousand years of fishing, anglers learned little more about tuna than those first Roman fishermen knew. Until quite recently, that is.

BLUEFIN

There are a number of different species of tuna around the world and all of them are pelagic, which means they travel endlessly on or near the surface of open seas. But the largest and most impressive of them all is the bluefin, which probably reaches its greatest size in the waters on the North American side of the Atlantic Ocean and which Yankee boat captains call the "horse mackerel." The largest bluefin, *Thunnus thynnus*, of which there is an actual record

was captured off New Jersey. It measured about 14 feet long and weighed 1600 pounds. It is also on record that in one season a single fisherman in the same area harpooned 30 tuna that averaged about 1000 pounds. Though such enormous fish do exist, the average size of a bluefin would be somewhere between 200 and 250 pounds.

The bluefin is almost worldwide in distribution, since it's found on both sides of the Atlantic and in the Pacific as well. In Europe it ranges from Norway southward to the Mediterranean Sea and there is excellent fishing in Danish waters during mid-August. It occurs also off the African coast southward from Gibraltar to the Cape of Good Hope. On the Atlantic coast of America its general range is from the central Caribbean northward to Newfoundland. Later on we will pinpoint the wanderings of the bluefin more specifically in this area.

All of the tuna are most efficient and relentless beasts of prey, and large quantities of food are required just to keep them alive. Since the bluefin is by far the largest of the tuna, it is also the most voracious eating machine of all.

Tuna are schooling fish that feed principally on smaller schooling fish. The tuna, for example, is one of the chief enemies of its own relative, the mackerel, and also of menhaden and herring. They will even attack dogfish sharks and whole dogfish weighing as much as 8 pounds have been found in the stomachs of bluefins. Tuna, in fact, feed on any schools of smaller fish they

Landing a giant bluefin tuna at Soldier's Rip near Wedgeport, Nova Scotia. This is a great bluefin hot spot. (*Photos by Nova Scotia Film Bureau*)

find. And they consume vast quantities of squid as well. There is no doubt that their appearance in any local waters and their movements across the ocean are governed by the abundance or absence of fish on which they depend.

But as terrible as tuna surely seem to smaller fish, even the largest bluefins are preyed upon by killer whales. The killers are known to seize them by the back, near the head, thus to cut the spinal cord and kill them instantly. At other times, bluefins have been found stranded in shallow water from which they could not escape. Apparently they reach this predicament by pursuing smaller fishes or perhaps while fleeing from killer whales.

Although fishermen have hunted tuna for food during the past twenty centuries, it was only in the past fifty years that anglers have sought tuna for sport. The records are most obscure on who caught the first bluefin on hook and line, but one of the first was a Wedgeport schoolmaster who ventured out into Liverpool Bay, Nova Scotia, in a rowboat. The year was 1871.

This pioneer, Thomas Pattilo, had only 32 fathoms of ordinary cod line wound on a swivel reel of unreliable design. He used a steel hook ⅜-inch thick, 8 inches long, and with a 3-inch shank. Then with a single companion to do the rowing he went fishing.

Pattilo quickly hooked a monster tuna, which towed his boat across the harbor much faster than his friend could row in the other direction —until it hurtled head on into a fleet of herring netters. One netter was swamped and the rest were scattered in confusion. One of the angry herring fishermen finally cut Pattilo's line and thus his first tuna escaped.

But on the next attempt, there were no herring fishermen nearby and at the cost of blistered hands and an aching back, Pattilo achieved complete success. Somehow, in spite of his crude tackle, he boated a tuna which weighed over 600 pounds and thereby set some kind of a bluefin fishing milestone.

It is only fitting that the present world's record tuna should have been taken in the same water as Pattilo's outstanding catch. In 1950, Commander Duncan M. Hodgson was fishing in an open 16-foot dory manned by Percy MacRitchie, a veteran guide. They had a strong strike, and in the next eighty minutes the fish towed their craft more than 12 miles. The tuna was eventually beached, however, and when weighed nine hours later (after much loss of blood) it still weighed 977 pounds. It was 9 feet 9 inches.

For reasons which bluefin fishermen know better than anyone else, tuna fishing can become a pure addiction although it usually is more hard work than it is a lively sport. Because of their streamlined body proportions and ample dimen-

Landing a giant bluefin tuna at Bimini, Bahamas.
(*Photo by Miami News Bureau*)

sions, bluefins have been called the torpedoes of the sea and that is an apt description. They certainly are among the speediest fishes on earth, and they have been observed keeping pace with a ship that was logging 8 knots. And the bluefins did seem to be in a hurry.

Their bullet-shaped heads and oblong bodies seem to cut through the water with a minimum of drag. Their dorsal and pelvic fins fit into grooves as the fish propel themselves forward with a quick motion of powerful, crescent-shaped tails. A taut, mucus-covered skin with minute scales slides easily through the water.

Since bluefins are pelagic as we mentioned before, they are constantly chasing or following such smaller migratory fishes as menhaden. Another favorite on the tuna's diet is the unique and graceful flying fish. It has been said that when chasing a flying fish, a tuna will estimate its trajectory and then capture it when it reenters the sea. That means that a tuna would have to be moving far faster than the 8 knots mentioned before.

The bluefin's weakness for flying fish inspired

a curious method of angling which is called the tuna-plane or the kite-fishing technique. It was first devised by captain George Farnsworth of Avalon, California, and it since has been adapted to fishing elsewhere.

Just after World War II, Harlan Major, a fishing writer, learned about the kite-fishing technique and introduced it to the East. He met Tommy Gifford, a game fish guide from Montauk, New York, and immediately Gifford accepted the idea. Before long he boated the first white marlin, the first tuna and the first broadbill sword fish ever taken on kites along the Atlantic coast. Since then he has flown his kite successfully for sailfish as well as these other species in almost all eastern United States waters, as well as those of Nova Scotia, Bimini, Cat Cay, Cuba, Puerto Rico and Jamaica.

As you can guess, the angler's line is fastened by a clothes pin to the kite string and the bait skips over the surface of the water in a manner tantalizing to many of the big game fish. The technique can be used when trolling or (if there is a wind) when still-fishing.

"The kite will account for more fish than any other method of presenting bait," Gifford claims. "I'd say it is four or five to one over an outrigger with live bait and maybe as much as eight to one over an outrigger when trolling dead bait."

An average angler's best chance to catch a big bluefin is to intercept one of its annual migrations at one of the regular fishing ports along our coast. He can charter a boat at any of these places. The cost for a whole party will run somewhere between $50 and $150 a day. Later we will discuss the exact—or nearly exact—times when the schools of tuna reach various ports.

Once a fisherman has chartered a boat, the method most universally used to catch bluefins is to chum for them. Menhaden, herring or mackerel are ground up into an oily "liquor" and slowly spilled over the transom of the boat into the sea. As this chum dissolves into the tide, it's figured to lure the big tuna close to the stern of the boat where a bait is waiting for them.

A bluefin bait can be a strange contraption indeed. The backbones are removed from 6 to 10 herring which weigh about a pound apiece. They are then spaced about a foot apart and tied to a piece of tarred cord. The cord is attached to a light string about 15 feet long which in turn is tied to a 15-foot bamboo pole. The angler's hook, which is buried inside one of the herring near the end of the string, can be any size from 6/0 to 12/0.

A deckhand or first mate stands in the stern of the boat, alternately raising and lowering the long pole, thereby causing the herring to skip along the tops of the waves as the tuna come near. This is to simulate an actual school of herring in flight.

If all goes well, a striking tuna will swirl up behind the teaser and grab it. He may gulp only one of the herring or he may take all of them. If the angler is lucky, the gulp will include the herring which has his hook imbedded in it.

When the tuna makes the first run, it usually sounds, breaking the light cord which attaches the string of herring to the bamboo pole. That is the moment when an angler sets his hook. It's an exciting moment which he had better enjoy to the fullest because from that point on it is nothing but pure, backbreaking drudgery.

When a giant bluefin is solidly hooked, he will make one terrific run after another trying to free himself. He'll shake and shudder and frequently tow even a heavy boat for many miles. And if not handled skillfully, he can snap an angler's rod and line with apparent ease.

There is another technique that is most effective at times and charter-boat captains use it

Bluefin at the dock in Bimini. (*Photo by Miami News Bureau*)

at slack tide with the boat completely adrift. A 1-pound herring is hooked through the back and dropped astern. Just above the wire leader a toy balloon is attached with a light piece of string and small safety-pin swivel. Occasionally the balloon can be moved up or down on the line to change the depth of the bait. If and when the tuna strikes, the balloon simply disintegrates and the long hard fight is on.

The proper line size for bluefin is 39-thread (or even 79), but since other fish (white marlin, sailfish, wahoo) are often taken in the same water a boat captain may recommend that his more experienced customers use 24-thread line.

In 1949, however, Guy Stoddard of Miami, who was aboard Captain Tom Gifford's boat, proved that tuna could be taken on 15-thread line. He caught two on this light tackle and one of those, a 435-pounder, was for a time the world's record.

With either the 24- or 39-thread tackle, a 15-foot size 11 piano-wire leader is used and the most common hook size in Atlantic waters is 12/0.

In 1935, Michael Lerner, a big game fishing and hunting pioneer with experience in many parts of the globe, went to Nova Scotia for a whirl at the fabled swordfishing thereabouts. On his way back to Yarmouth to catch the scheduled ferryboat for Boston, he stopped for gas near Wedgeport. He happened to have his big game fishing gear in the car and that led to fishing talk with the gas station attendant and a group of cronies who had gathered there.

Lerner's ears almost popped when he heard about the 1000-pound bluefin tuna that the natives said were regularly harpooned at the mouth of the Tusket River and at Soldier's Rip, a tidal channel so named because a troop transport once foundered there off Wedgeport.

"How far out is this fishing?" Mike asked.

"Only about an hour's run in a lobster boat," someone answered.

Without further conversation, Mike canceled his reservation on the Boston boat, rigged a crude fighting chair in the stern of a lobster boat and went tuna fishing.

That first day out he caught two tuna. Two days later he caught another bluefin, but business called him back to New York. The business transacted, he was back in Wedgeport again a week later and in the next eight days of fishing he boated 21 large tuna which weighed 3677 pounds! As a result of this effort and of Lerner's salesmanship, he convinced several commercial fishermen and lobstermen to rig their boats for sport fishing. And a number of years later the International Tuna Cup match was organized in the tiny lobster town of Wedgeport.

Like moths to a flame, big game anglers came from all four corners of the globe to match their skills and muscles with giant bluefin tuna every September. And they had astounding action. Even though the matches do not exist anymore (because in recent years the bluefins wouldn't cooperate and wouldn't guarantee to arrive at Soldier's Rip at the same time as the fishermen who traveled from as far away as Havana, Cape Town and Lisbon), it was one of the most colorful events in saltwater fishing history and no chapter on tuna fishing can be complete without it.

Many of the strange experiences and memorable incidents which illustrate the extreme addiction of tuna fishermen have survived the Wedgeport tuna tournament. In one of the earlier tournaments, Louis Mowbray, curator of Bermuda's famous Government Aquarium, was a member of the British Empire Team. Actually he was a member of the team eight times and the captain twice. But it was in 1956 that he hooked a 614-pound bluefin, fought it for six grueling hours and for the last hour on a reel without handles! The handles simply broke off. Mowbray stuck it out until the fish was landed.

In North American waters the giant bluefin is found at various times of the year all along the Atlantic coast from the Bahamas and Cuba northward to Newfoundland. They cruise in a roughly circular migration which begins with spawning somewhere in the Straits of Florida, that vast, deep blue "meadow" area between Key West and Havana.

Let's examine the sometimes devious route of this circular migration which has been fairly well pinpointed and compiled by various marine biologists and by the reports of cooperating fishermen.

The journey usually begins in March or April on the Straits of Florida spawning grounds. Traveling northward from there the 500-pound bluefin tuna usually pass Cat Cay and Bimini in the Bahamas in May and June. They reach Montauk Point, Long Island, and the Rhode Island coast in late June and early July. Of all tuna summering grounds (including Cape Cod Bay), Wedgeport, Nova Scotia, has always had the biggest concentration of tuna from August through September. Occasionally, large concentrations are found as far north as Newfoundland. As the winter months arrive the bluefins begin their southward migration, which carries them past Bermuda and on to the Lesser Antilles.

The winter migration continues in a westerly direction off the Venezuelan coast and by February the fish are running past Jamaica. A possible spawning ground may be in the Windward Passage between Cuba and Haiti. Scientists believe that some tuna head north through the passage and also up the Old Bahama Channel and Mona Passage, which is between the Dominican Republic and Puerto Rico, northward toward Cat Cay and Bimini.

Another spawning ground is suspected south of Cuba, but so far it is unconfirmed. The most recent reports on bluefin movements was the sighting recently of large concentrations in the Gulf of Mexico, especially south of the Mississippi Delta region.

Perhaps much of the lure of fishing for the giant horse mackerel anywhere in his range is the fact that many potential record specimens still swim in the sea. As recently as 1957, Captain Mark Connelly harpooned an 1100-pounder a short distance southwest of Block Island. A 1225-pounder was harpooned off the coast of Rhode Island and there is an old record of one giant bluefin which was taken off Narragansett Pier, Rhode Island, just before the turn of the century. It is said to have weighed 1500 pounds and was divided among all of the popular hotels which were then clustered about the pier.

A fisherman's best bet to break into the 1000-pound bracket or just to get a jumbo bluefin for the first time would be to concentrate in the Bimini or Cat Cay region during mid-May. That is the period when the largest bluefins of all seem to be migrating along the eastern edge of the Gulf Stream past the Bahamas. Charter boats are available there.

Besides the bluefin, there are several other species of tuna which anglers agree are among the world's great saltwater game fishes, but scientists are not in such complete agreement on their classification. There is the yellowfin tuna, for example, which some marine biologists believe is the same as the Pacific yellowfin tuna.

Others do not. And then there is the Allison tuna which other marine biologists believe is only the yellowfin tuna. And in addition, there is the blackfin tuna, generally known as *Parathunnus atlanticus*.

But specific scientific identifications are seldom of great interest to anglers so we'll consider the yellowfin and the Allison as one and the same here.

YELLOWFIN

Not nearly as much is known about the habits and migrations of the yellowfin as his larger cousin the bluefin and perhaps that explains why they are never encountered by fishermen in such appreciable numbers. A few are taken off our Florida coast from the area around the sea buoys of Government Cut, off Miami Beach, northward about as far as Fort Pierce. The first fish appear in midwinter, usually remain through May and they appear to prefer the green water just inside the Gulf Stream. The average weight in this area is less than 100 pounds, but yellowfins quite possibly grow to 400 pounds.

Like all the tuna, yellowfins strike hard on strip bait and feathers. Once hooked, they prefer to fight a deep fight.

Fifteen- or 24-thread line is generally accepted as adequate, although more experienced anglers take them on 9-thread line. And like all the tuna, this one feeds on smaller fish and it is a good fish to eat itself.

The yellowfin when fresh out of the sea and still alive is brilliantly iridescent, with a golden or bright yellow stripe along the flank. They have yellow fins, a bluish black back and whitish or pearl bellies, but soon after death the bright colors fade and the yellow colors disappear completely.

No doubt the yellowfin (or his kin) is completely international because it is found in tropical parts of all oceans—in waters from 60 to 85 degrees. It probably will not tolerate either colder or warmer waters than these and it seems to gather where there is a meeting of one or more different ocean currents.

The record yellowfin as recognized by the International Game Fish Association weighed 266 pounds 8 ounces and measured 6 feet 10½ inches in length. It was caught in 1959 off Kona, Hawaii.

BLACKFIN

The blackfin tuna, which is also called long-finned albacore, albacore, black tunny and little tunny, is one of the most beautiful of the tunas and one of the most handsome fishes in the sea. Its distinguishing characteristics are a pair of long pectoral fins which extend to the back of the front dorsal. The broad, bright, yellow band around its middle may not be present, but on some individuals it is an extremely brilliant color.

Blackfins swim in small compact schools. They approach shore erratically at times, but in large numbers. During some years they seldom appear at all. The average size is less than 15 pounds, but the fish possibly attain a length of 3 feet and a weight of 35 pounds in American waters. A 44½-pounder was boated near Cape Town, South Africa, in 1957.

Once while fishing off Bermuda with Ken Foree, popular outdoor editor of the Dallas *News,* we ran into waters full of blackfins. Ken caught a pair of blackfins which weighed 18 pounds apiece and which almost tore his arms from the sockets when they struck. Then he hooked another which I would judge weighed twice that much. But the tackle on which this blackfin was hooked was much too light and it broke off very quickly.

"I'm almost glad it escaped," Ken said. "My backbone couldn't stand another."

The strike of a blackfin is hard and sudden and its first run is always a long one. It fights strongly and deep. Since it is generally caught while fishing for other fishes, the tackle is most often too heavy or too light. Ordinarily, 6/9 tackle is ample.

A blackfin tuna swims deep and it's caught in greatest numbers on weighted line with strip bait, spoons or block-tin squids. Once a school has been located, it is possible to catch quite a number of fish on casting tackle with deep-running lures. Just as many other ocean fish do, blackfins will often follow a hooked fish.

This writer has taken only one blackfin and although it weighed only 9 pounds, the catch will not be forgotten soon. We were fishing far off Bermuda's south shore and had located a school of tuna. Promptly I hooked one on spinning gear and 10-pound monofilament line. But an hour later, the fish still wasn't ready to gaff.

And when it *was* finally gaffed, it felt like a reprieve from a long sentence at bard labor.

Chapter Seven

THE JACKS, FISH THAT FIGHT FISHERMEN

The jack crevalle, *Caranx hippos,* is the commonest member of a large family of fishes. It's also one of the most dogged, rugged, untiring game fishes an angler is ever likely to meet. It frequents the green waters between the Gulf Stream and the Atlantic shoreline and it thrives completely across the Gulf of Mexico and down the Central American coast. It likes tidal bays or channels and it especially prefers hard sand bottoms where inlet currents scour out small crustaceans or harbor schools of smaller fishes. The crevalle also ranges along southern beaches just beyond the breakers in schools which vary from 5 or 6 to 30 or 40 individuals.

From the smallest sizes to the largest, the jack is always a school fish and all individuals in a school will be of very nearly the same size or age group. A 15-pounder is considered an extremely good jack and the record for Florida waters is a 38-pounder taken by Arthur Cannon in 1951. In 1955, Lloyd Miller caught a 15½-pounder when fly-casting in the vicinity of Miami. It's possible that in extreme cases, jack crevalle will reach 40 or 45 pounds.

More than any other fishes, jacks have often proved a terrible disappointment to fishermen in southern saltwaters. For a moment or two the fisherman thinks he has hooked a record-size

Unusually large amberjack just hoisted aboard off Miami, Florida. This is one of the strongest fish in the sea. (*Photo by Miami News Bureau*)

Yellowtail jack taken off Bermuda.

number of large jacks are hooked, but only a small percentage of them are landed by bridge fishermen.

The best lures of all for jacks, however, are the yellow feather jigs and bucktails in ¼-ounce spinning size, or yellow streamer flies. In either case it's best to use a fast, whippy retrieve.

Ordinarily it isn't very hard to find jacks. They'll find you. If you cruise very long in Florida shallow waters, you're almost certain to find a school of them feeding in frenzied, violent fashion on the surface. If you can somehow keep up with them and manage a cast or two into the school, you're almost certain to have a strike no matter which lure you're using. However, there are a few exceptions to this.

Occasionally, jacks will gather for long periods of time in areas where mullet or small menhaden are extremely plentiful. At these times the jacks can become selective and pass up many of the natural or artificial baits which are otherwise effective. The best way to tempt such temperamental jacks is to try a small darting or wounded minnow type of surface plug. It should be hurried and skipped across the surface as rapidly and erratically as possible.

More than once, jacks have been a nuisance to me. While fishing the lagoons of Costa Rica's Caribbean coast, Tom McNally and I found tarpon in unbelievable numbers. But still it was almost impossible to deliver our lures to the feeding tarpon. On every cast a small jack would grab our fly or plug the instant it struck the water. It would then be necessary to play the jack, land it and release it before making another cast to the tarpon. And usually a jack would grab the next cast, too.

The jack family is distributed in warm and temperate waters completely around the world. Some of the jacks, such as scads and bumpers, are only small forage-size fish while others, like the Pacific yellowtail and the Hawaiian ulua, reach big game proportions. Some jacks travel in deep water while others live on the surface. Some of them are hardly fit to eat—and the crevalle would probably fit in this category—while others, such as the pompano, are among the finest food fishes of all. But no matter how varied are their habits and their eating qualities, one characteristic is certainly true of all of them: they belong to the toughest and most powerful clan in or out of the ocean. And the biggest and

snook or channel bass or maybe even an extralarge trout, but then eventually he feels the steady throbbing or pulsating on his line and he realizes he has hooked a jack. Then later he reels in a jack of only 3 or 4 pounds which was fighting like a 15-pound trout. It can be a terrible disappointment.

Still, every fisherman should catch several large-size jack crevalles simply for the education involved. It's good conversation material. And a good muscle builder, too.

There's little doubt that for strain and endurance no fish in shallow inshore water can measure up to the jack crevalle. Although he's certainly of light tackle size, he can be strong enough to take out much of the sport of light tackle fishing. It's just too strong for its own good. And if you should hook a big one on light tackle you have a day-long job on your hands. Or you can cut your own line.

A jack is as obliging as he is tough. He will strike a wide variety of baits, either trolled or cast, furiously and with the suddenness of a sledgehammer blow. He takes surface plugs and deep-running lures equally well and seems to have a preference for yellow. He will take cut baits and live shrimp fished either on or close to the bottom around bridges and pilings. Quite a

Jack crevalle from Parismina River, Costa Rica. Angler here is Tom McNally, popular Outdoor Editor of the Chicago *Tribune*.

toughest of them all is the amberjack, *Seriola lalandi.*

The world's record amberjack is a 120½-pounder taken in 1955 off Hawaii's Kona coast. The largest Atlantic fish is a 119½-pounder. But it's possible that amberjacks of more than twice that size exist in the waters of the world.

A red snapper fisherman working out of Panama City, Florida, hand-lined an amberfish recently which weighed 146 pounds. But he admitted that he'd lost several others which were considerably larger. From time to time many offshore fishermen in the Gulf of Mexico hook, but are unable to stop or to turn, large fish before they vanish with all the line from a reel. In nearly all cases these are amberjacks.

At times bay and inshore fishermen along the Florida coast, and Louisiana coast around Grand Isle, encounter schools of baby amberjacks which

will average about 18 inches or slightly more in length. Finding and catching these fish is pretty much like finding and catching jack crevalle of the same size.

Ordinarily the larger amberjacks stay close to the outer reefs along our shores and in water from 30 to about 140 feet deep. They prefer the larger, more precipitous reefs which are punctuated with coral caves. Wherever you can find such environment you can usually also find amberjacks. Occasionally charter boats encounter amberjacks around patches of floating weeds in the Gulf Stream while fishing for sailfish.

It isn't a difficult matter to tie into a big amberjack. There are a number of charter boats which specialize in amberjack fishing and it is a good idea to charter such a boat out of Panama City, Miami or Key West. All of these cities are very near to good amberjack water.

Two important methods are used to catch the big amberfish. One is to troll parallel to the reefs, either with live fish, cut bait or with large feather jigs. Perhaps a better and more productive method, especially if the day is reasonably calm, is to drift-fish along the outer reef while using live grunts or live yellowtails for bait. An angler is almost certain to hook several amberjack in a day's time by fishing in this manner. His only problem is to land them.

Suitable tackle should be heavy with at least 24-thread line because the amberjack's fight is a deep-down, relentless, boring effort. Once a jack gets into a cave or a hole in the reef, there is nothing to do but break the line.

Amberjacks seem to be more plentiful on the offshore reefs during winter and spring and it's believed that they move to deeper waters during late summer and fall.

Although amberjack fishing always verges more toward hard labor than it does to fast, exhilarating sport, it has a great fascination for many fishermen because the species grows to such unusual size. And every time an angler wets a line in amberjack water, he has as good a chance as anyone to hook a new world's record fish.

The amberjack is not a bad food fish; its flavor is extremely delicious when smoked. But in Cuba its flesh is considered poisonous and it is against the law to buy or sell amberjacks on that island. In the Bahamas, on the other hand, it is very highly regarded as food.

Another fish which plays fishermen is the horse-eye jack, *Caranx latus,* which is occasionally taken in Florida waters but which is most common in the Bahamas. Its distinguishing characteristic is a large yellow eye and prominent scutes along the lateral line. Unlike the crevalle jack and another cousin, the blue runner, it prefers reefs and offshore waters almost exclusively.

Like the other jacks the horse-eye is a school fish that actively feeds upon small fishes, shrimp and crustaceans. Its average size is about 2 pounds, but it attains a length of 3 feet and a weight of more than 25 pounds. A 10- or 15-pounder, however, is a large horse-eye and a fish of that size can give any angler's tackle a good workout. Horse-eyes will take either dead or live bait fished on the bottom and they will strike either trolled or cast strip baits, feather jigs and spoons.

Because of its appearance, the blue runner has often been called a cross between a bluefish and a crevalle jack but of course there is no foundation for this belief. Actually the blue runner, *Caranx crysos,* is thinner and more streamlined than most of his cousins.

The blue runner ranges along our east coast northward as far as North Carolina, but it is most abundant along the west coast of Florida northward to Biloxi and Mobile Bay. It's present along the beaches, usually on a flood tide when it comes in close to feed on smaller fishes, shrimp and other aquatic life both on the surface and on the bottom. At this time it's also within easy reach of the skiff and bridge fisherman.

A school fish, the blue runner strikes hard on small block-tin squid, on shiny spoons, feather jigs and strip bait. It's a hard fighter for its size and casting, fly or spinning tackle is perfect for this species. A blue runner will average about a pound or pound and a half in weight, but on rare occasions it reaches a length of 24 inches and a weight of 6 pounds.

Besides being valuable to light tackle fishermen as a game fish, the blue runner is also an excellent bait for many of the larger offshore fishes.

Another jack that is often confused with the blue runner is the runner, *Caranx ruber.* It ranges throughout the West Indies and occasionally strays as far north as North Carolina. Unlike the blue runner it is a restless fish which inhabits open water and evidently travels very widely. It's found in great numbers around the Dry Tortugas where it is taken by trolling with small strips of cut bait, with spoons or feather jigs. Runners rarely exceed 15 or 16 inches in length, but on light tackle they are extremely strong and active fish.

Although most jacks are completely unsophisticated in their feeding habits, there is one member of the family—the pompano—which is extremely shy and wary. At times it is almost impossible to approach within casting range of the pompano let alone to tempt him to take a lure.

The pompano, *Trachinotus carolinus,* is taken in good numbers along both coasts of Florida, but its exact range elsewhere hasn't been too clearly defined. A number of them are taken around Cuba and some of the other Caribbean islands, but beyond that nothing much is known.

Most Florida pompano are taken by surf casting in the region from Miami northward to Jacksonville via a unique crossed-bait-trials technique. The bait is usually a sand flea, which is a small crustacean about an inch long. The surf caster can easily find and dig a supply of these flea-shaped baits because they are left behind in the surf by each receding wave. The angler then

Al Rotolo has hooked a heavy jack near Smith Light off Key West. This is a great hot spot for trophy jacks. (*Photo by George Laycock*)

George Laycock with crevalle jacks taken near Smith Shoal off Key West, Florida. (*Photo by George Laycock*)

must catch them before they burrow into the wet sand.

Any of the standard kinds of surf tackle or spinning surf tackle are used, plus a pyramid sinker and a No. 1 hook with a nylon leader.

In this crossed-bait-trials technique the object is to make one cast at an angle to the beach and then retrieve the bait slowly so that the sinker leaves a trail across the sandy bottom. That completed, the fisherman walks farther down the beach and makes another cast designed to cross the trail made by his first retrieve. He then retrieves slowly to make another sinker trail which intersects and crosses the first one.

The final step is to make a cast and try to place the bait at the junction of the two sinker trails, and then to wait and see what happens. In theory, at least, a pompano is figured to have an acute sense of smell and it's further believed that once he discovers one of the sinker trails he will follow it right to the sand flea bait. It does sound ridiculous and although I have never tried it, I understand that it works very well. At least Florida's east coast fishermen catch plenty of pompano this way and if they are unable to find enough sand fleas, shrimp or chunks of clam work almost as well.

Another pompano technique used both by bridge and boat fishermen is jigging. Fishing from bridges, they simply lower a small ⅛-ounce, white or yellow feather jig to the bottom and then jiggle it up and down. No retrieve is made unless an angler intends to move to another spot. He just jigs the bait up and down regularly.

Using spinning gear, which is the most effective of all for pompano, boat fishermen depend on a slightly different technique. The idea is to make a cast, allow the jig to reach the bottom and then to retrieve it ever so slowly just by raising the rod tip and then reeling fast enough to retrieve slack as the rod tip is lowered again.

Pompano are known to be year-round residents of southern Florida waters but they are easiest to catch during migrations north along the coast. The migration along the east coast usually begins in February or March. Along the west coast it's a little later. Pompano arrive in Louisiana and Texas waters in April or May or sometimes as late as June.

These splendid food fishes are seldom taken in water more than 10 feet deep and when they are actively feeding they are seldom farther than 100 yards from shore. During calm weather they tend to remain in deeper waters—or at least not too many of them are taken at that time. But when the surf is fairly heavy, pompano often move right in among the breakers to catch sand fleas and coquinas. Also look for pompano just inside inlets and passes on an incoming tide and just outside the same areas on an outgoing tide.

A 2-pound pompano is a good one, but occasionally they reach 4 or 5 pounds and a length of 20 inches. They're best known as a table fish, but once hooked, a pompano is extremely game. The meat is rich, oily, and it has an incomparable flavor when fresh.

In certain isolated gullies and depressions in the reefs along Florida's east coast, fishermen frequently find another extremely game member of the jack family. It's the African pompano, *Hynnis cubensis*. For the fisherman or charter-boat captain lucky enough to find one of these depressions, there is much excellent fishing in store because these Africans run in small schools and they will strike with abandon, one after another.

The African is a typical tough member of the jack family. It strikes the same kinds of baits and fights the same kind of dogged, throbbing battle. Fairly stout tackle should be used when fishing over a pompano hole because these fish attain a length of almost 36 inches and a weight of about 40 pounds. The average will run between 10 and 15 pounds, however.

Among the smaller Africans, the first signs of the dorsal and anal fins are continued into delicate filaments which stream out behind them but which are almost always lacking in the larger fish, perhaps because they are worn off against rocks and coral. The African pompano is edible, but the flavor of its flesh isn't nearly as delicious as that of the common pompano.

Perhaps the most beautiful member of the jack family is the rainbow runner, *Elagatis bipinnulatus,* which is also called the Spanish jack or Pacific jack. It's most frequently taken in the open-ocean currents or on the extreme outside edges of reefs by fishermen trolling for other species of fish. Its average size is only a few pounds but it does reach a length of 36 inches and a weight of more than 10 pounds.

I've caught rainbow runners in large numbers on the open Pacific off Quepos, Costa Rica, up to 12 or 13 pounds. They were terrific fighters and a few of them made exciting jumps. These fish were taken on everything from yellow feather jigs to streamer flies and bass popping bugs. Elsewhere they've been known to strike extremely large cut strips of bait or large metal spoons.

Practically nothing is known of the life history or the wanderings of the rainbow runner which is elongated in shape and marked with bright blue and yellow stripes which fade quickly after the fish is landed.

Chapter Eight

GRAY GHOST ON THE FLATS

BONEFISH, PERMIT

BONEFISH

My friend John Moxley is the perfect fishing companion. Bad weather, hardship and even reluctant fish seldom disturb his calm and good humor. But best of all he "wears" his great enthusiasm for fishing so that anyone can spot it as easily as a diamond in a dustbin.

John and I had fished pretty much around the world together, for everything from barbels in Tanganyika to Dolly Varden trout in British Columbia, but somehow John had never met the bonefish. He'd read about them, of course, but hadn't seen one alive until the blazing-hot day that Jesús Miró Alejandro Juan Sánchez, our caramel-colored Mayan boatman, deposited us on a vast mud flat inside the strange and remote Boca Paila.

"There," Jesús said with a sweeping gesture, "you see the macabi, the bonefish."

We saw the bonefish, indeed, because the flats were almost working alive with them. And the sight was all the more exciting because we'd traveled far and by a devious route to reach the place. From San Antonio we'd buzzed across the border to Mexico City and then on to Mérida, the whitewashed capital of Yucatán. From Mérida it was an hour's hop to Cozumel, a slumbering Gulf island surrounded by blue sea.

At Cozumel we had to charter a vintage sailing vessel, the *Pez Vela*, to return to the Yucatán mainland and to Boca Paila. It was a wild and woolly crossing over a rough sea which will not be soon forgotten.

Boca Paila is a shallow bay completely protected from the Gulf by a barrier reef and a shifting sandbar. If our route to reach the place seems complicated, it's only because no roads penetrate the eastern Yucatán wilderness. You reach Boca Paila this way or not at all.

"It was worth every bit of travel." John smiled as he advanced confidently toward the nearest tailing fish. "Bonefish here I come!" He carried a light spinning outfit with a Phillips wiggle jig on the business end.

"Good luck," I said, wading calf-deep into the lukewarm water not too far away.

A school of bones turned slowly toward John, leaving a wake of milky silt behind them. The minute they were in range, John aimed, cast and . . . the bones flushed like a frightened covey of quail. John quickly retrieved his empty lure.

A few minutes later I noticed from the corner of my eye that the same thing happened again. Then two, three, four more times it happened while I landed a pair of 3-pounders, releasing each one. That's when John came sloshing in my direction.

"What in the hell," he asked, "am I doing wrong?" He really had a hangdog look.

"Cast far enough ahead of and away from the bones so as not to alarm them," I said.

"Here," I continued, "where they probably haven't seen a fisherman before, you can cast fairly close. But never, absolutely never, cast behind or into a school.

"Your lure should be delivered so that it can be retrieved just ahead of the feeding school. Do that as slowly as you can, without snagging on the bottom, and you should get action." I guess I sounded like an elementary school teacher.

As any bonefisherman knows, that advice was greatly oversimplified. But it's a good place to begin, and ten minutes later from across the flat, John gave a loud yahoo you could have heard thirty miles away in Cozumel. In the same instant his rod bent dangerously and a silvery ghostlike fish went streaking across the flat with all the stops pulled out.

"Yahoo!" John shouted again.

Before that busy afternoon was finished, John had hooked ten bones, of which he landed eight, and had spooked ten times that many. But in the process he suddenly discovered the knack, or the secret, of presenting a lure or a bait to a bonefish. And at the same time a whole new world of fishing pleasure was opened up to him, because bonefish are certainly among the finest game fish on the face of the earth.

They're neither the strongest fish nor the fastest, but they rate high on both counts. Bonefish never jump. They are wary, mildly unpredictable and splendid long-distance runners once they're hooked. And most of all they're widely available in many warm saltwaters of the Americas.

Here is one fish you see before, during and after the strike. If you happen to be a serious trout fisherman somehow transplanted to the salt, the odds are good that the bonefish will become your favorite fish. I've known completely addicted trout fishermen who never again raised a rod for trout after dueling with the first bonefish. The thrill is contagious.

Bones belong to a vast breed of herringlike fishes, which means that the ladyfish and tarpon are among their first cousins. But except for slight similarities in appearance and structure, they're different from their more acrobatic relatives in everything from general behavior to feeding habits.

It has been said and written that bones are strictly shallow-water feeders, but I don't be-lieve it. Recently in British Honduras, our party caught them in numbers in a deep channel among mangrove "islands" while casting both jigs and live bait for other species of fish. Most bonefish of the Hawaiian Islands are also taken in deep water. But I'll admit that they spend long periods in shallow waters, on alcohol-clear flats, and during these periods they usually seem to be feeding or cruising in search of food. Since this is the only time that fishermen really see them, it's easy to assume that they feed exclusively in such a shallow habitat.

But the point still remains, for all practical purposes, that the best and only place to fish for bones is in completely transparent water from a few inches to no more than 2 or 3 feet deep. In such environment as that, any fish is bound to be skittish and timid. Obviously an angler must use a careful, cautious approach to hook them.

In heavily fished areas, bonefish do become sophisticated and therefore extra caution is necessary to score. Perhaps this accounts for the widely circulated idea that bonefish are only for experts—that they're hard to fool, hard to hook

Successful bonefishermen near Marathon in the Florida Keys. Fish were taken on fly rods. (*Photo by Miami News Bureau*)

and hard to land once hooked. But little of this is true.

"I haven't found bones especially hard to fool," Phil Francis once told me, "not even with artificials."

Phil is one of the busiest and best anglers in Florida. He was one of a handful of light-tackle pioneers in that state and although there is no way to confirm it, he would be high on the list of anglers who have caught the most bonefish. That includes the largest bonefish taken anywhere on light spinning tackle in 1953 in *Field & Stream's* annual contest.

"They're no tougher to trick than most other fish in clear water," Phil says. "Naturally it's easier to fool small ones than big ones. But even the old-timers become careless and their antics when chasing a bit of hardware can be ridiculous to see."

Here's how a bonefish behaves on the flats. Generally he cruises against or angles into the tide, digging and grubbing in the mud bottom for crabs, shellfish, mollusks or whatever. Sometimes an individual seems to pick up every object he finds, mouthing it before he either swallows or spits it out again. Maybe it's this habit of sampling everything that makes him grab an artificial lure that has none of the "odor" or "feel" of a live critter.

Still another misconception often repeated is that bonefish feed only on a rising tide, but that just isn't the case. It *is* likely that they prefer to feed on a rising tide on a certain flat, or maybe on a whole chain of flats. But elsewhere they prefer falling tides or even slack tides. Just as there are certain flats where fishing is most productive at high tide, so are others most "alive" during a retreating tide and still others are best during half tide.

But no matter what the tide, fishing for bones, which is as much hunting as fishing, is a fascinating game of wits and testing one's eyesight. Except for that incident in a British Honduras channel, I've never caught a bonefish I didn't spot beforehand. Sometimes it is only a gray or dark shadow that an angler sees. Just as often it's the tip of a tail, or maybe even the whole tail breaking the surface as a bone moves about with his snout poking into the mud. In either case there's a definite knack to spotting the movement. It's tricky at first, but all at once an angler with average eyesight catches on; from

that day hence he can spot most of the bones within his range. The more spotting experience, the better.

Except on the dullest days, both beginners and veterans of the flats find that glasses which reduce glare are absolutely invaluable to reduce eyestrain as well as to reveal fish "camouflaged" underwater. I'd say such glasses are almost as important as a reel in bonefishing.

Bonefish can be taken in good weather or bad weather (with a sudden cold spell having the worst effect), but the ideal time to see them, as well as to catch them, is in early morning or late evening when the surface is slick and calm. Then their antics are more readily visible for longer distances. And if you happen to have the low sun at your back, there's an added advantage, because the same sun is in the eye of the bone. That seems to make him less selective when following your lure.

These gray ghosts or white foxes (as implied by the scientific name, *Albula vulpes*) are sometimes as curious as fish can be. Often they follow lures they have no intention of striking and this can grow gray hairs on any angler. On days when this happens frequently, the pressure and the suspense becomes so great you can hardly stand it. But the characteristic curiosity goes even farther. When poling across a flat, I've flushed bones, only to see them run, make a wide circle and come up behind the skiff to see what chased them in the first place. Occasionally a follower can be caught.

No bonefish, or macabi (Spanish) or banana fish (from the tapered snout?) or boneyhead (as on Grand Cayman Island) or sanducha (as the Cubans call it) is as impressive in appearance as it is game. It's odd-looking rather than formidable as are tarpon and marlin. The color is white chromium, shading to pale olive on the back. But most distinctive is the armor-plated, abrasion-resistant head with a pointed, almost piglike snout. Inside the head is a matched set of grinders stout enough to convert the toughest crab shell into digestible vitamins. This mechanism can also, in time, reduce a fishhook to basic metal.

Even the most garrulous guides of the Florida Keys speak softly when roving across bonefish flats. This might be an indication of a bone's keen hearing, but most ichthyologists doubt it's *that* keen. Still, a bone will react to the slightest

The Overseas Highway, US 1, passes hundreds of square miles of bonefish flats from Key Largo to Key West. Light-colored areas are shallow flats. (*Photo by Florida State News Bureau*)

scuffling or vibration from a boat. The eyesight is extremely sharp too. And from the manner a hungry bone can locate live bait from far, far away, it's obvious that it has a most acute sense of smell. Which brings us to baits and how to use them.

There's a technique with which anybody can catch a bonefish if he can first locate the fish. It is far from the most exciting way, but it *is* deadly. Simply bait up with a fresh shrimp, alive or dead, and then toss it ahead of, and up-tide of, a feeding fish. Then just sit back and wait for the bone to find it, which he will surely do. It may be tiresome and nerve-racking, but if your purpose is to catch a bonefish by any means, this is your best bet.

Bonefish can even be baited. Sometimes a few shrimp are scattered about a flat to attract them and to start them feeding. Then all at once a bone picks up a shrimp that happens to have a hook embedded in it. The fisherman raises his rod sharply and the reel sings.

Still another baiting technique is to take a live conch and crush the shell, leaving the meat inside. Eventually bones will find it and, seemingly frustrated at being unable to eat the contents, will become aroused and search frantically about for something they *can* swallow. Perhaps what they finally settle for is a bait or a bucktail jig.

Light spinning tackle—say a 6-foot, fairly stiff rod with 6- or 8-pound test line on the reel—is the best bet for an average angler, no matter whether he's using live bait or counterfeits. If it's bait, he just casts it ahead of his fish as described before and thereby tests his patience. If it's an artificial, he casts and tries to retrieve it in a rather slow, enticing manner beyond the bonefish's snout. Bones have been hooked on a variety of lures, but only a few are very effective and the jig, from ⅛ to ¼ ounce in size, is far ahead of all the rest.

Naturally all jigs in those sizes are not suitable. A productive flat may contain everything from ribbon grass and oyster beds to coral tips and fans, so a lure must be designed to wiggle through these obstacles as well as run shallow rather than deep when retrieved in a slow, erratic manner. In other words, the metal head of the jig must be flattened horizontally rather than be round or bullet-shaped, for the best performance.

The first of these flat-bodied jigs I ever tried was a homemade model with orange bucktail and peacock herl tail. It was designed by Captain Bill Smith of Islamorada, Florida, and it was deadly. Now there's a similar lure on the market called "Wiggle Jig." Manufactured by the Phillips Fly and Tackle Company of Alexandria, Pennsylvania, it's the most reliable of all commercial bonefish lures available nowadays.

Another type of spinning jig with a dished-out or concave head, and with a marabou tail, was recently reported as very effective on grassy Bahamas flats by Al McClane, fishing editor of *Field & Stream*. It should work elsewhere, too.

Phil Francis has been able to take bones on the same type of pickled pork frog used by freshwater bass fishermen, and some moderate success has attended the use of the new, soft

plastic lures also meant for freshwater species. It might be that more experimentation with the plastics would be worthwhile.

Fly fishing for bonefish differs from spinning only in the basic tackle used. The approach, the presentation of the lure and the retrieve are virtually the same. You simply substitute a fly for a jig or chunk of bait. And the best fly almost wherever it's used is a Pink Shrimp, also made by Phillips. The fly was inspired by author-angler Joe Brooks, who possibly has taken more bones on flies than any other angler alive.

Other effective fly patterns are the hackle or bucktail streamers in size 1 or 1/0, perhaps in all white or all yellow, with or without plastic "heads" and eyes. In areas where bones seem especially spooky, a streamer dropped gently in the water will cause much less alarm than any heavier spinning lures.

Catching a bonefish on a fly isn't a feat beyond the ability of an average fisherman. It's unfortunate that this is a common impression. An angler *does* need somewhat different equipment for fly-casting the salt, but with that equipment and the ability to use it, he can catch as many bonefish as a spincaster.

The critical item of either spinning or fly-casting tackle is the reel. (*But this point is true and vitally important when fishing for most species of saltwater game fish.*) It must be well built and sturdy enough to take a terrible beating. It must have a smooth, entirely dependable drag. And it must have sufficiently large line capacity. The reel is the critical item of tackle.

For bonefish particularly, you need a spinning reel spool that can hold 200 yards of 6-pound line. It doesn't hurt to have even more, because you could conceivably hook a permit that might run even farther and faster. A good trick is to tie a short length of 8-pound or 10-pound nylon between the lure and the regular 6-pound line with a blood knot. This arrangement will stand more wear and tear when a bonefish is hooked.

The fly-fisherman will want a big, single-action reel, such as one of the larger Medalists, to hold 200 yards of 18-pound to 20-pound backing line as well as the casting line.

You do not need a guide to catch bonefish, but if you can afford it, why not engage one? An experienced guide can save plenty of valuable time lost by searching about, which means you can spend more time fishing. He will also

Angler on a bonefish flat—Tom McNally at Grand Cayman Island. Many bones here.

eliminate much uncertainty by knowing which flats are best at which times of day. And of course a guide can eliminate much of the drudgery of the sport, such as poling a skiff across the flats, obtaining bait, etc. But, even so, a guide isn't necessary, particularly if you are an adventuresome sort of angler.

According to Phil Francis: "I've had my most exciting days with bones in the Florida Keys. I'd maybe rent a boat at Key Largo and ask the liveryman where the bones had been active. He'd tell me and I'd go looking for them. A few times I've been blanked, but usually I have plenty of action."

If you're fishing alone, you have two choices. Stand in your boat and drift with the wind across the flats—or put on a pair of sneakers and go wading. In either case, watch the water all around you with relaxed eyes (if that's possible), trying to look *through* the water rather than studying the surface. Again it's well to emphasize that polaroid glasses are invaluable. When you spot anything, even a shadow or an unidentifiable movement, make a cast just in case. You'll make mistakes and cast at ghosts, but they're worth the occasions when a shadow suddenly reacts like a genuine, live bonefish.

With only a few exceptions, the various great game fish we've discussed are hard, vicious strikers. Sometimes every fish in a school (as I've seen among dolphin, jacks, mackerel, tarpon) will race for the bait. I've seen schools of bonefish do it too, but only rarely. Nine days in ten they're dainty rather than savage strikers, a good point to remember, because it's so easy to strike too swiftly when you can see the whole show. With most other fishes, it's more common not to strike swiftly enough.

Playing and landing a hooked bonefish isn't too difficult and sometimes it's not even too ex-

Bonefishermen on a Bermuda beach. Author (left) and Joe Brooks, internationally known angler.

citing. There's nothing to do but hold the rod high overhead. The structure and texture of a bone's mouth is such that a hook seldom pulls out, so if you allow your fish to make its first long run with only a light drag, half the battle is won. Other runs will follow, but they're progressively shorter and weaker and you can progressively tighten the drag.

The gray ghost is an internationalist who has been caught in such widely separated latitudes as South Africa, Japan, Cape Hatteras and the Red Sea. But it's in the warm shallows of tropical America that the species is most abundant, or at least most available to fishermen.

Bones grow big and ultrasophisticated around Bermuda, where they're seen most often along white sand beaches. Live bait is the proper medicine here. They're not so big, but far more numerous in the Bahamas. The flats encircling Grand Bahama Island, especially at West End, are great and so are most of those about huge, lonely Andros Island to the south. Not so well known are Crab Creek on Munjack and the mossy flats of Angel Fish Creek on Little Abaco Island.

Add also these hot spots in the Bahamas: Green Turtle Cay and Sandy Point on Great Abaco Island, Cat Cays; the Biminis; Harbour Island, Spanish Wells and Rock Sound on Eleuthera; Pot Cay and near Andros Town on Andros Island. No doubt there are others still to be "discovered."

I've caught bones off Grand Cayman and at Cuba's wonderful Isle of Pines when visiting there was a happier experience than it would be now. Fidel Castro seized the fishing fleets as quickly as the banks and sugar mills. Elsewhere around mainland Cuba there is extraordinary bonefishing, with many suitable waters on the south and east coasts of the island all but unexplored. Some fishing also exists around Puerto Rico (around the island's southwest quadrant, mostly), the Virgin and Windward islands and along the Mexican coast.

But even though the modern bonefisherman is a widely ranging species, the Florida Keys region—from Key Largo southward to the Dry Tortugas—remains the Mecca of the most serious and devoted. Fishing may be better elsewhere, but this is where it all began and this is where nearly all return someday.

In 1909 the Matecumbe Club was built at a spot on Upper Matecumbe Key now known as Islamorada. It was built by a dozen anglers interested in bonefish and nothing else. Irvin S. Cobb was an early guest there. At the same place, exactly forty years later, Joe Brooks began to demonstrate for writers, photographers, guides and fisherman alike that Keys bones were great light tackle and fly-rod fish. His demonstrations started an avalanche of visiting fishermen. So the tradition has grown.

But no matter what the locale, every bonefisherman eventually finds that the sport is far more than just finding and catching the elusive gray ghosts. It's feeling the warm water wash your feet as you stroll across a strange aquatic pasture. It's stopping to watch sea urchins in the ribbon grass or guitar-shaped ray making a jet stream in its frantic dash to escape. It might be the sight of roseate spoonbills flying to roost in a sunset or the more formidable spectacle of a sawfish meandering across your path.

Bonefishing is all these things—and more.

PERMIT

Not too many years ago, the permit (*Trachinotus goodei*), which is the largest member of the pompano family, was scarcely known to fishermen. But in recent seasons the growing number of bonefishermen who spin- and fly-cast the vast flats around the Florida Keys have found it a frequent resident of many of the finest bonefish waters. It's encountered on many flats between Government Cut at Miami Beach and the Dry Tortugas. Elsewhere it's found on flats encircling Cuba and along the Central American coast from Yucatan southward to Nicaragua.

The permit likes its flats a little deeper than does a bonefish. It also likes them to be closer to deep water. But it can be caught on these flats in the same manner as a bonefish, which means with crabs, crawfish, conch or hermit crabs for bait.

But a permit is incredibly shy, spooky and completely unpredictable. Unlike the more accommodating bone, it does not appear to frequent the same flats day in and day out. Although permit will, on occasion, take such artificial lures as bonefish jigs and streamer flies, only a relatively few of them have been taken in this manner.

When a permit is hooked, there is no tougher,

The Mexican Pompano, or Permit, is but one of many species caught by charter boats working out of Tampa and vicinity. (*Photo by Florida State News Bureau*)

faster fish anywhere in the lukewarm shallows. The first run is followed by one after another of equally long runs until a fisherman believes he has hooked a fish several times its size. The average size of a permit is between 10 and 15 pounds but there are 30- and 40-pounders available. Perhaps they even grow in excess of 60 pounds, if anybody cares to tackle anything so formidable.

Although the permit is most exciting to catch on shallow flats, a fisherman's best bet is to look for him elsewhere. The channels or passes, and the deep waterholes of bays along both Florida coasts are the best specific types of water to search. On the east coast, permit range northward as far as Fort Pierce. On the west coast, where the species is popularly known as the Mexican pompano, it ranges northward past Panama City, Apalachicola and Pensacola, and maybe completely across the Gulf Coast to Brownsville, Texas.

Chapter Nine

THE DEEP AND DELICIOUS FISH
SNAPPERS, GROUPERS

SNAPPERS

One of the wildest, woolliest nights I've ever spent, developed because I wanted to please a Cuban cook.

I was fishing aboard Vic Barothy's houseboat, the *Jucaro*, off the Isle of Pines, which then was an angler's haven but now is a vast concentration camp. Vic and I had spent several great days of light-tackle fishing for tarpon and bonefish. But when we returned to the houseboat one evening, chef Albert Whittaker confronted us.

"Them boney fish," he began, "are good for nothing. You never bring back no eatin' fish."

"Why don't you just catch some eating fish, yourself?" Vic suggested.

"That I do, sir," Albert smiled. "Tonight."

Somehow I wound up in the skiff with Albert an hour or two after dark. We outboarded from the moored houseboat to a nameless tidal river. Albert had heavy boat fishing tackle and I had my saltwater spinning outfit with a Sea Star reel. Between us was a supply of dead mullet for bait.

"I figures," Albert said, "that we drifts these mullets with the tide and right away we gets customers."

Albert surely figured right.

After baiting up, the cook gave a mighty heave and the mullet plunked noisily far out in the black. For a few seconds nothing happened, then Albert's reel fairly whistled as line raced away.

"I has him," Albert announced.

What Albert had at the other end of the line was almost more than he could handle. He grunted and groaned like a wrestler in a headlock and it was a long, long time before he began to move his fish toward the boat. But eventually by persistence and brute strength, Albert managed to land the fish, a mangrove snapper of over 20 pounds. And the minute it was in the boat, it bit right through his thumb when he tried to remove the hook.

Vic, who was sleeping soundly on the houseboat, said he heard Albert holler several hundred yards away.

But that was only the beginning. A few minutes later I hooked a big snapper, which broke off when it managed to get into the mangrove jungle at the edge of the channel. As soon as I replaced my hook and bait, I had another strike and ten or fifteen minutes later landed it. It was a snapper of about 12 pounds.

"That," Albert said, sucking his thumb, "is what I call eatin' fish."

In that same instant his reel screamed and he barely caught his rod on its way overboard.

In the next hour we were besieged by snappers. But then a school of small tarpon moved into the channel and on almost every cast they would grab the mullet before the snappers could get to them. It was really crazy the way they cavorted and performed out in the darkness. One tarpon almost jumped in Albert's face and that's when he said he had enough.

"Let's go home now," is the way he put it. "Tarpon just ain't no good to eat."

But that isn't the only memorable experience I've had with mangrove snappers. Here is a fine fish which is widely distributed along both Florida coasts, on many offshore reefs and inside waters around mangrove shores throughout the Caribbean. Probably the mangrove is the gamest member of a large family of snappers which live around the world. It's almost as strong as any jack of equal size, and it's a clever fish besides.

Ichthyologists assure us that fish behave or react by instinct or by impulse alone. But many snappers seem to be able to think, especially in heavily fished waters.

Fish for snappers in wilderness waters such as the numerous tidal rivers of Andros Island,

Author with a 4-pound mangrove snapper caught on a Bermuda reef. Fish was chummed close to the boat with hog-mouthed fry.

Bahamas, or at night, and the snappers may actually strike with abandon. But try them around the docks which they frequent in great numbers in busy Florida fishing areas and all but the smallest specimens ignore everything, live or artificial, which contains a hook.

Mangrove snappers seem to thrive in numerous environments, over deep and shallow reefs, in the surf, in bays and lagoons, in creeks and rivers and occasionally they will even ascend into fairly fresh water. Any mangrove snapper prefers cover and, as the name suggests, will often be found under mangrove roots along deep mangrove shorelines. Channel markers, bridges, piers and docks are also favorite hiding places.

The average mangrove snapper taken on hook and line in Florida waters will weigh only a pound or less, but the species becomes more wary and more wise with each ounce of weight it gains. A 5-pound snapper is an extremely good one and 10-pounders are quite rare in Florida. Twenty-five to 30 pounds is about the maximum for the species.

Where fishing pressure is fairly light, the mangrove will strike a variety of surface plugs as well as deep-running plugs, trolled feathers and strips of natural bait. It will also take a yellow or red streamer fly when it is cast in close to mangrove banks.

A particularly effective pattern of streamer fly is that which has a heavy lead-wrapped body which permits it to sink quickly before being retrieved. Mangroves will also take almost anything in the line of natural bait, but they seem to prefer shrimp above all other items.

Although mangroves remain meticulously close to cover or to shade during daylight hours, they do begin to cruise out into the open as soon as night falls. During the day an angler should keep his cast close to any of the likely places mentioned before, casting beyond a reef and drawing his lure or bait over the top of it. In the case of fishing mangrove shorelines, the lure or bait should be delivered as far back underneath the overhanging branches as possible.

The mangrove snappers found around piers and docks are wise almost beyond belief. They will feed upon anything that is thrown overboard, except a morsel that has a hook in it. Many a first-time visitor to Florida has had the experience of dropping bits of fish to the snappers, including one that has a completely hidden hook. Invariably the snappers will eat all but that one morsel.

Although the mangrove is quite game, no special tackle is needed to catch the fish. Ordinary casting, spinning or fly-casting tackle are adequate. When fishing especially for snappers, I use 8- or 10-pound line and a wire leader about 15 inches long. No matter whether the bait is natural or artificial, it's necessary to strike immediately and try to horse the fish away from protective cover. A large percentage of the larger snappers hooked escape by dodging back into a coral formation or into the mangrove roots. Then there is nothing left to do but break the line.

Except around piers and docks, chumming for mangrove snappers can be an extremely effective method. I've seen it work a number of times and particularly well off the Bermuda reefs. The idea is to toss bits of mullet, whole hog-mouthed fry or shrimp chum into the water, a small amount at a time until the snappers arrive to eat the free handout.

Ordinarily, snapper waters are clear enough so that you can see the fish approach and begin to feed. As more and more fish appear, increase the amount of chum until they begin to compete recklessly among themselves for the food. Then without interrupting the chumming, toss in one piece with a hook attached.

It's a good idea to use monofilament line with a small hook and without a sinker. Make the snapper forget his natural caution and beat his brethren in the race for a free dinner by making the bait look as much like the free-floating pieces of chum as possible.

It is interesting to note here that mangrove snappers have what is called a "feeding line." (So do amberjacks and a few other species.) When not aroused, a snapper may seem completely pale in color. But a black or dark diagonal line which runs across the face and through the eyes begins to develop as soon as the mangrove snapper begins to feed. And the more actively it feeds (as on chum tossed overboard), the longer and darker the feeding line becomes.

However, chumming can be a nuisance, and often it requires large amounts of bait. Anyway, there's another method which is sometimes quite effective in taking larger snappers. This also requires a good supply of either dead or live mullet.

Using a hook as large as 4/0, cast out a mullet and let it settle into likely snapper water. Ordinarily you will feel the inevitable biting and nibbling of small snappers. But ignore these. Do not strike. If the nibbles stop, reel in your line and put on a fresh bait. Then cast it again. Eventually a larger snapper than the nibblers will come along, chase the smaller snappers away and take your bait. The theory here is that a large snapper can't stand by indefinitely while smaller fish enjoy a free meal.

Snappers will take feather and bucktail jigs on occasion, especially at night. But it has been said that any snapper, once it reaches a foot in length, can tell every artificial lure by its trade name, catalog number, size and retail price. Perhaps that's the reason why they seem to prefer the most bedraggled, chewed-up jig it's possible to find.

While fishing in Florida's Marco Pass area, I assembled quite a stringer of snappers with an Upperman bucktail jig from which all the paint had been chipped and on which only a few strands of white bucktail remained.

Besides the mangrove, fishermen frequently meet four other members of the snapper family; the red, mutton, schoolmaster and lane snappers. The mutton snapper is caught along both Florida coasts, but it is much more numerous along the east side. It's an extremely beautiful fish which can make chameleonlike changes of color, ranging from pale pink to lemon yellow and olive green. It's caught offshore, most often on hard or rocky bottoms where it mingles with groupers and other common bottom fish.

The average mutton snapper may only weigh 2 pounds, but occasionally it runs as long as 2 feet and as heavy as 25 pounds. Like all the other snappers, its flesh is white, firm and among the best available in the sea. It's excellent when cooked in almost any fashion, and it's especially good in chowder.

Occasionally the schoolmaster snapper is caught inshore around the Florida Keys, but more often it's found around Florida Keys outer reefs. It reaches its greatest abundance in Bahamas waters.

Toothed like the mangrove snapper and even more wary about striking, it will sometimes take streamer flies. But it much prefers live shrimp or cut bait. Grayish in color with lemon fins, it strikes hard and fights stubbornly in the manner

Anglers on charter bottom-fishing boat. Catch will include snappers, groupers, grunts, rockfish. (Photo by Florida State News Bureau)

of its cousin. The schoolmaster will only average a pound or so in weight. Ordinarily those found on the reef will run larger than those found inshore around bridges and piers. The top recorded weight in Florida waters is about 8 pounds.

The brilliantly colored lane snapper is seldom found farther north than Big Pine Key in Florida waters. It's quite numerous in the Dry Tortugas and reaches its greatest abundance in Cuban waters and along the Yucatán coast of the Gulf of Mexico. The lane is a school fish which seems to prefer sandy bottoms where tidal currents are fairly strong. It also likes to loiter in deep cuts or channels close to the mangroves.

In the Marquesas Keys—west of Key West—and in the Dry Tortugas, large schools of small lanes are known to cruise about in sheltered waters. These cruisers usually average less than a pound. A 2-pounder is a large lane snapper and probably the maximum weight is about 4 pounds.

Lanes will strike quite a number of different artificial lures including surface plugs, bass bugs and small, deep-running spoons. They will take streamer flies with complete abandon and seem unable to resist either a live or a dead shrimp. Light fly tackle is perfect for these fish because of their small size and their willingness to take small lures. Many fishermen consider it the most delicious of all fishes on the table.

More than likely, red snappers are the most abundant of all members of the snapper family. They're also among the most stupid, and nothing more than a stout handline and a supply of meat is necessary to catch them, once a school or a bank of red snappers has been located. These snapper concentrations or banks are scattered all through the Gulf of Mexico, and snapper smacks with large crews aboard fish for them almost the year around in extremely deep offshore waters. In an average year they land about 4 million pounds of this delicious fish. The average size will be about 5 pounds, but reds have been known to reach 40 and 45 pounds.

Along the east coast of Florida from Fort Pierce northward to the St. Marys River, red snappers are also found on offshore banks, but farther south along the Florida east coast the species is replaced on the reefs by mutton snappers. Although a handline is the most handy and effective way to catch snappers, it is possible to use fairly heavy boat tackle, with a heavy sinker to reach the bottom quickly. They will strike at cut bait, shrimp, fish entrails or almost anything of this sort.

The flesh of the red snapper is white, firm, delicate and world famous. It can be cooked in any manner, but it is best when poached or baked and served with a tart cream sauce.

Bottom fishermen in the Caribbean and the extreme southern Florida Keys encounter still another snapper, the dog snapper which may weigh more than 100 pounds. It's found in company with groupers in deep water along outer reefs.

GROUPERS

Groupers of one species or another are found from North Carolina southward to South America. Here they provide an incalculable amount of sport and high quality food for bottom fishermen. Some groupers such as the Warsaw run to prodigious size, reaching several hundred pounds in weight, while others are quite small. But the most common in South Atlantic and Caribbean waters is the red grouper.

Brown or brownish rather than red in exterior color, this heavy-bodied grouper is named because the inside of its mouth is a bright orange-red. It's plentiful around most Florida inshore and offshore reefs and sometimes on hard or rocky bottoms in between. Although it will only average about a pound in sheltered water, it may average 5 pounds or more around offshore reefs. The maximum weight of a red grouper will be about 40 or 45 pounds and a 40-pounder will be about 3 feet long.

Reef fishermen can hardly help but catch groupers because this fish will take cut bait thumped along the bottom and it will strike at feathers or other lures trolled over rock patches or coral heads. Red groupers feed on small fishes, shrimp, crayfish, crabs, in fact on anything. The species isn't exactly notable for its lively fighting qualities, but it is extremely strong and on light or medium tackle becomes quite a sturdy opponent.

I have taken red groupers, including some good ones up to 12 and 15 pounds, while casting with jigs along mangrove shorelines. It is only possible to land a small percentage of the big reds hooked in this manner because they immediately dive back into the protective cover of the mangrove roots and then it's all over.

Red groupers are extremely tasty, but they should be skinned and filleted before preparing for the table. The meat is excellent for chowder.

The Nassau grouper is most common in southern Florida waters, particularly in the Keys area. It's taken only infrequently north of Tampa and Fort Pierce, and in those areas, only on the deepest offshore reefs. It has a habit of schooling up with red and mutton snappers. As in all groupers, the mouth is extremely large and it contains several sharp caninelike teeth. In deep offshore waters it will average about 5 or 10 pounds and it attains a maximum length of about 3 feet and weight of about 40 pounds.

The Nassau contains small scales which are set tightly in a tough skin. In deep places it can easily be chummed up close to the boat and held there as long as it's possible to provide a free meal with pieces of chopped chum. Although this is strictly a bottom fish, it will occasionally rise and become hooked on trolled spoons or large jigs. Most Nassau groupers are caught, however, on trolled whole fish or on chunks of cut bait.

The black grouper is found completely around Florida, at many points along both coasts. On the west coast where it is most abundant, it is the most numerous fish, except perhaps for the mullet. It will average less than 5 pounds in size, but quite often it's caught in 10- to 50-pound sizes. It attains a known weight of 60 pounds and possibly much more.

Along Florida's west coast, the black grouper never ventures very far from reefs, hard bottoms, or rocky bank areas. Here the best bait is a live shiner, a live yellowtail or a live grunt. It's wise to use stiff rods and fairly heavy tackle because the black grouper has a nasty habit of boring deep into underwater caves as soon as it is hooked.

On the east coast and particularly along the Keys, the black grouper is caught by trolling with strip baits, spoons or feathered jigs. Its strike is very hard and sudden. After the strike, it immediately bores straight down to find protection in a reef or rock pile. Trolling tackle should include at least 30-pound test line and maybe more because once the black gets into a hole it's difficult to pry it loose. Sometimes drift fishing with small live fish, crabs, crayfish or shrimp is effective, but extremely heavy tackle must be used to horse the fish upward immediately after the strike.

The yellow grouper is one of the smallest and most beautiful members of the family. It exists in an almost endless number of color phases which makes it extremely difficult to distinguish from other groupers, from rock hind and even from other rockfish. The yellow grouper seldom wanders very far from offshore reefs, and it is most abundant in the Bahamas where it is caught by still-fishing or by trolling. It is less frequently taken in the Florida Keys.

Another resident of the offshore reefs which bottom fishermen frequently catch is the multi-colored and spotted rock hind. Its red spots are a distinguishing characteristic and these spots never change, even though the rest of the body frequently changes from gray to green or olive and brown. The average size of the rock hind would be less than 2 pounds, and it is doubtful that the fish ever exceeds 8 pounds in weight. It's most abundant in the Florida Keys, but it is occasionally taken along the lower east coast from Palm Beach to Miami.

From the standpoint of size, one of the most impressive fishes in our warm saltwaters and all over the Gulf of Mexico is the spotted jewfish. A resident of rocky offshore reefs, tideways and deep holes, the jewfish also likes the shelter of pilings, bridge abutments, underwater caves and offshore drilling rigs. Occasionally it is also found under the roots of mangroves in tidal channels. It's extremely abundant in the Florida Keys area and in many places along the Florida, Alabama, Mississippi and Louisiana Gulf Coast. Another hot spot is the Florida Ten Thousand Islands area. So is the Panama City area.

Jewfish will average from 15 to about 25 pounds. They have been taken up to 700 pounds on cut bait and shrimp fished right on the bottom. Although the jewfish would seem to be slow and sluggish, it strikes readily at feather jigs and strip baits trolled near the surface, over either inshore or offshore reefs. The strike of a large jewfish is sudden, and it feels as if the

This 225-pound jewfish was taken near Key West. (Photo by Florida State News Bureau)

bait had become hung on the bottom.

Among the best live baits for jewfish are grunt, yellowtails, catfish and crayfish. It goes without saying that extremely heavy tackle is necessary to raise these giants from the bottom. Fishermen who make jewfishing a specialty use ¼-inch manila rope with a heavy chain leader and hand-forged hooks. A good spot to tie into a jewfish is on the outer east end of a rocky pier or jetty.

There are quite a number of other fishes which might be included in the deep and delicious category and which bottom fishermen are certain to encounter in our warm saltwaters on the Atlantic side of North America. Actually, the list is too long to describe in any detail. But some of the more common species are: the grunts, of which there are 14 species in Florida waters; the southern and grass porgy; the margate fish, which is sometimes called pompom; the gaff-topsail catfish; the porkfish, hogfish, and squirrelfish. All of these are extremely good to eat and on light tackle are great fun to catch.

Chapter Ten

THE MYSTERIOUS STRIPERS

Years ago this writer spent many weekends on singing trout streams with Sid Rowbotham. And a more serious, devoted, zealous, fanatic trout fisherman never lived than old Sid. He was one of the best anglers ever to wade Michigan's elegant Au Sable and Boardman rivers, but suddenly one day his career as a trout fisherman came to an abrupt end. It happened because he went to visit his brand-new son-in-law in Providence, Rhode Island.

The son-in-law simply took old Sid surf-casting one golden evening and as luck would have it, he connected with a hefty striped bass just as twilight fell on the ocean. In that instant the old boy was hooked as surely as the bass he caught. He never picked up his fly rod again, at least not to catch trout.

Sid Rowbotham wasn't the first fisherman ever to jump the fence because striped bass have a habit of unsettling otherwise average fishermen. Striper fishermen trudge miles and miles along sandy shorelines to reach a bit of booming surf, just on mere rumor that striped bass have gathered there. It also causes them to creep and crawl over barnacle-encrusted rocks without regard for life or limb. Many will fish day and night until fatigue alone causes them to doze for an hour or so before returning to the beaches. It causes the faithful to mire and slide on muddy riverbanks or precarious jetties and to spend long hours on the slippery deck of a boat tossed by high seas.

Let it be understood, however, that the antics of a striper fan no matter how strange or how strenuous they seem, are far more wholesome than those of a spectator sportsman. It's a wise man who chooses fishing—any kind of fishing— to becoming part of the howling mob at a baseball or football game. He'll live a longer and healthier life.

It's easy to pinpoint the reasons for a striper's tremendous appeal to fishermen. There are other fish which grow bigger and still others which fight harder. A few are more handsome, and some are more difficult to catch. A very, very few are better on the table, but not many species rate so high in all these categories. A striped bass is a great game fish which has almost everything.

You can take stripers from the beach or by trolling for them offshore. You can catch them in protected tidal waters and inlets, and on all types of lures from tiny flies to thick chunks of crab. If the striper has one most outstanding characteristic, it's in the vast number of ways you can fish for him and the great variety of tackle you can use.

Say, for example, you're a heavy-tackle man trolling offshore. Usually a big spoon or plug will tie you into a big fish. If you like light tackle— if you are a flycaster or spinning fan—the inshore bays, channels and estuaries of many coastal rivers will give you all the action you need. In addition, it's even possible to still-fish for stripers from an anchored boat, from a beach or pier, using anything for bait from shedder crabs, squid and eels to sandworms, shrimp or clams. The striper will eat anything he can swallow.

But no method of catching stripers packs all the high adventure and excitement of casting for them in the wild, wind-whipped surf. This can mean fishing with natural baits or with such counterfeits as metal squids, wobbling spoons, eel-skin jigs or an assortment of plugs too numerous to list. It's true enough that surf-casting for stripers can be a heartbreaking proposition because it's so uncertain. The stripers have little regard for time and tides and a fisherman's convictions. Still, one of the greatest thrills which saltwater angling has to offer is the hooking, playing and landing of a large striped bass while chest-deep in surf.

As long ago as colonial times the striper was held in highest esteem. In 1634, William Wood set a rough pattern for modern outdoor scribes when he wrote: "The basse is one of the best fishes in the countrye and although men are soon wearied with other fish yet they are never with the basse. It is a delicate, fine, fat, fast fish having a bone in its head which contains a saucer full of marrow, sweet and good, pleasant to the pallat and wholesome to the stomach."

But it wasn't until after the Civil War that sport fishing for stripers, or for any other species, became popular on our east coast. During the 1870s a number of famous old fishing clubs were organized. Among these were the Cuttyhunk Club, the Squibnocket, Pasque Island, West Island and Cohasset Narrows clubs. Only the Cuttyhunk clubhouse still remains today, but for several generations the fisher-members and their guests lived high, practiced the fine art of chumming and managed to catch many a fine striped bass on tackle far more crude than striper fishermen use today.

One peculiar but most interesting feature of most striped bass clubs was that each one contained a large roost of pigeons. But the pigeons were not used for shooting, a favorite sport of the time, but rather for communication with the mainland. Most of the club members were businessmen in New York, and this was the manner in which they conducted business while enjoying the fishing at the club.

But unaccountably, striped bass almost vanished from the New England coast during the early 1900s and these colorful old clubs gradually disintegrated. And of course, the fishermen disappeared along with their clubhouses.

Even though striped bass or rockfish, *Roccus saxatilis,* have been taken since colonial times, very little is known about their habits and their life history. After they "disappeared," no one retained much interest in them. But after the stripers reappeared in great numbers along the Atlantic coast in 1936, interest suddenly revived. Fisheries biologists at federal, state and local levels were encouraged to find out something about them.

But it wasn't quite that easy. For one thing, the sea is a vast void in which a fish can hide. Of course that complicates the biologist's task. And there were politicians to deal with, never an easy matter, because they controlled the money to do the job. But it's typical, I suppose, that politicians should drag their feet over providing money for a matter so economically and aesthetically important as the striped bass fishery on our east coast.

One of the most dramatic incidents in the history of American fish management involved the striped bass, and it occurred as long ago as 1879. Details are somewhat lacking today, but it's known that a number of small striped bass were seined from the Navesink River in New Jersey and transported across the continent to San Francisco Bay. Only 435 fish survived the transcontinental trip. Twenty years later the Pacific commercial catch of stripers alone reached 1,234,000 pounds. In 1915, some 1,785,000 pounds were marketed from waters where they never existed before!

This interocean transfer seems almost impossible to modern biologists, who now have the equipment to do such a thing easily. But in 1879 there were no aerated tank cars and so the fish were transported in anything available. Water in milk cans and makeshift aquariums had to be changed frequently and manually. It was also agitated by hand to keep the fish alive. And when the shipment passed the Mississippi, a few of the stripers were tossed in that river, according to an old account, "just for luck."

There isn't any way to estimate the number of stripers in Pacific coast waters today because commercial netting was forbidden since 1935, and the striper has been considered a game spe-

Surf casting in Oregon Inlet, North Carolina. (Photo by North Carolina News Bureau)

cies ever since. But it is known that the original planting has extended over a major part of the west coast from San Diego northward as far as the Columbia River in Washington. Today's stripers are even caught in fringe waters of the Gulf of Mexico, but here their activity seems to be confined entirely to fresh or brackish water.

Alabama Sportsmen find them in goodly numbers in the Coosa and Tallapoosa rivers, sometimes 100 miles from the Gulf itself. There are similar situations in Louisiana and Mississippi, and perhaps these river populations are the result of numerous indiscriminate plantings of small stripers made during the late 1800s.

A striper's normal natural range is on the Atlantic seaboard from northern Florida northward to the Gulf of St. Lawrence. Between these two points, the fish can be found in a vast number of different situations, from the muddy waters of the Santee-Cooper drainages in South Carolina to the cold, noisy surf on some Maine beaches. Part of the population of striped bass in this normal range migrates over great distances; other stripers seem to migrate very little. And those which do migrate, do so in patterns which biologists still are unable to describe with any accuracy.

Here are some examples of the striper's contrasting behavior. In the St. Johns River of Florida lives a population of sedentary stripers which doesn't seem to travel at all. In the St. Lawrence River the bass seem to make short journeys up- and downstream, but they rarely leave the river. There are similar native schools in Nova Scotia and New Brunswick.

Recent studies have revealed that young fish spawned in the Hudson River rarely travel farther than Long Island Sound. In Chesapeake Bay, which is the largest hatching area for stripers, there are "groups" of fish which appear to remain or to circulate in the bay area throughout the year. But strangest of all the nonmigratory stripers are those which live in the Santee-Cooper drainage area of South Carolina. Stripers have always lived in these rivers, but until recently (after two giant dams were built to form Lakes Moultrie and Marion) they were able to return each year to saltwater. Now the stripers are landlocked, they are spawning successfully and reproducing in vast numbers in an entirely freshwater environment.

But the most mysterious and perhaps the biggest striped bass of all are those which migrate long distances up and down the coast. No one has been able to completely predict their movements and perhaps no one ever will. What marine biologists suspect, though, is that schools swimming out from Chesapeake Bay, Delaware Bay and from the Virginia Capes region join together with other passing, northbound schools. Probably they spend the summer in New England or even as far north as the Maritime Provinces only to return south again as autumn comes.

There are many excellent examples of the striper's unpredictability, but one of the best concerns the vast concentration that appeared year after year off Old Man's Rip near Nantucket Island, Massachusetts. Few of these fish were ever smaller than 20 pounds and most were quite a bit larger. These fish appeared to arrive in springtime and they remained nearby until late November.

But just about the time when research biologists decided to begin a tagging program in the region, the fish abruptly changed their habits and they haven't schooled in this area since.

Generally, it can be said that stripers follow the sun. They go northward as water temperatures increase and then they return south again as water temperatures fall. Most fishermen, however, do not care where stripers came from. They are far more interested in where to find them on the days they spend fishing.

Because stripers can be taken in so many varied situations, a fisherman must choose from a bewildering array of tackle. Of course everything depends upon the type of fishing he plans to do. For surf fishing, a good rod will have a 30-inch butt, 7-foot tip of from 10 to 16 ounces. The reel should be able to hold 200 yards of from 20- to 45-pound test line. It can be either a large, saltwater spinning reel or a casting reel with a star drag.

For boat fishing, use a regular boat rod with an 18-inch butt, or 5- to 6-foot tip of from 5 to 10 ounces, a reel which can hold 150 to 200 yards of 20- to 45-pound test line, 5/o to 7/o hooks on 24-inch wire or heavy nylon leaders. In addition, an angler should have a supply of 1- to 6-ounce sinkers, plus bait which can be sandworms, bloodworms, soft-shell crabs, squid, menhaden or plugs.

Since these fish seem to enjoy the environment of turbulence—of white water smashing against solid ground—a good spot to look for them is along rocky cliffs, breakwaters or at any similar places where the wave action is violent. Here a light tackle fan can have plenty of action spinning or fly casting from shore. The ideal spinning outfit includes a rod from 6 to 8 feet long, a reel that can hold about 200 yards of 10- or 12-pound monofilament, and for artificial lures, a supply of small feathers, plugs, eel skins and spinners. The spinners can be used with worms and other live bait. For using live bait, a 2/o to 6/o hook is just about right. Of course, this same spinning tackle can also be used for trolling or casting from a boat.

It's worth noting here that the largest striped bass ever taken on fly-casting tackle was a 29½-pounder taken by Joe Brooks at Coos Bay, Oregon. His tackle included a 9-foot 6-inch, 6⅝-ounce fly rod, and a single-action reel, containing 100 yards of braided 14-pound test nylon backing and a forward taper GAF fly line.

It's fortunate for fishermen that striped bass will attack or eat anything which swims, creeps or crawls in saltwater. While artificial lures can incite a bass into striking either through anger or curiosity, natural bait depends upon one thing—hunger. If the striper happens to be feeding, some natural live bait will probably work out best of all. If he is not actively feeding it's entirely possible that he will most often strike an artificial lure. Of course, there are times when it doesn't make any difference which is presented because everything from sooty terns to cigarette lighters have been found in their stomachs.

Sometimes successful striper fishing depends very much on an efficient system of intelligence as well as knowing the habits of the fish and how to use your tackle. In such hard-fished areas as Montauk, Narragansett, Cape Cod and elsewhere along the Atlantic seaboard, it's possible to keep in constant touch with the times of striped bass arrivals. Although many serious striper fishermen try to maintain strict secrecy when they find schooling fish or when they know a run has arrived, this information is bound to leak out. It's too hard to conceal the concentrations of fishermen and beach buggies along any popular area of coastline. It's also possible to keep track of striper movements and migrations by calling bait and tackle dealers on the spot or by carefully watching the outdoor columns in the local newspapers.

There aren't really any shortcuts to successful fishing, especially in the surf, except perhaps to imitate exactly the technique of an expert striper fishermen and/or to study the beach at an extreme low tide. At this time an ideal observation point is from the top of a car or beach buggy, or high on a sand dune. Then while the sea is at its lowest ebb and the ripping currents are still, it's possible to examine conformation of the bottom and so locate the haunts of feeding stripers. It's good to note any sudden drop-offs, holes, offshore bars, gullies or cuts. It's also well to make a mental note (or even to draw a simple map) of eelgrass beds and mussel-studded bottoms. Also keep in mind any mud flats (where sea worms are likely to be plentiful) and all points where tide rips will develop as soon as the tide begins to flood again.

Striped bass are indeed partial to so-called "live" water. They are powerful, robust and quite at home in swirling ocean currents or in a breaking surf. Perhaps it's because these turbulent areas hold masses of smaller fish in a kind of suspension. Although there are exceptions to the rule, the smaller stripers generally come closer inshore to forage. The larger bass either wait until night falls or they approach the shore via

String of striped bass taken in South Carolina's Cooper River.

gullies or cuts, which an angler is fortunate to have located before the flood tide begins.

Pockets of white water or any obvious depressions in the surf line are apt to hold the largest bass of all. It's worth repeating that stripers do not like still water and it's a clever fisherman who looks for such turbulent areas as those scoured by strong currents, or choppy because of the most violent tide rips.

There are a number of unmistakable signs that striped bass are feeding in a given vicinity. Some old-time surf casters insist that they can locate feeding bass by smelling them. Maybe they can. Anyway, it's believed that the fresh and pleasant scent that is given off when a striper is first landed is the same odor that can be distinguished simply by walking along a beach.

On other occasions the feeding of bass is betrayed by telltale bulges on the surface and the sudden skittering of small baitfishes. The appearance of a slick in otherwise choppy waters is also worthy of investigation, and no fisherman ever fails to keep an eye on schools of menhaden as they drift along, even though apparently unmolested by larger fish.

The most dramatic evidence of feeding bass is the sudden gathering of such seabirds as terns and gulls. Occasionally, it's possible to find them circling and diving like intercepters locked in combat. And chances are that underneath them, squid are squirting out of the water or mackerel are scattering nervously all about. Somewhere beneath all this activity is a school of striped bass.

Of course, birds gather when other fishes besides stripers are attacking the bait fish but few other species feed so noisily. Big bass slash and boil on the surface, sometimes swapping ends and slapping the water with strong, broad tails. Usually it's possible to see clearly the barred flanks of the feeding fish, but waste no time watching them. Get to the spot as quickly as you can and cast right into the center of the feeding. In such a situation, the odds are greatly in favor of the angler hooking a fish no matter what lure he casts.

There are about as many opinions on the best time of day or night to go striper fishing as there are striper fishermen, but the truth is that it's a twenty-four-hour proposition and the bass are likely to arrive on the scene at any time. At certain seasons, especially in spring and fall, daylight casting tends to be more productive than it is in midsummer. Along most of the Atlantic seaboard it doesn't pay to spend much time fishing at midday during most of July and throughout August. Quite a number of veteran surf casters would vote for a flood tide—no matter what the month—either very early in the morning or at dusk as being the most ideal period.

Not too many striper fishermen will agree on which bait is consistently the best. However, a consensus in the Cape Cod region might reveal that block-tin squids, bullhead jigs and small plugs will work best for fish in the 2- to 10-pound class. But where the stripers are running larger than 10 pounds, much larger squid and the largest size in surf plugs or large rigged eels or eel skins are usually preferred.

When casting at night, many anglers use large jointed plugs that operate just on or under the surface. Some prefer the noisy poppers, darters and splashing-type plugs.

One of the greatest striped bass killers of all, for day or night along the Atlantic seaboard, is an aromatic but hard-to-cast combination of artificial and natural baits called the rigged eel or eel skin. There are all sorts of ways to prepare this bait, but the most common is to take an eel skin and to rig it onto a lead-head jig or some other casting weight. Either way, it should be retrieved slowly along the bottom. The best way to give an exciting and undulating motion to the eel skin is simply to raise and lower the rod tip during the retrieve. The rig should be made to actually bounce and crawl along the bottom.

One variation of the eel bait is simplicity itself: String a length of leader completely through the eel, attaching 2 or 3 or 4 hooks at intervals and then wrap a strip of lead around the eel's head to make it sink and to give it casting weight. An eel rigged in this way should be retrieved in the same manner as the eel skin and jig combination.

Landing a good striper in a heavy surf is not an easy or uncomplicated matter. Beginners too often make the mistake of trying to drag a fish through the inshore breakers. This usually results in a broken line, a snapped leader or straightened hooks.

It's always important to let the surf work for you instead of against you. Pump the bass shoreward on each crest of a wave but allow it to

These big rockfish were caught from a pier at Virginia Beach, Virginia. (Photo by Va. Dept. of Conservation and Development)

slide back with the undertow. Then if your timing is correct you will find that it's possible to keep the fish coming on a wave that will eventually leave it high and dry on the beach. Now get there as fast as possible, grab the leader and pull the fish to a safe location far back from the water's edge. But never, absolutely never, try to remove the hook from a striper while it is still alive and kicking. Use a beer bottle, billy or piece of driftwood to whack it on the head. Trying to remove a plug from a flopping striper too often results in surgery to remove the hooks from the fisherman's hand.

But there are dangers to surf fishing other than removing the hook from a big striper bass. If you have ever watched sandpipers, some of the tiny shorebirds that scamper lightly along the edges of every beach, you may have noticed that even these tiny birds occasionally are caught unawares by towering, incoming breakers. Figuring that no surf caster on earth is as agile as a sandpiper, it's evident that everyone who fishes from the surf is likely to get ducked someday. It's not always a pleasant experience.

HOW TO SURF-CAST. (1) Put reel in free spool with drag adjusted for weight of lure. Left hand low on butt, and right hand just below reel with thumb holding spool. Lure should hang about 3 to 4 feet below rod tip. (2) Bring rod tip back by pushing left hand (on the butt) and pivoting rod on right hand. Overhand or sidearm swing can be used. (3) Cast forward as lure almost touches water behind you. Push with reel hand at same time pulling with hand holding butt. (4) Release spool so line flows freely. Timing will come only with experience. Thumbing reel is necessary to prevent backlashes. (5) When lure hits water take reel out of free spool. Shift rod butt to comfortable position between your legs or to rod holder, and move left hand up rod to just in front of reel. If squidding, start retrieve immediately. If bottom fishing, strip out several feet of line so bait will settle to bottom. When retrieving, level-wind line with left thumb so line will play out freely on next cast.

No matter how practiced they are, surf casters seem unable to resist the desire to wade in the surf and, once wading, they can't resist wading too deep. And no wonder, because often the best fishing lies near the outer extremity of the breaking surf. But great care must be taken not to be knocked down by the waves.

Never turn your back to an incoming wave and never let a wave catch you in the stomach. Keep a constant eye on incoming waves and meet them sideways with the legs braced to prevent being swept off your feet.

If you are knocked down by a wave, remember that the water tends to lift your feet and submerge your head. And this is true despite the fact that you may be wearing heavy waders, because the upper part of the body is heavier than the legs. But above all, in such an event, stay calm, paddle hard with your hands until you are able to regain your feet.

It isn't wise to wear hip boots because no matter how cautious the angler, the waves will eventually reach over the tops and, except in the middle of the summer when the water is fairly warm, wet feet and legs in the Atlantic will soon make any fisherman uncomfortable. The best outfit for surf fishing is a good pair of rubber waders, a waterproof jacket with a belt that will tighten about the waist and hold both waders and jacket snugly. Waders with felt soles are probably the best for slippery rocks since the felt affords a better grip than rubber. But better even than felt is a pair of cleats, such as ice fishermen use, worn on the outside of the wader shoe.

Besides his terminal tackle, a surfer should always carry a sharp knife, pliers, headlight for fishing early or late in the day or at night, sunglasses, chapstick, creepers for movement over slippery rock, a gaff, a surf belt, a sand spike and a billy. Sometimes a Coleman gasoline lantern is mighty valuable, too.

Surf casting is far more thrilling and a far more adventuresome method to catch striped bass than fishing from a boat. But still it probably isn't as effective in most places along the Atlantic seaboard. The boat fisherman, for instance, is not limited by how far he can cast. When a boat fisherman finds a school of fish he can stay right with it casting into the school and following it as it moves along. When no striped bass are in evidence, he can keep exploring and probing by bottom fishing, drifting, or trolling.

And nowadays, with the outboard motor so handy and so portable, trolling for striped bass in a variety of situations is a very easy matter.

Trolling is especially effective. An experienced charter-boat captain or guide needs only to troll across known gravel bars, past tide rips and wherever the current clashes with underwater boulders, rocks, old wrecks and piers. Shellfish beds are also extremely good striper grounds. In the Chesapeake Bay area, particularly, striper captains know all these locations as intimately as they know the backs of their hands. The best trolling lures are spoons, bullhead-type feathers, nylon and bucktail jigs perhaps with a strip of pork rind added. But no matter what tackle or what technique he decides to use, a trophy-hunting striper fisherman's best bet for a really big fish is in the vicinity of Cape Cod or such Massachusetts islands as Cuttyhunk, Martha's Vineyard, and Nantucket. The Narragansett, Charlestown and Newport Beach sections of Rhode Island, Montauk Point area on Long Island and the vicinity of Sandy Hook, New Jersey, are also good spots for stripers.

During midwinter a vast concentration of large bass with many over 50 pounds always gather in the area of Cape Hatteras, North Carolina, but fishing conditions here are such that neither surf casters or trollers have had very much luck with them. There is always the ugly combination of rough seas, extremely cold, damp weather, a multitude of weeds in the water and a disinclination of the fish to strike.

Here follows a state-by-state schedule of striped bass movements along the Atlantic seaboard:

In Massachusetts the best season usually begins early in May and lasts until November 30, and perhaps later during rare seasons when the weather permits and the fish remain. The largest stripers, which are called "bulls" but which invariably are females, arrive in the largest numbers along about July 1 on the mainland coast and about June 1 off Cuttyhunk and Martha's Vineyard. The cream of Massachusetts fishing usually occurs from mid to late fall in the offshore tide rips and reefs near Cuttyhunk and Martha's Vineyard.

The first casting and trolling for school fish around Cape Cod begins on May 1 and lasts until it is too cold or too uncomfortable to go out any longer. Ordinarily the first catches are made around Buzzards Bay and Falmouth. However, the best fishing doesn't begin until June or the first part of July and then it slacks off during midsummer only to improve again by mid-September.

Rhode Island has produced some of the greatest striper-fishing and some of the largest individual fish on the entire Atlantic coast. School stripers begin to arrive at such spots as Watch Hill, Weekapaug, Quonochontaug and Point Judith about mid-April and they remain until November. At Narragansett Bay, fishing begins about May 1 when the smaller school stripers arrive in great abundance. Later on, the trophy fish show up in such celebrated locations as Beavertail, Brenton Point, Newport and Sakonnet Point, which have produced many huge bass that were only a few pounds off the world's sport-fishing record. Block Island is another area not as well explored by striper fishermen as the Massachusetts Islands, but it does have great potential.

Located as it is on the northwest shore of Long Island Sound, Connecticut does not catch some of the best runs of large bass. However, it does have extremely good fishing for school stripers. As early as March some of them appear in the Thames River near Norwich and New London. A little later, bass begin to run in the Niantic estuary. Other Connecticut hot spots where fishing begins from mid-April to early May are around Greenwich, Cos Cob, Norwalk, Darien, Southport, the mouth of the Housatonic and Connecticut rivers, at Mystic and at Stonington.

Although the Hudson River is shamefully polluted and no government agency makes any serious attempt to improve the situation, it is still an important spawning ground for many of the school striped bass that are taken around Long Island and elsewhere along the New England coast. There is some light-tackle casting and trolling in the Hudson River itself as early as April 1. New York City anglers have much sport with school-size fish beginning at Flushing, Little Neck and Manhasset Bay, at Glencoe, near New Rochelle and Mamaroneck. Fishing the south shore of Long Island at Jamaica Bay and at the Rockaways is good in May and during some years holds good until November.

Montauk Point at the extreme tip of Long Island is one of the greatest striped bass fishing areas in the world. Here it is possible to catch them by surf casting or by chartering one of the special boats designed for use close to the wild and rocky surf. The biggest bull bass arrive here late in May and remain until mid-December.

Although Sandy Hook, New Jersey, ordinarily accounts for the largest striped bass taken in New Jersey coastal waters, there are a number of extremely good areas nearby. About April 1, fishing begins along the north shore of Delaware Bay. At the same time school stripers are available around Cape May and near Atlantic City, New Jersey. Barnegat Bay also has school stripers—sometimes throughout the summer and early fall months. The Manasquan River is a popular spot for night fishermen. Some extremely fine bull bass are taken in this area early in the summer and late in September. Other New Jersey striper areas extend from Sea Girt to Long Branch around Sea Bright, off Monmouth Beach and in the vicinity of the Raritan River mouth.

Striped bass fishing in Delaware waters isn't what it might be because of heavy pollution. Still some fine bass are taken in Delaware Bay occasionally as early as March 15 and lasting until Christmas. There is good fishing in Rehoboth Bay and Indian River Bay from April through December and in the Indian River inlet. This is the state's best known striper area, and surf casting for school fish gets under way on both sides of the inlet early in April. Here fishermen can continue to catch fish if they can stand the weather through January and February.

The best bass fishing areas in Maryland and the District of Columbia would include Chesapeake Bay and all the rivers that drain into it, such as the Susquehanna, Elk, Sassafras, Back, and Patapsco. There are also excellent trolling grounds around such well-known places as Rock Hall, Bloody Point, Poplar Island, Herring Bay, Tilghman Island, Sharps Island, Solomons Island and the Cedar Point area. Add also the Patuxent River.

In Virginia where striper fishing begins in March, the Rappahannock and York River areas are good. So is the vicinity of Norfolk and the James River estuary.

From Virginia southward the striped bass becomes more and more a river fish and most of the fishing is done in rivers themselves or in their mouths. Trolling is the most popular method, and surf casting, which is at its best in the New England area, is not practiced here to any extent. Some scattered catches are made by surf casters in spring and late fall, but it really isn't developed.

Stripers are found in most of the Carolina rivers and in Pamlico and Albemarle sounds. The largest striper of which there is any record was a 125-pounder netted here in 1891 at the mouth of the Chowan River. The rod and reel record, incidentally, is a 73-pounder taken in Massachusetts in 1913. Some good rivers in North Carolina where school stripers are taken regularly on fairly light tackle include the Pasquotank, the Tar, Roanoke, Chowan and Neuse.

Limited fishing exists in the Piscataqua and Hampton river systems of New Hampshire. In Maine there is a certain amount of fishing in Casco Bay, Penobscot Bay and near Kennebunkport. Ordinarily the fishing does not begin here until mid-June, and it is all over by the tag end of September.

On the Pacific coast the best striper fishing by far is available in San Francisco Bay and in the San Joaquin delta area. There the fish are found during the summer months off sandy beaches and rocky shorelines, sometimes within casting distance of the shore. The beaches immediately adjacent to the Golden Gate are the best, year in and year out, but occasional large runs are encountered as far south as Monterey and as far north as Bodega Bay. Stripers along the Pacific coast do not strike as great a variety of live and artificial bait as they do in the Atlantic. Or so it seems to anglers who have sampled both oceans. Off California they seem to prefer shrimp and anchovies to all other live baits and on occasion will take a variety of jointed wooden plugs fished fairly near to the surface after dark.

Stripers up to 78 pounds have been netted off the California coast, but anything over 20 pounds is an extremely fine fish. Some of the other good striper waters occur as far north as the Columbia River and Coos Bay, Oregon, is an extremely fine area to catch small school fish in large numbers.

Surf casting for striped bass along the North Carolina coast.

Chapter Eleven

BULL REDS, BLUES AND WEAKS

CHANNEL BASS, BLUEFISH, WEAKFISH

CHANNEL BASS

One of the thrills that should happen to every saltwater fisherman someday is to stand knee-deep in the pounding surf on North Carolina's Outer Banks when the channel bass are in. To complete this picture of Angler's Paradise Found, the big bass should be feeding so close to shore that their backs are half out of water. And the mullet on which they're feeding are sprayed right up on to the beach as they try to elude the big bass. This doesn't happen every day, but it does happen often enough to be worth plenty of waiting.

I'd waited many years myself until one magic morning in November. After two days of fruitless fishing, the big red channel bass appeared all at once. We spotted them first just south of the Cape Hatteras lighthouse and for a long time they fed in an area too far out from shore.

But suddenly somebody shouted: "Bulls on the beach!" And sixteen fishermen were casting into them all at once.

When a big channel bass strikes a bait it's something like a blacksmith striking an anvil. At least that's how it seemed to me. Almost in the same instant a knot that I had neglected to check was broken and my fish was gone. But the fishermen on both sides of me connected immediately and one of the wildest melees I've ever

watched ensued. It reminded me of a hockey game.

"Out of my way!" somebody hollered as he ran down the beach. "I've got a whale by the tail."

My hands were unsteady as I replaced the leader and attached a new lure to my line. But by the time I made another cast, almost half the fishermen wading in the surf nearby had tied into bass and were frantically dodging one another to keep from getting them tangled.

Before the morning was finished, reinforcements had arrived in beach buggies and more lines were tangled. Other anglers came in an airplane. But more than a hundred channel bass were landed and stacked like cordwood on the beach. Not one of the fish weighed less than 40 pounds and the largest ran about 59 pounds. As I said—it was a thrill that should happen to every fisherman some day.

This wonderful invasion of channel bass occurs several times a year in the vicinity of Cape Hatteras. Usually it happens in April and again in November, with the exact time depending on the weather. It isn't easy to be in the right spot at the right time and indeed it may seem impossible. I've known fishermen who traveled to the Cape for many, many years just to enjoy this brief phenomenon, but they still haven't hit the channel bass runs exactly right.

Channel bass, which are also called redfish, redhorse, red bass, red drum, drum, drumfish or red choppers, rank with the finest game fishes in American waters. They range from Barnegat Light southward all along our coast to Mexico and beyond. Although they seldom venture farther north than the New Jersey coast, they're among the most important fish for surf casters. But they're also taken by trolling, by casting with light tackle in warmwater bays, and they're even found on the same shallow flats that bonefish inhabit in south Florida waters.

A surf caster fishes for channel bass in the same manner that he would fish for stripers except that the redfish do not prefer such wild and turbulent water. Instead, they feed close to shore in a quieter environment, where they can search at leisure for crabs and other bottom food. Channel bass move so slowly and conspicuously while feeding that often they can be seen by a cautious fisherman. They give the impression of being sluggish—perhaps like carp—until they feel the sting of a hook. Instantly they're off in a tremendous surge of power which can melt a hundred yards of line or more from a reel.

Surf casting for the channel bass, which isn't a bass at all but belongs to the croaker family, can be done with either conventional gear or heavy spinning tackle. Since metal squids are very effective when casting to a feeding school, any bait-casting or wide-spool surf reel which can handle squids from 2½ to 4 ounces is suitable. Line testing 27 or 36 pounds is recommended, although an expert fisherman doesn't need it quite so heavy. When there is ample room to play a fish without fouling up anyone else, spinning tackle is excellent for this type of redfish squiding. Line of 10- to 12-pound test is stout enough and lures from 2 to 2½ ounces are excellent.

Most of the time spent surfing for channel bass will be bottom fishing for which any angler needs a supply of patience. For this he'll also need the same gear as for casting squid—a wide-spool surf casting reel or spinning tackle. On the wide spool use 36-pound test line and a 4-ounce pyramid sinker to keep the bait from rolling and traveling in the surf. Use an 18-inch steel leader and several ounces of cut mullet, sand crab or shrimp.

The ideal spinning outfit includes a saltwater reel with 150 to 200 yards of 12- or 15-pound test line, a 2-ounce pyramid sinker and a wire leader. Size 6/0 or 8/0 O'Shaughnessy hooks are fine during the April and November seasons because the fish run larger during these periods. Too often, smaller hooks fail to hold in the fish's mouth and a trophy is lost. This happens most frequently when the point of the hook becomes buried inside the bait. The best surf rods for redfish should be from 8 to 10 feet long, for normal surf casting and spinning.

It's wise to remember the channel bass habit of grubbing on the bottom, perhaps even of scavenging a meal that can be any kind of readily available fish, clams, crabs or shrimp. Their jaws are made to crush shellfish easily, to eat the meat and spit out the shell. Many old-time surf fishermen believe they can hear channel bass "drum" as they crunch shellfish close to the beach.

Casting into the crashing surf for channel bass at Nags Head, North Carolina. (*North Carolina State photo by Sebastian Sommer*)

Channel bass fishing anywhere is a feast or famine proposition and it's possible that a fisherman can wind up skunked even after a whole week of hard effort. On the other hand, a man can strike it hot from the first cast and proceed to enjoy uninterrupted good fishing through an entire weekend holiday. But more often than not, there will be a series of three or four very poor days followed by a day or two of the fastest sport.

Year in and year out the best channel bass fishing occurs along North Carolina's sunbleached Outer Banks. As actual real estate, the outer banks are about 200 miles of shining sand strip, rarely more than 3 miles wide, often a few hundred yards narrow and interrupted only by an inlet or two along the way. To the east is the Gulf Stream of the Atlantic Ocean. To the west are Pamlico Sound, Currituck Sound and a thousand pale blue bays. Channel bass exist on both sides of this strip of sand.

Before the autumnal equinox, storms and hurricanes are spawned in this lonely world of water and wind. But in wild spring gales or in autumn calm, the waters all around contain channel bass as well as many other species of fish. Some are resident and some are transient.

Not too many years ago the banks were inaccessible, but now two roads bring the entire area within easy driving distance of Norfolk or Raleigh, via a bridge from the mainland to Manteo (on Roanoke Island) and Nags Head. From Nags Head you can turn either north or south. Light planes can land on the beach, which is actually a 200-mile airstrip. Beach buggies can be rented at various places along the Outer Banks.

The first time I went to Cape Hatteras I used my station wagon but wound up pushing and digging it out of the sand more than half the time. After that I found navigation was much easier in a rented beach buggy.

The channel bass fishing calendar in the Outer Banks area runs something like this: The bass begin to move at Oregon Inlet, Ocracoke, Hatteras, Drum Inlet, Topsail and Morehead City in early April. By June the run has usually reached the peak. Later on, the hordes of bass move northward along the Atlantic coast and in early fall they return again—usually in October—on the southward migration. Both surf casters and boat fishermen have two chances at them in this area.

Channel bass have strange ways of affecting fishermen. In 1936, for example, an astute doctor told Grady Sheets that fishing and forgetting his business could be the best possible cure for his ulcers. So Sheets selected red-drum fishing. And since then he has taken over 4000 red drum over 20 pounds apiece. One day in a pouring rain at Drum Inlet, he landed 108 reds from 7 to 25 pounds, which probably makes him the world's champion. Anyway, he's *the* man to see for channel-bass fishing information. He has a boat and motor business in Winston-Salem.

But speaking of records and eyebrow-raising statistics, here's something interesting on the Outer Banks area. Ottis Purifoy operates a fleet of charter boats out of Morehead City and during one season, 6162 of his customers caught 112 tons of assorted fish on 1027 trips. That breaks down to about 316 pounds per trip of such assorted other fish as kingfish, albacore, dolphins and snappers as well as reds.

Most of the channel bass taken when trolling from boats run extremely large, from 40 to 60 pounds during the spring and fall months. The Pflueger Record spoon, size 7, is an excellent one for trolling and it has probably landed more bass than any other artificial lure ever made.

Farther south the Florida Bay area and the entire Ten Thousand Islands sector is one large channel bass nursery. Here the fish feed along the edges of banks and shell bars where small fishes, shrimp and assorted crustaceans are very plentiful. But even where natural "baits" are abundant the channel bass in Florida can be taken in numbers on jigs, and nylon lures or trolled spoons. I have also taken them on small plugs cast and retrieved near the bottom.

Channel bass show up almost everywhere in Florida waters. I've taken them while bottom-jigging the vicinity of Punta Rassa, Sanibel Island and Captiva Pass. Here the technique was simply to bounce a ¼-ounce yellow Upperman bucktail across the bottom of deeper portions of Punta Rassa Bay. Farther south in the Keys, near Islamorada, I found channel bass up to 8 pounds while searching the shallow, warmwater flats for bonefish. Although some jumbo reds are taken in the surf near Melbourne Beach, most of the Florida fishing is more tailored for the light-tackle enthusiast.

It's true that many channel bass are taken more or less accidentally while light-tackle fishing for other fish, but they can also be taken specifically. One especially good technique is to cast the edges of oyster bars and mangrove islands. Although nine days in ten the best bait is a ¼-ounce bucktail jig, there are certain times when the channel bass will strike savagely at a small surface plug or at a popping bug cast on a fly rod. Since his mouth is on the underside of his head and not especially designed for surface feeding, the top-water strike of a channel bass is unusually noisy and clumsy, but extremely thrilling.

Generally speaking, saltwater fish require a faster retrieve of any artificial lure than does the average freshwater fish, but the channel bass is an exception. For this species a lure needs to be worked very slowly, and this applies to spoons, jigs, plugs or flies. Assuming that the fisherman is using jigs, he should retrieve the lures by turning the reel handle very slowly while twitching the rod tip ever so slightly to make the jig bounce naturally on the bottom. Surface fishing must be especially slow and deliberate. Occasionally a fisherman will notice a roll behind a surface bait and the odds are good this is a channel bass. Even when the fish does roll it's important not to speed up the retrieve because the channel bass just needs more time to take a top water plug than a tarpon or a snook which share the same waters.

Except in the surf, no special tackle is needed for Florida channel bass except that all line guides, reels and hardware must be resistant to saltwater corrosion. A freshwater spinning outfit or casting outfit is ideal. The spinning outfit should include 8- or 10-pound line and the backing on the fly reel should have about 8- or 10-pound test. Such light gear is completely adequate. Although a wire leader is not absolutely essential for channel bass, it's wise to use one because snook frequently are encountered right along with channel bass.

There is extraordinary fishing for channel bass along the entire Gulf coast of Texas, probably with the best of it concentrated in the Galveston Bay area and in the Laguna Madre between Corpus Christi and Port Isabel. Here the fish are taken on a variety of natural baits from shrimp to cut mullet. But they take artificials just as well.

In recent years, Texas Gulf Coast fishermen have developed an interesting type of vehicle called a Water Scooter for fishing in the warm shallows of the Laguna Madre. Actually it's a

A 48-pound big bull channel bass taken near Oregon Inlet on North Carolina's Outer Banks. (*North Carolina State photo by Bill Gulley*)

shallow-draft skiff with a raised deck in the stern and a 10- to 18-hp outboard. An angler stands on the deck and steers the scooter from a standing position while he cruises about the bay in search of feeding channel bass. As soon as he finds them he cuts the motor and drifts as closely as possible to the school. Then he begins casting.

Since a Water Scooter can buzz along at up to 30 mph, a fisherman can cover plenty of water on a short fishing trip. And a small storage compartment on most of them permits carrying lunch, ice, spare tackle or bait. It's possible that this curious craft could well be adapted to use elsewhere.

A few channel bass exceeding 100 pounds in weight have been taken in commercial nets, but the world's record for hook and line was taken by Zack Waters, Jr., with an 83-pounder off Cape Charles, Virginia. That's a good record at which to aim for any fisherman.

Based purely on past performances, here are several super hot spots for a trophy channel bass: the point at Buxton on Hatteras Island, the sloughs some ten miles north of the light-house at the Cape, the north shore of Hatteras Inlet, the north shore of Ocracoke Inlet. And the best time of the year (over a period of many years) to hit any of these places has been November 15.

BLUEFISH

In 1874, in a report of the United States Commission of Fish and Fisheries, a professor, Spencer F. Baird, submitted the following description of bluefish:

"There is no parallel in the point of destructiveness of the bluefish among the marine species on our coast, whatever may be the case among some of the carnivorous fish of South American waters. The bluefish has been well likened to an animated chopping machine, the business of which is to cut to pieces and otherwise destroy as many fish as possible in a given space of time. All writers are unanimous in regard to the destructiveness of the bluefish. Going in large schools in pursuit of fish not much inferior to themselves in size, they move along like a pack of hungry wolves destroying everything before them. Their trail is marked by fragments of fish and by the stain of blood in the sea. And where the fish is too large to be swal-lowed whole, the hinder will be bitten off and the anterior part allowed to float away or sink. It is even maintained with great earnestness that such is the gluttony of the fish that when the stomach becomes full, the contents are disgorged and then again filled."

Except for the professor's point about destructiveness of the bluefish, it would be hard to find a more colorful and more exact description of the species. The bluefish *is* destructive only in that it consumes an extraordinary number of other fishes. But this destruction is only a facet of nature's savage balance in the sea. Other species are equally "destructive" but their destructiveness is not so evident to fishermen.

But destructive or not, bluefish are surely among the most voracious fish in the world. It is not at all unusual to find a school of small blue-fish chopping up and feeding on smaller bait fish while still another school of larger blues is systematically eating the small blues. They are, in fact, as cannibalistic as can be, but this characteristic only serves to rate them among the finest fish that swim, from an angler's point of view. It isn't hard to find an angler who considers the Atlantic bluefish the greatest fighting fish for its size on the face of the earth.

Bluefish have even been accused of attacking man, and perhaps there is some faint reason or background for these reports. During World War II, bluefish were said to attack fallen fliers along the coast of North Africa. While it is true that bluefish in the Mediterranean commonly reach a size of from 20 to 30 pounds, the reports have never been accredited. But when you consider that a whole school of these blues could suddenly appear in water where a man is foundering, and perhaps bleeding, it's easy to see how such a story would develop.

The bluefish is the only member of its family known to scientists and its scientific name is *Pomatomus saltatrix*. Its common names are almost too numerous to list, but some of those most frequently heard are skipjacks and snappers, both of which usually refer to small school fish of a pound or less. Years ago commercial fishermen called bluefish which weighed more than a pound, tailors, and this name still persists in many areas especially around Chesapeake Bay. Other old names include snapping mackerel, summer snappers and greenfish.

Blues seem to range completely over the At-

Anglers going offshore from Virginia Beach to fish for bluefish and channel bass.

lantic Ocean and in most adjoining waters. What appears to be a midget strain—5 pounds maximum—lives off the coast of Brazil. They have been weighed up to 45 pounds off the North African coast and the world's record fish recognized by the International Game Fish Association was a 20-pounder taken in 1951 off Montauk Point, New York. Before that the unofficial world's record was a 25-pounder hand-lined off the Cohasset Narrows Bridge in Massachusetts. There is also an authenticated record of a 24³⁄₁₆-pounder taken off São Miguel in the Azores in 1953 and it still stands as the world's record on rod and reel. Any fish over 10 pounds no matter where it's caught is worth bragging about.

The largest blue ever taken by a surf caster was an 18-pounder caught at Jones Beach, Long Island, in the summer of 1952 by Bob Clyne of Richmond Hill, New York.

Much has been written and much more could be written about the strange cycles that govern the population of bluefish in Atlantic waters. Years of great scarcity follow summers of the greatest abundance. What causes these fluctuations isn't known or even partially known by anyone. There are many theories on the subject, but they are nothing more than theories, and further mention of the cycling process here is of no value to fishermen.

But back in the mid 1930s, there occurred a bluefish run that was the greatest ever recorded by fishermen along the Carolina coast. At that time fishermen lucky enough to be on the scene saw as much as 15 miles of beach churned to a froth by vast schools of blues feeding on baby menhaden. Millions and millions of blues were so eager in their pursuit of the smaller fishes that every receding wave left windrows of them flopping on the sand. Perhaps this kind of run will never happen again, but everyone who has ever hooked a bluefish hopes that it does.

It's a good estimate that every bluefish will eat several times its own weight in food every day. A fisherman's main problem is where to find them. Blues are great travelers and they move with incredible speed from place to place along a coastline. Even when they are on a wild feeding rampage, they appear and disappear in flurries with a speed that makes it impossible for even the fastest fishing boat to keep pace. They are school fish of course, and they travel in group as small as 50 up to more than any angler can

count. And curiously enough, all the fish in a single school vary very little in weight; sometimes only an ounce or two separates the largest from the smallest among thousands.

Blues follow a fairly definite migratory pattern, going north in the springtime and then south in winter much as do striped bass who share some of the same waters. While traveling they are always on the prowl for mossbunkers or menhaden, which are their favorite foods. But they will not pass up any species of smaller fish, including smaller bluefish, as we pointed out before. They're here today and gone tomorrow and whenever they are in a particular area, every serious fisherman thereabouts hurries to get in on the great fishing that usually follows.

There is plenty of room for argument but perhaps the blue is most directly responsible for the strange vehicle known as the beach buggy. As long age as the era of Model Ts, fishermen were building custom conversions of these cars for use on sandy beaches. Today most of the vehicles have four-wheel drive and they are equipped to carry fishermen and everything they need for a short holiday near the surf. Most contain a couple of crowded bunks and a compact galley.

Equipped with oversize, low pressure tires, these beach buggies can be taken anywhere along a shoreline which is not too rough and rocky. Fishermen simply cruise the beaches in their buggies watching for fish feeding close to shore or for the wildly circling schools of gulls which somehow gather whenever a school of bluefish comes boiling to the surface. Almost as handy as the beach buggy are binoculars, which permit a fisherman to detect gulls much farther away and to scan a larger area of the water's surface while sitting in one place.

There are three major ways to take bluefish and all are deadly when the critters can be found in numbers. Trolling is the most effective of all because it is possible to fish four lines—two of them on outriggers—all at one time. And each of the four lines can drag a different bait: say an eel skin on one, a metal squid on another, a spoon on a third line and a feather jig on the fourth. Of course, all of these lures will take bluefish and the minute a school is located it's possible to have fish on all four of them at once. Unless the anglers are alert and on their toes it will result in an impossible snarl-up of lines.

When a school of blues is located by trolling,

it's best not to push right into the middle of them. A far better idea is to troll quickly around the fringes of the feeding fish, picking up only those fish on the perimeter and thereby not alarming the whole school. Of course, it's fairly easy to locate the main body of the school because of the surface disturbance and because of the birds that will usually be working overhead.

It's always a good idea to try to combine casting light lures with trolling. If a regular medium spinning outfit or even a saltwater fly casting outfit is handy, one fisherman can start dropping streamer flies or block-tin squids or jigs around the edge of the school as the boat draws near. Nine times in ten the caster will get a strike on every cast, and once hooked on this kind of light tackle, the bluefish is a performer almost without comparison.

Serious bluefishermen, almost no matter where you find them, are particularly adept in the traditional and fine art of chumming. Chumming has been mentioned elsewhere in this book, but it approaches its greatest effectiveness with bluefish, at least more so than with most other Atlantic game fishes. The idea is to anchor in a suitable spot offshore and there start distributing big gobs of ground-up menhaden overboard. If all works according to plan, the blues will scent the chum as it drifts down-tide and they will follow the "spoor" right up to the boat. As soon as the school is within casting distance, the anglers begin to cast with block-tin squids or pieces of cut bait. As long as the chum holds out, it is possible to keep the school within close enough range to hook a blue on virtually every cast.

Chumming is as fascinating a technique as it is effective. First there is the suspense involved in whether the fish will react to the chum or not. Then once they are in range, it's possible to use the lightest kind of tackle because the fish are near enough to see and are right on the surface. I've known fishermen to use extremely light fly rods with surface bass bugs which the blues chew to pieces in no time at all. A 5-pound blue on a fly rod is like a pair of bulls in a pottery factory.

Quite a few bluefish spend the winter along the east coast of Florida from Biscayne Bay north to Cape Canaveral. There are also small schools of them wandering about the Florida Keys and north along the west coast as far as Tampa Bay.

Usually they're concentrated around any inlet near the Gulf Stream and they are noticeably absent from any muddy or silt-laden river mouths.

From Florida the bluefish seem to follow the Gulf Stream northward so that they are too far offshore while passing Georgia and South Carolina to be readily available to fishermen. However, there are a few little-known fishing spots in Georgia such as the Cumberland Island beaches, Jekyll Island, Sea Island, St. Simons Island and the Sapelo Island region. Some blues are also caught off Beaufort, South Carolina.

Somewhere in the vicinity of Cape Fear, North Carolina, the large schools of bluefish seem to desert the Gulf Stream and to move closer to shore on a course which carries them as far north on occasion as Cape Cod. During April and May they're in numbers off the North Carolina coast and by June, usually, they reach the New Jersey coast around Barnegat Light. In every area, trollers usually catch the first fish and from them the word of the bluefish run is spread. There's surf fishing for blues from Cape Hatteras to Cape Charles, Virginia, and northward beyond Cape May, New Jersey, which begins in April or May and which lasts throughout the summer. However, the best sport of all seems to begin during the main fall migration southward.

From September through November there is fast surf fishing in the Montauk area and especially in the Cape May area.

But no matter when or where you find your bluefish and no matter how you're fishing for them, keep this one important rule in mind: Retrieve your lure swiftly, almost as fast as you can reel. If you happen to be in the center of a school of feeding blues, you'll have a strike almost as soon as your squid hits the water.

There's never any doubt about a bluefish strike. It hits like a rocket going full speed ahead and it will hook itself even before you can react and raise your rod tip. And once it's on the line, a blue will leap and cavort and perform like few other fishes in the sea.

Bluefishing may mean trolling for hours on end without the sign of a fish. Or it may mean driving along a beach that seems empty of any marine life. But when you do find your blues, it will be worth all the waiting and all the traveling and all the time that you have invested.

WEAKFISH OR SEA TROUT

Long before it became associated with rockets, the space age and astronauts, Cocoa, Florida, was famous for another reason. The local Chamber of Commerce liked to call the place "The Saltwater Trout Capital of the World." And the truth is, they have good reason to do so.

Year after year, more than 1000 spotted weakfish, or saltwater trout, in the 6- to 12-pound class were taken just a short drive from town. And year after year the spotted weakfish division in *Field & Stream* magazine's annual fishing contest has been dominated by entries from the Cocoa and Cocoa Beach area.

But Cocoa is not unique. It's only one of dozens of towns along our south Atlantic and Gulf Coast which depend on weakfish for a good part of their economy. It happens that weaks are the most abundant game species and among the most popular fishes in all America's vast saltwaters.

Weakfish, which are called sea trout most often, really belong to the croaker family instead. This means they are related to the drum, the croakers, the spots, the California white sea bass and the totuava, rather than to the freshwater trout family. One or more of three species of weaks are found all along our coast from Cape Cod to Brownsville, Texas. The spotted sea trout, *Cynoscion nebulosus,* is the most important of the group. It is taken in abundance from North Carolina to around the tip of Florida, with the center of the greatest fishing existing along the Gulf of Mexico.

The gray trout, *Cynoscion regalis,* is taken in greatest quantities in North Carolina waters and its range extends northward to Rhode Island. It's especially abundant and is sometimes called the tide runner in Great Peconic Bay, Long Island, and the Mullica River, New Jersey. It is scarce in Florida waters and extremely rare in the Gulf.

Cleaning a typical catch of spotted weakfish taken in a morning's casting in the Laguna Madre near Port Isabel, Texas.

A third species and of least importance is the white or sand trout, *Cynoscion arenarius,* which is found only on the west coast of Florida and in the Gulf of Mexico. It is small and reaches a maximum of 16 or 17 inches in length.

The gray weakfish grows slightly larger than the spotted weakfish. The largest gray ever taken on rod and reel is a 17½-pounder from the Mullica River. The largest spotted weakfish is a 15$\frac{3}{16}$-pounder taken from the Indian River near Fort Pierce, Florida. Fish of both species of over 25 pounds have been taken by commercial fishermen and it is possible that a sport fisherman could catch a 20-pounder in either species. Now let's look at the spotted weakfish first.

It's a handsome fish and an extremely good one on the table but otherwise it isn't very impressive. Spotted weakfish do not belong in the same class with such game species as snook or bonefish or channel bass as far as being clever and hard to catch. Most of the time, they're extremely easy to catch. While many of the other well-known, southern game fish are durable, tough and agile, the spotted weak is almost delicate, with fragile jaws. It never jumps and it's really not a very strong or exciting fighter.

But no matter whether weaks bore you or excite you, they're tremendously abundant and available. These two qualities more than make up for the lack of fighting abilities. Weaks are, in fact, the old standbys of thousands of southern saltwater anglers.

The range of the spotted sea trout includes Florida's entire east coast. The biggest specimens come from the lagoons along the middle East coast which stretch from Palm Beach north to Melbourne. They are especially numerous in Florida Bay and all along the Gulf Coast, particularly at such places as Cedar Key, Tampa Bay, Charlotte Harbor and Pine Island Sound. Westward from Florida they are found in the vicinity of Mobile Bay, near Biloxi, at scattered points along the Louisiana coast, and they become very abundant in Galveston Bay and in the vast lukewarm Laguna Madre, which extends from Corpus Christi to Port Isabel, Texas.

Almost no matter where they're found, spotted weaks are partial to grassy bottoms in bays, lagoons, sounds, on flats and in almost any water from 2 to 6 or 7 feet deep. On a rising tide they fan out across shallow grass flats to feed on shrimp and small fishes. Later they retreat again to deeper flats and holes as the tide recedes. At certain periods they feed along beaches of the Gulf Coast, congregating around inlets and passes where the food supply is greatest. At these times schools of them are so dense that they seem to swim flank-to-flank in the water.

Spotted weaks are especially sensitive to abrupt changes in the weather. They may leave the shallow flats during very hot or very cold weather and spend longer periods in deeper water. But as soon as the weather levels out and a series of mild days begin to build up, they return again to the same flats where fishermen find them easiest to catch. If the weather remains warm they will roam the flats almost the year round.

Weakfish tackle can be and should be extremely light. For one thing, there is no better way to lose a trout after he's hooked than to horse him, because his soft mouth rips very readily. And from a sporting point of view, only the lightest kind of gear gives the fish an opportunity to show what little it can do. Its most spectacular effort is a series of wallows on the surface and this tactic sometimes will permit the trout to spit out the hook.

It's a happy coincidence that the most sporting tackle for weakfish is also the most efficient. At times it seems freshwater spinning tackle was designed for this species, even more than for most of the freshwater fishes. You could travel around the world and not find a fish better suited to this kind of gear. Running a close second is a light fly casting outfit.

Spinning tackle is so well adapted to trout fishing that the commercial anglers who work the Texas and Louisiana Gulf Coast areas use the fixed-spool reel to account for almost half of their entire catch.

By far the largest percentage of weakfish are taken on such naturals as shrimp, minnows or cut bait and of these, shrimp has accounted for 90 percent of all fish taken. The simplest way to use shrimp is to impale a large one on a bare hook and cast it out with light spinning tackle. Retrieve it as slowly as possible in good weakfish waters. A good supply of shrimp is necessary because these critters are not tough enough to stay on the hook during rough use. But there are a number of clever shrimp hook-harnesses on the market which make this tactic much easier.

Surf casting near Cape Hatteras, North Carolina. This is great water for channel bass and weakfish. (*North Carolina State photo by Bill Gulley*)

More and more fishermen have discovered that buying and using live bait is absolutely unnecessary and just an extra expense. Small bucktails or small jigs are every bit as deadly and in most cases far more deadly than any live bait. The best jig is a ⅛- or ¼-ounce size in yellow or white. There will be days when it is possible to use 2 jigs in tandem and therefore catch two trout at the same time. Still another extremely productive technique is to tie a streamer fly or a tiny, $\frac{1}{16}$-ounce jig on a length of leader behind a heavier jig, which serves as the necessary casting weight.

Jigs work equally well whether the trout are in deep or shallow water, over sandy or grassy bottoms. Many good weakfish waters in lagoons and flats are frequently cluttered with loose floating grass and at these times jigs are among the only lures that can be fished without continually fouling up. There are a number of jigs with piano-wire weed guides on the market and a

supply of these should be in every trout fisherman's tackle box.

The best retrieve for weakfish is a medium speed. This permits the jig to bounce lightly along a sandy or shell bottom. Or if the bottom is grassy, it's best to retrieve just a few inches above the tips of the grass. Sometimes it will be necessary to vary the retrieve, either to speed it up or to slow it down, but in most cases weakfish are not too particular.

Virtually every fish that lives in saltwater has a habit of giving an angler his money's worth, and there are occasions when even the sea trout puts on a decent performance. These are the times when weaks are feeding busily over the shallowest flats and they occur more often at dusk or even after dark than in daylight. Then the trout will strike top-water lures with considerable enthusiasm.

It doesn't make any difference whether the lures are plunkers, darters, injured minnows or popping bugs, just so long as they're retrieved slowly and noisily. A weak will usually swirl or roll several times before striking, in which case a slight increase in speed on the retrieve usually makes the rolling fish take the plug. Some very large spotted weaks have been taken by casting with darter plugs around pilings and channel markers after dark.

Although only a few saltwater species will regularly strike those freshwater lures with "built-in" actions, the spotted weakfish is not so particular. Most of the standard wobbling plugs that are so well known to bass fishermen will take trout at least part of the time. They are not nearly as good as jigs, however, but there are days when they will work almost as well.

A freshwater bass fisherman can also have the time of his life using a fly rod and small popping bugs, or wounded-minnow type plugs on the surface. The color or the shape of the bug makes no difference, but the size 1 or 1/o worked slowly, with loud pops and gurgled on the surface, would seem to be ideal. Once while fishing in San Carlos Bay at night, we had action as long as my supply of bass bugs held out. But between the spotted trout and the ladyfish which attacked on almost every cast, we were able to get back to camp and to bed early.

The sand trout, which sometimes shares the same waters as the spotted trout, is a much harder fighter for his size, but he does run considerably smaller. A 2-pound sand is an extremely good fish. Ordinarily the sand stays closer to the bottom in deeper water than his spotted cousin. It seldom ventures out onto the flats. It may be caught by casting small jigs across channels and then retrieving them along the bottom. Sand trout prefer the slowest retrieve as a rule and will even take a jig that is dragged rather than bumped across the bottom.

Although the goings on around Cape Canaveral have a resounding effect around the world, it hasn't affected the trout fishing around nearby Cocoa. This is still the best place for an angler with a trophy trout in mind. It's fertile and it's productive because the area is surrounded by many hundreds of square miles of flats that are protected from deep water. And close by, the trout have a choice of sand, mud, rock, seashell or grass bottoms. Oyster beds, pilings and broken-down docks are everywhere and the biggest weaks of all like to gather in such places.

There is also much evidence to prove that the best fishing occurs from a new moon to the full moon and from a high tide to a low tide. In other words, two hours before and one hour after the change.

A good way to spot big trout in the Cocoa area—as it is elsewhere—is to watch the pelicans. As soon as the trout begin feeding across the flats, whole schools of mullet flush crazily ahead of them, sometimes jumping clear of the water. That's the signal for pelicans to stream out of the mangroves and dive onto the mullet, which are sandwiched between two perils. It's at this time that an angler must carefully watch his plug or he's likely to hook a pelican instead of a trout.

Weakfish are seldom more available than they are in the vicinity of Cocoa. In many places it's possible just to pull a car off the road along Sykes Creek, the Banana or Indian rivers and then wade out and begin casting. It's handy to have a guide and a boat, but it really isn't necessary. Even the wind and the weather isn't a bad problem here because during a strong northern blow—common in winter—it's possible to fish in the Barge Canal, which runs east and west across Merritt Island. The canal is about 12 feet deep and when bad weather moves the trout into this canal, the concentration there is unbelievable.

As elsewhere, the regular fishermen at Cocoa are finding that the biggest weaks are most active after dark. Night anglers use two different techniques. One is to drift and cast with a surface plug or a plug that resembles a needlefish. The second method is to drift while using jumbo shrimp, live needlefish, mullet or balaos and to allow these baits to travel freely with the tide. A large float counter-balanced with an egg sinker is used to keep the bait about two feet below the surface.

When a trout strikes, the fisherman allows it to run and doesn't try to set the hook until the fish stops and begins a second run. This is the same technique that is used all over Florida from causeways and bridges.

Just as weakfish have a fondness for mullet and needlefish, so do the porpoises of Florida inshore waters have a fondness for weakfish. As soon as porpoises appear over the grassy flats, it's a wise fisherman who seeks his weakfishing elsewhere.

The gray trout, or gray squeteague, shecutts, squit, chickwick on sea trout, which reaches its greatest abundance north of Virginia, is a somewhat stronger fighter than the spotted sea trout. It does have the same tender mouth, however, and in general the same methods are used to catch it.

Weakfish usually arrive in northern waters in numbers early in May. The first fish appear in Peconic Bay, Long Island, about the middle of May and it's during that period that all available charter boats are booked far in advance. The typical method of fishing is to use such live bait as sandworms and squid or shrimp and then to chum the weaks into range. Although the weakfish is essentially a bottom feeder, it can be attracted close to a boat and held there by persistent chumming.

Gray trout can be taken equally well both day and night in the small bays off the New Jersey, Long Island and Connecticut coasts. A typical technique of many charter-boat captains in this vicinity is to watch for schools of shiners, menhaden and other baitfish during daylight and then to return to the same area after dark. Almost always a large school of weakfish will have moved into the vicinity. The mouth of an inlet to a bay is always a good spot for weaks at high tide and again during the outgoing tide. Any coves in these bays are also good fishing areas.

Many fine weakfish are taken from mid-August to mid-September by trolling with a small bucktail fly, a spoon or a feather jig. A sinker of sufficient weight is added to troll the bait at a depth of from 10 to 15 feet, which is the zone where weakfish are most likely to be hooked. It's always a good idea, if several weaks are hooked in one area, to drop the anchor overboard and to start chumming and or casting thereabouts. Be careful to lower the anchor gently and then allow the lure to sink to about 15 feet before retrieving it very slowly.

There are periods, especially in midsummer, when bottom fishing with a slack line and using worms for bait is most productive. With a slack line the weakfish will usually hook itself. Always give the fish plenty of time to mouth the bait before striking and then do so firmly rather than abruptly. Some of the better baits for bottom fishing are shrimp, bloodworms, sandworms, squid and shedder crabs.

Breakwaters and docks are always good places to prospect for weakfish during the middle of the summer and especially on midsummer nights. It's often possible to find small fish skittering and racing wildly along the surface with no indication that larger fish are following them. Ordinarily this is a sign that weakfish are about, because they do not splash water or boil to the surface as do striped bass, bluefish and most other larger fish when chasing minnows.

Chapter Twelve

ATLANTIC GRAB BAG

COD, POLLACK, BLACK DRUM, SHEEPSHEAD, BLACK SEA BASS, TAUTOG, PORGY, FLUKE, FLOUNDER, HALIBUT, WHITING

CODFISH

Most saltwater anglers, and especially those who live along the north Atlantic seaboard, have good reason to despise cold weather and the winter season. High winds, rough seas and a stinging salt breeze make any kind of fishing an extremely unpleasant proposition.

Of course most sane fishermen stay home, but cod fishermen are not particularly sane and they even wait until winter for what they consider the best fishing of all. On some of the very worst days of January and February a surprising number of "codballs" will leave the comfort of warm living rooms to suffer on cold and slippery boat decks just to catch a mess of cod.

The codfish, which is found on both sides of the Atlantic Ocean, is one of the most important fish in the world. Early American colonists depended on cod for food and for part of their income. The species was so highly considered that it is pictured on the Colonial Seal of Massachusetts. And today the figure of a codfish still hangs in the Bay State legislature.

On the North American side of the Atlantic,

cod range from the Arctic Ocean southward to Virginia. They prefer cold, deep water and inhabit certain offshore banks almost the year round. South of Cape Cod they are sometimes found inshore, especially from November to April. An exception is Coxes Ledge off Block Island where cod may be found in July and August, but generally speaking they are most plentiful in water from 50 to over 250 feet deep.

Cod are extraordinary travelers. One fish tagged in Iceland was later caught off Newfoundland 2000 miles away. All codfish seem to make extensive migrations, to forage for food and to spawn. In addition, there are shoreward movements in the fall and again in the spring. Tagging has revealed that most of the cod caught in New Jersey and New York waters come from the Nantucket Shoals area where they spend the summer.

The brown-spotted, yellow-bellied, chin-whiskered cod is known by many names, including Atlantic cod, black cod, rock cod and scrod. Its scientific name is *Gadus callaris*. But by any name, no expensive or elaborate tackle is necessary to catch the species. The cost of a winter fishing trip on a party boat, for instance, may be as low as five or six dollars a day, bait included.

Cod are not terrific fighters, but still you need strong tackle rather than elaborate tackle be cause you have to contend with strong tides, deep water, heavy sinkers and rocky bottoms. Many fishermen prefer a simple, stiff, two-piece boat rod and still others use only their regular surf rods. Freshwater tackle is completely out of place on a codfish party boat.

The reel should hold 200 yards of monofilament line testing about 30 or 40 pounds. The best hooks are size 7/o or 8/o in Sproat or O'Shaughnessy types. These are knotted onto heavier (than the line) test nylon leaders, each about 24 inches long, then to a spreader or to a three-way swivel.

Two hooks are often used with the bottom hook tied about a foot above the sinker and the top hook just about 2 or 3 feet above the first hook. Sinkers from a half to one pound are sometimes necessary to reach bottom depending on the depth of the water, the velocity of the current, and the tide.

Virtually any bait is good enough for codfish, and the lengthy list of possibles would include clams, shrimp, lobsters, mussels, conchs, starfish, sea urchins, sea cucumbers, worms or any pieces of cut bait. The bait most often provided aboard party boats is the surf clam or skimmer. The entire "innards" of a couple of these large clams are placed on a single hook. Codfish entrails also can be used in a pinch.

I have never fished for cod in North American waters, but I have done so in the Arctic Ocean off Hammerfest, Norway. No live bait is used there. On calm evenings under the midnight sun, the skipper would only allow our boat to drift while we bounced half-pound, shiny, silvery, metal jigs up and down along the bottom. As soon as we began to locate fish, the skipper pitched an anchor overboard and we would concentrate on that area. There we would catch cod as quickly as we could get our jigs to the bottom and begin the slow jigging routine. But it was hard work.

These Norwegian codfish averaged about 4 pounds and we caught several of them to 20 or 25 pounds. I see no reason why this same fishing technique would not work just as well in North American waters.

Some of the best codfishing along the Atlantic seaboard occurs almost within sight of New York City. Many party boats are based at such nearby ports as Sheepshead Bay, Canarsie, Freeport and Montauk. Still other boats fish out of bases along the New Jersey coast. During mild winters they go out almost daily, even through January and February, but the most fruitful fishing occurs in November, December, March and April.

Most of the party boats, at least the larger ones, have such comforts as heated cabins and small coffee shops on board. Many of these also rent fishing tackle. Even when the weather is worst, it can actually be a pleasant change of pace to go codfishing.

More important even than tackle, perhaps, for codfishing is good warm clothing. The winter fisherman should wear woolen or insulated underwear, heavy outer clothing, a cap with earmuffs, large-size boots or overshoes which can accommodate extra pairs of woolen stockings, waterproofed gloves and waterproofed parkas or foul-weather gear. The more raw and cold the day becomes, the more important it is to be dressed properly.

The average cod taken by American anglers will run about 4 pounds. The International Game Fish Association recognizes a 74$\frac{1}{4}$-pounder taken at Boothbay Harbor, Maine, in 1960 as the largest sport fishing catch. However, trawlers captured a 211$\frac{1}{2}$-pounder off Massachusetts in 1895.

Cod prefer rocky, pebbly bottoms or mussel beds. Near New York, the Cholera Bank, Angler Banks and 17 Fathoms are the best known areas. Cod are also always found around sunken, offshore wrecks.

POLLACK

Winter codfishermen sometimes encounter a bonus in the cod's close relative, the pollack. Often this fish frequents the same waters. Sometimes called Boston bluefish, its scientific name is *Pollachius virens* and it ranges from about Cape May, New Jersey, to Nova Scotia and perhaps beyond.

Ordinarily pollack are taken on the same tackle and by the same methods as are cod along most of the Atlantic seaboard. Unlike its cousin, however, it has the fortunate habit of rising to the surface just before dark and just before day-break at certain times of the year to forage actively for small fish. At these periods pollack become excellent light tackle fish and the fisherman who finds them on the surface, either while surf casting or while fishing from a boat, is lucky indeed.

Perhaps the best pollack fishing of all occurs in October and lasts well into November. This is a foggy time of the year along the Atlantic coast and visibility can be poor, but that makes no difference. The presence of pollack is always easy to tell because of the wild commotion they make while chasing small fish on the surface. In addition, they are usually accompanied by sea gulls, which feed and circle just above them.

Surface-feeding pollack, which will average 5 pounds but which may reach 20 or 30 pounds, will strike at a number of different artificial lures. Large saltwater darting plugs are effective, and so are feather jigs and bucktails when retrieved with short sharp jerks.

Occasionally during periods of very calm weather, pollack feed actively and extensively on the surface at night. It's a most lucky fisherman who encounters them at this time.

Here's the charter-boat dock—one end of it—in Sheepshead Bay. I took this one because of the sign.

BLACK DRUM

The black drum, *Pogonias cromis,* can be found anywhere from the shores of Long Island to the mouth of the Rio Grande. It is one of our most important commercial species and the annual catch has reached 2,000,000 pounds. But it is also a rather important sport species along the Atlantic coast.

The drum, which is closely related to the sheepshead or freshwater drum, is quite a heavyweight. The largest known specimen weighed 146 pounds. The largest specimen taken on sport fishing tackle was a 94¼-pounder taken in 1957 near Cape Charles, Virginia. A number of 50- and 60-pounders are taken every year.

Aside from its game and food qualities, the black drum is a most interesting fish. It may be the best musician of the entire family of drums and croakers to which it belongs. Anglers who have always supposed that fish are silent creatures are surprised to learn that many of them have voices so loud that they can actually be heard a considerable distance above the surface of the water. These vocal efforts, in the case of the drum, are produced by the vibrations of special bandlike muscles against a taut air bladder.

The black drum is now believed to be the origin of the old Indian legends in the Pascagoula Bay country. According to these tales, mysterious and supernatural music, variously described as sweet, plaintive and low, could be heard coming from the water on summer evenings. The Indians didn't know what to make of it, but fishermen now know that these sounds only indicated the presence of large schools of drums.

Whether drumming indicates spawning and sexual activity or whether it's an expression of feeding contentment is uncertain. But some biologists do believe that the fish are most vocal during their spawning migrations. The males are said to drum very loudly, while the females have softer voices.

The black drum has such large and competent pharyngeal teeth that it is obvious its favorite fare is shellfish. In Texas it has a reputation as an oyster pirate, but the truth is, it prefers a small clam that is very abundant in the shallow bays along the Gulf Coast. These clam beds are well known to fishermen as the best places to look for black drum.

Drums suck the clams up and out of the mud in which they burrow. Then they crush the shells. Although they swallow many shell fragments along with the meat, some parts of the shell are discarded. Apparently, black drum are great gluttons, and when feeding they stand on their heads with their tails out of the shallow water, oblivious to all but the business at hand. Lucky fishermen frequently find them in this tailing position.

On the Texas coast, drums spend a great deal of time in shallow inshore bays both in summer and winter. Sometimes the water in the passages to the deeper bays becomes so shallow that they have difficulty passing through and often they are badly cut when passing over these oyster "reefs."

Drums are caught over the entire Florida coast but are most numerous over the state's north Atlantic coast. Small or puppy drums are caught there throughout the year, but the best fishing for larger fish begins sometime in March.

Whenever fishing in known black drum waters, the tackle should be heavy. A fisherman should use an extremely heavy wire leader because nylon leaders are no match for the oyster beds that drums frequent. Drums are also caught from bridges, piers and along certain coarse sand beaches.

Northward from Florida some of the hot spots for black drum are in the vicinity of the Sea Islands of Georgia, near Beaufort, South Carolina, at various points inside North Carolina's Outer Banks and in the vicinity of Cape Charles, Virginia.

The flesh of large black drum is considered by many to be coarse and tasteless, yet the fish is held in high esteem around St. Augustine, Florida, where it is the main ingredient in delicious chowder and baked drum dishes. Black drum should always be filleted and skinned. But skinning is never an easy matter.

SHEEPSHEAD

The sheepshead, *Archosargus probatocephalus,* of the Atlantic and Gulf coasts may be found anywhere from Texas to the Bay of Fundy but it is abundant only in the southern half of the Atlantic Coast. Greatest abundance of all occurs along the northwest coast of Florida.

As a senior member—in size—of the porgy family, the sheepshead is closely related to the familiar scup or porgy which is an important commercial fish northward from Virginia. It is not to be confused with the freshwater sheepshead that is a member of the drum or croaker family.

The sheepshead is most often captured around wharves, breakwaters and sunken wrecks, where it finds abundant food. It has a weakness for crabs, oysters and other shellfish which it crushes easily with its strong bridgework. In inlets it moves in and out with the tide and, at least in the southern part of this range, does not seem to migrate extensively. During the spawning season, which occurs in the spring, sheepshead assemble into schools and move into shallow water to deposit their eggs. Many are caught at this time.

The largest sheepshead of record weighed about 20 pounds, but the average is only about 2 pounds. The larger fish should be filleted and the smaller ones cooked whole. The meat is white, tender and very pleasantly flavored.

A fisherman should look for sheepshead along rocky, irregular bottoms, over reefs not too far from shore, and in inside channels. The most notable physical characteristics of the fish are the sheeplike lips and the protruding teeth. The inside of the mouth is equipped with grinding teeth which permit easy feeding on such bivalves as mussels and barnacles.

Sometimes the sheepshead is so fast in taking live bait that it is very difficult to hook and in some areas its nickname is bait-stealer. Over reefs it will quickly seize baits the minute they are dropped to the bottom. One very exciting way to catch sheepshead is to thoroughly chum an area with shrimp or bits of shellfish and after the sheepshead have begun to feed actively, to cast with small ¼-ounce jigs. On light tackle it becomes a sporty fish and fights extremely hard, for its size.

BLACK SEA BASS

From June through August the black sea bass (or black bass, sea bass or chowder fish), *Centropristes striatus,* is rather plentiful along our eastern seaboard. It is usually found in shallow water over rocky formations with weeds, ledges, sandbars and reefs close at hand. During dog days in many areas, the black sea bass is the only really abundant fish, except perhaps for the fluke. That's an important point for the striper or bluefish or trout fisherman to keep in mind because he can always find bass even when these other glamour species are uncooperative.

Averaging only a pound or two apiece, but occasionally reaching 8 or 9 pounds, the black sea bass is a strong fighter and always a pleasure to catch. On light tackle they never seem to stop fighting even after they are in the boat. They can inflict nasty cuts on a fisherman's hands with their very sharp fins. The best way to handle this fish and to remove the hook is either to hold it firmly by the lower lip or to put fingers into the eyes to grip it solidly enough.

Black sea bass seem to prefer sea clams or squid, but actually they will take almost anything that is offered in the way of bait. What's more, they attack the bait with a rush and swallow it immediately so that hooking them is never a difficult proposition. Ordinarily the larger bass are taken while bottom fishing from boats and the smaller ones are caught while fishing from shore. It isn't necessary to use heavy tackle, and the standard hook is a 2/0, 3/0 or 4/0 O'Shaughnessy tied to a nylon leader about 18 inches long. The sinker should be from about ½ to 1½ ounces in weight. Most fishermen use two or three baited hooks at one time.

The flesh of the sea bass is white, sweet and firm and may be prepared as any other panfish. The large ones can be filleted and smaller ones cooked whole. In either case, they are doubly tasty when served with hush puppies. The sea bass, as one of its local names indicates, is excellent for chowder.

TAUTOG

The tautog, *Tautoga onitis*, is a member of the family *Labridae* which consists of about 400 species that live mostly in tropical and subtropical regions. Of the western Atlantic species that are of interest to sport fishermen, only the tautog regularly ranges north of North Carolina.

Nature has equipped this fish with plenty of teeth. It has extremely strong choppers in its jaws and powerful, conical teeth far back in its mouth. With this double-barreled apparatus, the tautog feeds on the hardest of crustaceans and shellfish along the Atlantic coast. About the middle of May the tautog begins to move from

deep water to feed and spawn in the big bays and inlets along our middle Atlantic coast. This is a good time to begin fishing for the species.

There are two good reasons for using fairly heavy tackle for the tautog. It is necessary to use considerable force to set the hook, and the fish, as soon as it is hooked, will almost certainly try to take refuge among any rocks or underwater obstacles it can find. The tautog rod should be a 6-footer with a 10-ounce tip, and the reel should hold at least 150 yards of 30-pound test line. This may seem a bit heavy for a fish that averages only 3 or 4 pounds and seldom grows more than 20 pounds, but once a tautog reaches sanctuary among the rocks, there isn't any way he can be horsed out.

The first fishing of the season is usually done from small boats or party boats and of course the best water to explore is that over rocky ledges, among rocks and shoals, in weed and rock areas and over mussel bars. It isn't any use to look for tautog very far from this type of habitat.

Early in the season a tautog is also a fairly reliable target for surf casters. An especially good spot to find them is where the flood tide covers up an isolated area of rock. It doesn't have to be an especially large area because half an acre of rocky "island" will hide quite a number of tautog.

The most consistent fishing is in April and early May and then again from September until the end of October. When either very warm or very cold weather arrives, this species goes into deeper water and does not return again until either spring or fall. In winter and summer it's found on the bottom in from 50 to 150 feet of water. Occasionally it will rise to chum but since this is not a very consistent technique it's seldom practical.

Occasionally shore fishing is very productive. Tautog swim along rocky and weedy shores, hunting for food, and sometimes along such shores there are certain holes in which they congregate. Should any fisherman be fortunate enough to find such a place, he should make a firm mental note of it because it will afford fast fishing throughout the season and maybe for many seasons to come.

A wide variety of baits are acceptable to these fish, but one of the best is a piece of cut crab. Sea worms, squid and cut fish are also fairly good at times.

The tautog is often called blackfish, which is confusing because blackfish is also another name for the pilot whale.

PORGY

The northern porgy, *Stenotomus chrysops,* which is also called scup or northern scup, ranges from Maine southward all along the Atlantic coast to South Carolina. The southern porgy, *Stenotomus aculeatus,* which is also called scup or southern scup, maiden, fair maid and ironsides, ranges from North Carolina to the Florida Keys and over to Texas. Porgies are most abundant in southeast waters, but they are highly prized as a food fish everywhere.

The best fishing season for porgies runs from May through October. Throughout the summer and fall, special porgy boats drift back and forth over long-established fishing grounds and on good days these boats are literally filled up with porgies. The fish caught at sea weigh from 1 to 3 pounds and those taken in shallower bay waters usually weigh less than a pound. They bite best when the tide is slack or early during an incoming tide.

Strictly bottom feeders, they are found over shellfish beds, on sandy bottoms, around wrecks, reefs and at the entrance to bays. Scups take one bait about as well as any other, but they do prefer shrimp, skimmers, crabs, small pieces of squid and soft-shell clams. Skimmers, perhaps because they are most plentiful, are the favorite baits of most summer fishermen.

But no matter what the bait, a specialized fishing technique is necessary to catch porgies. The first trick is to find the bottom. Then lower your line and give quick, short jerks of the rod tip up and down, being careful that the bait does not rise higher than a foot above the bottom. Care should be taken not to move the bait too swiftly.

It should be mentioned that since porgies have extremely small mouths, the bait should be small so that it can easily be swallowed. Once hooked, a porgy is a stubborn little fighter because it turns broadside to the boat and bores to the bottom for all its worth.

Porgies along our Atlantic coast practically never exceed 4 or 5 pounds in weight. But while fishing the reefs off Bermuda, our party caught a number of them more than 10 pounds apiece. One was a 12-pounder.

SUMMER FLOUNDER (FLUKE)

The summer flounder or fluke, *Paralichthys dentatus,* actually a halibut, dwells along the shallow shoreline waters from Cape Cod to Georgia, but probably it is most numerous from New York to North Carolina. It frequents both the sandy and the muddy bottoms of the Atlantic seaboard and often is captured in muddy bottoms and estuaries where the water is only moderately brackish.

Like all the other flatfish of both oceans of North America, the summer flounder has its eyes and its color on one side. In the case of the summer flounder, this happens to be the left side as opposed to the winter flounder (a true flounder), which has them on the right side.

The fluke is remarkable for its ability to camouflage itself against any background on which it lives. If placed on a red background it becomes red; on blue it becomes blue, and so on through all the colors anyone could use on the bottom of an aquarium.

Unusually large porgy taken while bottom fishing off Bermuda.

Party boat returning to Sheepshead Bay after a day of flounder fishing in the Atlantic off the coast of New Jersey. Occasionally a boat will get into a school of blues or porgy or hit a few stripers.

Although the flesh of this flounder is dry, it has a good flavor, which is brought out best when the fish is fried or baked. It is one source of fillet of sole.

The fluke is a rather curious fish that will investigate any silvery or flashing movement in the water. It may not necessarily strike such an object but it will at least investigate, and most of the time it will suck the object into its mouth. If it happens to be a lure, the fluke may be hooked, but the fisherman must strike back immediately before it is spit out again. In no way does this summer flounder resemble any of the classic game fish, but still it is quite a strong and vigorous fighter. It feeds on both the bottom and the top and is caught in a variety of circumstances.

The summer flounder occasionally reaches a weight of 25 pounds but the average size would be closer to 2 or 3 pounds. The best way to find out if and where flounders are striking is to watch the outdoor columns in local newspapers. However, another good idea is to go fishing after a bright, calm day or two following a bad storm. Some fishes strike very well during heavy weather, but fluke are among the species that are notorious for feeding after a storm.

Another good time to fish for fluke is just before dusk and just after dark. During this period they are most likely to come to the surface and it is possible to have much sport with them by casting ⅛- or ¼-ounce feather or bucktail jigs.

Cast these lures and retrieve them as slowly as possible and use a wire leader. One variation to the technique is to cast the jig behind a large wooden float, setting the jig about 3 or 3½ feet deep, and retrieving the combination in very slow, sharp jerks.

WINTER FLOUNDER

The winter or blackback flounder, *Pseudopleuronectes americanus*, inhabits shallow water and occurs from northern Labrador to Cape Lookout where it is found only during the coldest winters. Though absent during the summer it is fairly abundant in winter in Chesapeake Bay.

Like all the other flatfish it swims and rests on one side, in this case on its left side. It is caught in a similar manner to the summer flounder and is taken best on similar light tackle. New England flounder fishing usually begins in March and lasts until the end of May. During this period the best spots to fish are in the "bottom holes" in the middle or near the mouth of a bay. The best period is on the outgoing or ebb tide. Fishing is productive until the tide changes and begins to come in.

Usually in June the blackbacks seem to vanish, or at least go out to sea and stop striking until fall. But they return again in September or October and are plentiful along North Atlantic beaches and bays until it's too late and too unpleasant to fish for them any longer.

There isn't any reason to use heavy tackle for winter flounder. A reel that holds 100 yards of 15- or 20-pound test line is good enough. Hooks in sizes 8, 9 or 10 with a 10-inch cone leader are sufficient. The best baits are blood- and sandworms, night crawlers, soft- or hard-shell clams, mussels or tapeworms. The ribbon worm or nemertine will often catch fish when all other baits fail. It is frail and brittle, reddish in color, and it's found by digging into mud flats at low tide. But you must use these worms on the same day they are procured, as it is difficult to keep them alive more than a few hours.

ATLANTIC HALIBUT

Only a few such fishes as the swordfish, marlin, some sharks and the tuna exceed the Atlantic halibut in size. It's the largest member of the flatfish family. Its scientific name is *Hippoglossus hippoglossus*.

This cold-water flatfish inhabits all of the

northern seas, ranging southward along the European coast from Norway to France and southward along our Atlantic coast to New Jersey. Like the winter flounder, its eyes and color are on the right side of the body.

Although the large halibut that are brought into New England ports range in length from only about 4 to 6 feet and in weight from 50 to 200 pounds, some weighing 300 and 400 pounds are taken almost every year. A 9-foot 2-inch jumbo weighing 625 pounds after it was dressed was caught about fifty miles from Thatcher Island, Massachusetts, in 1917.

The Atlantic halibut is a most voracious fish. It feeds mostly on crabs, lobster, clams and mussels. It even is able to capture seabirds occasionally and it is well-known as a scavenger of the refuse thrown from vessels at sea.

Although most Atlantic halibut are taken by commercial fishermen on set lines, it is possible to take them on sport-fishing tackle. They will strike a variety of baits; particularly throughout the spring and summer, which seems to be spawning time along the New England Coast. But once a halibut is hooked, it's a long hard drawn-out struggle rather than an exciting fight.

WHITING

The whiting, *Menticirrhus saxatilis*, often called kingfish, varies with the weather. It should not be confused with the much larger King mackerel, which is a mackerel; the whiting belongs to the

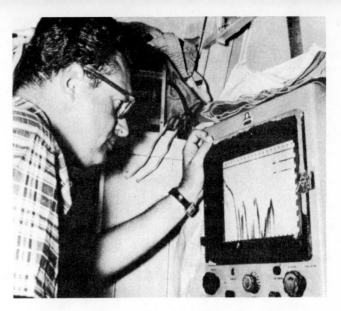

An extremely helpful device to locate shoals, banks, etc., in the Atlantic is a fathometer or depth recorder.

drum family of fishes, which includes the weakfish, channel bass, croakers and others. It is found along the Atlantic coast from Maine to Florida, but is common in the northern half of this range only in the summer.

During May, June, July and August, surf fishing for the whiting is extremely popular and it is rather good along the New Jersey and Long Island shorelines. The best time to fish for the species in this region is during high tide, as it follows the surge inward toward shore. It is also caught during a flood tide in bays and inlets.

Southward from North Carolina the whiting disappears from shallow inshore waters only during cold spells, but it reappears again as soon as the weather begins to warm up. In the Carolinas this species and at least one close—and barely distinguishable—relative are taken in abundance along the shore in about 4 fathoms of water late in winter or early spring.

The whiting is a light-tackle fish and an angler is most likely to be successful when he uses shrimp, crabs, small mollusks, worms or small fish for bait. It is possible to take them on artificials occasionally, especially on yellow feather jigs, but the bait fisherman ordinarily will have far better luck. Whitings usually run only from 12 to 18 inches in length, but they rate extremely high as food fish. A 6-pounder is about tops for the species. It is believed that the largest whiting feed most actively at night.

A "jetty rat" friend of mine, Ely Slotkin, casting the typical tin squid off a jetty at Manhattan Beach in Brooklyn. We were after stripers that foggy morning.

Chapter Thirteen

OFFSHORE FISHES OF THE PACIFIC COAST

CALIFORNIA YELLOWTAIL, PACIFIC JACK MACKEREL, BLACK SEA BASS, KELP BASS, TUNA, ALBACORE, WHITE SEA BASS, BONITO, SHEEPSHEAD, BOCACCIO, OCEAN WHITEFISH, HALIBUT

The saltwaters that completely surround the continent of North America are wonderfully full of hundreds of species of fighting game fish. But too often the emphasis has been on Atlantic coast fish and fishing, with special emphasis on the waters of Florida. Somehow, the fishing off our Pacific coast has never been publicized nearly enough.

Californians never really discovered the amazing angling at their own doorstep until relatively recent times. In 1927 there were only about 250 registered, saltwater sport fishing boats along the entire California coast. Twenty years later there were only 286, which doesn't represent any appreciable growth in enthusiasm. But by 1953 a vast change had taken place. Interest in ocean angling mushroomed and more than 2000 charter or party boats were in business. Californians at last discovered the rich marine resource at their fingertips.

The best qualified ichthyologists figure that there are about 30,000 to 35,000 different kinds of fishes living in the world today. Of these about 18,000 or 20,000 are marine fishes while

the remainder inhabit freshwaters. As many as 100 to 200 fishes completely new to science are discovered each year throughout the world.

About 550 different species of the world's total have been found in California saltwaters alone. Many of these are offshore fishes, with which we're concerned in this chapter. Some live near the surface of the open sea and these are called pelagic fishes. Others stay on the floor of the sea and these deep ones are called demersal species. Still others prefer living just halfway in between and they are called mid-depth fishes.

It is interesting to note that much of the time the body color of a fish is a dead giveaway as to the depth at which he normally lives—in the Pacific or Atlantic. Bright or multicolored species usually inhabit inshore waters shallower than 150 feet. Brown, red or black colors are typical for fishes that live on or near the bottom in moderate to deep water. Offshore surface dwellers are usually blue or gray above and white underneath. And finally, those that live at the middle depths, several hundred feet beneath the surface, often have light organs on their bodies or are aluminum-colored with crimson fins. Of course there are exceptions, but these are good basic facts to remember.

The roster of California marine fishes includes some interesting and strange characters as well as many of the popular game species. For example, there's the flatfish that makes a slow successful stalk along the bottom and then rears up to strike its prey like a cobra. In this manner it can capture crabs and the like with unusual skill. Another strange one is the goatfish, which has tastebud-equipped chin whiskers with which it sweeps the bottom in search of dinner. Anglerfishes dangle enticing lures from built-in fishing rods and the attracted victims are helpless to escape against the "current" created when the anglerfish opens its oversized mouth.

Senoritas actually operate fish delousing stations at specific localities in and around kelp beds. Sheepshead, kelp bass and quite an array of other fishes periodically take advantage of the senoritas' services and swim close by for a complete "examination." Usually several senoritas perform the overhaul at one time. The patient cooperates by languidly raising his fins, flipping gill covers or even by opening his mouth at the appropriate time. So long as the senoritas are near their delousing stations, they are safe from attack, but the instant they wander away, they become fair game for all other fishes.

The State of California has been a pioneer in the conservation and management of saltwater fishes and that is worth a tip of any angler's hat. As long ago as 1931, bag limits and size limits were placed on certain popular game fishes. Closed seasons on some species in danger were inaugurated as early as 1901. Also, California is one of only a handful of states that require a valid angling license to fish in salt water.

Now, let's investigate some of the more important game fishes that cruise in Pacific offshore waters, with emphasis on California.

CALIFORNIA YELLOWTAIL

One of the most handsome fishes of the Pacific Ocean is the California yellowtail, *Seriola dorsalis*, which is one of ten members of the international jack family known to inhabit North American waters. Only two are ever found in great abundance here and these are the yellow-

tail and the jack mackerel. In one year as many as 250,000 yellowtails were taken by sport fishermen alone. The commercial catch sometimes runs into several hundred tons annually.

Most of the yellowtails caught along our Pacific Coast originate in the area around Cedros Island off Baja California. Here yellowtails will spawn when they are about two or three years old and when they weigh from 7 to 10 pounds. A three-year-old female may carry and lay 1,500,000 eggs during the spawning season, which normally runs from June through September. The most activity occurs in early August. Yellowtails are great migrators and once they reach maturity they travel long distances, averaging as much as 200–300 miles to reach California waters.

Yellowtails have been reported from Monterey Bay to Cape San Lucas, Baja California, and north again throughout almost the entire Gulf of California. In recent years they have been caught only rarely north of Point Conception.

Most California yellowtails will weigh between 10 and 20 pounds and be between three and seven years old when hooked. The largest recorded specimen was an 80-pounder taken near Guadalupe Island several years ago.

Ordinarily yellowtails are not delicate in their feeding habits. They will forage avidly on anchovies and sardines in southern California waters. Further south they also include pelagic red crabs, squid and similar items in their diet. Because they will take such a variety of forage fishes, they can also be caught on a wide variety of live baits.

Ordinarily yellowtails are found in greatest abundance around the offshore islands, but at times they are abundant around the kelp beds along the southern California coast. When trolling for albacore during midsummer, an angler frequently receives a bonus of yellowtails if he will only drift or troll past floating patches of kelp with a Japanese feather, a nickel-finish spoon or an artificial squid. Generally yellowtails strike best on a fast troll rather than a slow troll.

During the summer and early fall months large schools of yellowtails are frequently observed "breezing" near the surface of the water. That means they're cruising aimlessly about— or seem to be. In winter and in early spring,

Landing a yellowtail off the coast of southern California. (*Photo by John Gartner*)

however, they're usually found deep, and practically never on the surface.

Fishermen have often seen yellowtails behave in an especially peculiar manner. For lack of a better title, this sport can be called "let's attack the shark." A dozen or more yellowtails will find a shark, usually a blue shark, and then appear to attack the critter from all sides—nudging, pulling at its fins, biting and bumping it. But appearances are deceiving; the shark is not really in trouble. The yellowtails, are only removing external parasities from the shark's body. It's at this particular time that a lure cast near the yellowtails will bring almost an immediate strike.

PACIFIC JACK MACKEREL

Jack mackerel, *Trachurus symmetricus*, have been caught along the North American mainland coast from British Columbia to Acapulco, Mexico, but probably they are rare south of Magdalena Bay, Baja California. On several occasions they have been taken as far as six hundred miles off the coast of southern California. They are an entirely pelagic, schooling species, most often found near the surface and in close proximity to the mainland shore, to islands, or hovering above offshore banks.

It is certainly a bonanza for Pacific coast fishermen when schools of large jack mackerel suddenly appear and become abundant in any given area. At such times the only really dependable bait seems to be a large live anchovy, which is fished very near the surface and usually on a small hook and light monofilament line.

The jack is an excellent fish for the light spinning enthusiast.

But jack mackerel have very weak mouths and they often wage a strong enough fight to tear loose from the hook. Still others are lost when fishermen attempt to hoist them aboard without the use of a net or a gaff. By far the best jack fishing period off California is usually from July through September. Occasionally the fish appear in numbers as early as May.

The catch from southern California party boats sometimes reaches 200,000 jacks in a single season, but they're extremely prolific and a single female will normally spawn more than once during the season. The eggs—only about $\frac{1}{25}$-inch in diameter—float freely in the upper layers of the ocean, usually within 300 feet of the surface. At average ocean temperatures, the eggs hatch in only 4 to 5 days. The spawning takes place over an extensive area as far as 80 to 250 miles from shore.

The Pacific jack mackerel—also called jack mackerel, mackerel jack, horse mackerel and Spanish mackerel—does not grow to very impressive size. A 20- to 22-inch fish is a good one, and the longest on authentic record is a 32-inch fish that weighed slightly more than 5 pounds.

A similar fish, the Pacific mackerel, *Pneumatophorus japonicus diego*, is often confused with the Pacific jack mackerel. It's also a pelagic, schooling species known to range from the Gulf of Alaska to Banderas Bay, Mexico, and it seldom will weigh more than a pound or measure much more than 14 inches in length. The largest

Pacific mackerel on record measured 25 inches and weighed 6½ pounds.

When Pacific mackerel are really abundant anywhere along the coast, they eventually are considered pests by most boat fishermen. Once attracted to the free-lunch counter found in the water around nearly every party boat during actual fishing, a battle of wits between fisherman and mackerel usually follows. Most fishermen try to keep from catching them. But they eventually become so exasperated that they eventually up-anchor and move to another spot.

Mackerel will take a wide assortment of lures and live bait. They readily strike small jigs, small spoons, small spinners, plugs, cut bait and live bait. And the truth is that it's difficult to find a fish that will be more active on extremely small tackle. But such a fish can be a nuisance when the anglers on a crowded passenger boat are looking for larger game.

Still, when mackerel are abundant, fishing is good the year round both for mackerel and for the larger species which feed on them.

For a fisherman who likes to spin with extremely light gear, this mackerel is made to order because it's very easy to attract the fish. A man simply chums for them by grinding up any smaller fish, such as sardines or anchovies, and allowing the bits of chum to drift away with the tide.

BLACK SEA BASS

The black sea bass or California bass or California jewfish or giant bass, *Stereolepis gigas*, is one of the most imposing fishes along the Pacific coast. It is a veritable giant and a genuine member of the bass family, which includes striped bass, kelp bass, certain other saltwater basses, groupers and cabrilla. It ranges from Monterey, California, southward and into the Gulf of California.

These fish are most abundant at Anacapa, San Nicolas and Los Coronados islands and between Oceanside and San Clemente on the mainland. Normally they prefer a rocky bottom just outside of a kelp bed where the water varies between 19 and 25 fathoms deep. Fishermen along the coast, however, know that they can frequently be found in inshore areas from 5 to 10 fathoms deep where the bottom is sandy. But these inshore blacks average smaller in size.

From all that marine biologists have been able to determine, black sea bass do not mature until they are eleven to about thirteen years old. At this age a fish will weigh between 50 and 60 pounds. In August 1958 a 320-pound female that was about ready to spawn was found carrying an estimated 60,000,000 eggs that weighed 47 pounds. The main spawning season for this species occurs from July to September.

From their size and extremely bulky shape, black sea bass would appear to be slow and clumsy. Actually they are capable of catching some of the fastest fishes in the Pacific in a short chase. The fact that they are fairly swift swimmers is evident in the wide variety of items found in their stomachs. Included on a bass's diet would be mackerel scad, jack mackerel, sheepshead, ocean whitefish, sand bass, cancer crabs or red crabs. Once the stinger of a stingray was found inside the air bladder of a large bass. It had become imbedded there after piercing the stomach.

The mouth of a large bass is yawning enough to consume a medium-size fish in a single gulp. Black sea bass probably exceed 7 feet 6 inches in length and 600 pounds in size. The largest known single specimen is a 514-pounder that was just

Typical catch of yellowtails, white sea bass and Pacific barracuda made at Todos Santos Bay, Baja California.

over 7 feet long. There's no way to estimate the age of this fish, but California biologists recently examined a 435-pounder and determined that it was between seventy-two and seventy-five years old.

There isn't any shortcut to landing a black sea bass once he is hooked. The tackle recommended by the most experienced anglers will give an idea of the type of struggle this large, brown, bottom-dwelling fish can wage. Most sea bass specialists use a double-built swordfish or marlin rod with a 22-ounce tip; a number 14/0 hook; about 500 yards of 70-pound test line on a 10/0 (600-yard capacity) heavy-duty, deep-sea reel, and wire or cable leader testing about 100 to 150 pounds and about 6 feet 6 inches long.

The bait can be almost anything, but one of the favorites is a small barracuda or mackerel, split and then tied to the line with a section of nylon. This is done to hide the hook as much as possible since the point is left embedded near the tail. Besides mackerel and barracuda, the black sea bass will readily take sand dabs, smaller bass, large sardines, queenfish or a fillet of any of the other fishes that live in the same water. The bait need not be fresh and there are some anglers who prefer to use it after it's a bit ripe from sitting in the sun.

Sometimes the strike is barely noticeable, but it's a wise fisherman who plays out a small amount of line anyway, say from 10 to 15 feet, just in case. As soon as this much slack is taken up and the line taut, he should set the hook as sharply as possible.

The secret to landing this species, which will average around 200 pounds, is to maintain all the pressure the tackle will stand. If the fish is given any slack at all, it will shake its head violently from side to side and there can be only a sad ending to this kind of action. Either the hook will be pulled free or the line will snap. The black sea bass doesn't know any "fancy Dan" tactics; it only likes to find a strong toehold on the bottom and hold it.

Sport fishermen can well afford to copy a trick used by some market fishermen to catch big blacks. The tail is chopped off a large live sardine or jack mackerel or ocean whitefish, when using these smaller fish as bass bait. The idea is to inhibit the swimming ability of the baitfish and at the same time to permit the release of blood into the water where a hungry bass may be lurking. More often than not he'll sniff it out.

KELP BASS

Although kelp bass, *Paralabrax clathratus*, also known as rock bass, sand bass, calico bass, bull bass and cabrilla, do not compare in size to their cousins, the black sea bass, they are nonetheless an extremely fine game species. But there is evidence that this almost entirely sedentary fish is becoming more scarce every year, even though commercial fishing has been prohibited since 1953. And a size limit, which is still in effect, was imposed on kelp bass at the same time.

As can be deduced from the name, kelp bass are mostly caught around kelp beds—on live anchovies or sardines fished near or just under the surface. In recent years, more and more fishermen have been catching them on trolled plugs, spoons and streamer flies because these fish will readily take a great variety of artificial lures. The best catches seem to be made with yellow or brown plugs or on streamer flies in the same colors. But more important than the type of bait

Good catch of barracudas taken near Santa Monica by Carl Davis and Lee Blythe of Malibu.

used is the knowledge that kelp bass are almost never caught—and never even seen—by skin divers very far away from a kelp bed. Also, many of the kelp beds where bass are most plentiful are not visible from the surface of the water.

Kelp bass are distributed from San Francisco southward to the vicinity of Abreojos Point, Baja California. They are not abundant north of Point Conception, California, but at kelp beds elsewhere within their known range, they are usually the most abundant game species in residence.

Calico bass, a common name for smaller kelp bass, can be caught practically the year round. But from May to October is best for the larger fish, which are frequently called bull bass.

Probably kelp bass have been caught up to 20 pounds and even more, but the largest record completely authenticated is a 12½-pounder. Anything over 4 or 5 pounds is an extremely fine catch on light tackle. And the species itself is probably one of the most interesting a light tackle fan will find along the Pacific coast.

The kelp bass and black sea bass have a number of cousins along the Pacific coast which are especially worthy of mention here. First, is the broomtail grouper, *Mycteroperca xenarchus*. This colorful, spotted fish is also called the garrupa (in Mexico), gray broomtail, pinto broomtail or spotted broomtail. It's found over deep reefs and in greatest abundance south of San Quintín bay and is especially plentiful in scattered spots off Baja California. It can be taken on strip baits, live baits or on spoon lures trolled at from 6 to 8 knots. The broomtail grouper has been caught up to 75 pounds, but the odds are good that it grows much larger.

Another cousin of the bass, which reaches 125 pounds and 3 feet 6 inches in length, is the gulf grouper or garrupa de baya, *Mycteroperca jordani*. It's less colorful than the broomtail, but is more abundant south of San Quintín bay and in the Gulf of California. Only a very few have been taken north of San Diego. Largely a bottom feeder on live bait, it will on occasion take an artificial 4/o or 6/o lure trolled very slowly.

The sand bass, *Paralabrax nebulifer,* can be taken the year round southward from Monterey on various kinds of strip baits, live anchovies, queenfish, small sardines, shrimp and mussels. It feeds directly on the bottom and occasionally reaches almost 2 feet in length. The spotted bass, *Paralabrax maculatofasciatus,* which is also called spotted cabrilla or pinto cabrilla, reaches about 1½ feet in length. It ranges from Point Conception, California, southward in nearly all bays, sloughs and stream entrances to Mazatlán, Mexico, and beyond. It also is taken on a wide variety of live and cut baits.

PACIFIC BLUEFIN TUNA

One of the most important events each year for many a California sportsman begins when someone suddenly reports: "Tuna off San Diego!"

As soon as the word spreads that great schools are streaming north toward Catalina waters, hundreds of party boats, charter boats and private craft will suddenly appear and roam these offshore waters. And the excitement, which follows from the docks of San Diego and Newport Beach to Long Beach and Los Angeles, is certainly something to see, because all at once these offshore waters are filled with ravenous schools of bluefin tuna making their annual and mysterious northern migration.

There are big tuna and small ones, but it makes no difference to most sportsmen. Even the 20- to 30-pounders can strip a reel in seconds and that's solid excitement no matter how you look at it. One fisherman called a Pacific bluefin a miniature submarine out of control, and no description fits the critter any better.

The famous California party boats are excellent vehicles for catching many of the species of fish found offshore but they're never more convenient than during the bluefin tuna run. All of them contain ample bait tanks, for example, which can hold an average of 15 pounds of live anchovies for each angler. And when the tuna are really active these anchovies are used up rapidly.

When tuna are "in," party boats always leave the dock long before dawn. The entire trip out to the tuna "grounds" is a time for vast speculation. Every experienced boat captain knows too well the vagaries of bluefins. He knows that some days the deep blue channel will be alive with their feeding antics, but suddenly next day they are gone. New and bigger schools can appear and disappear with almost magical suddenness, and every fisherman on board is hopeful that this will be the day.

If it happens to be one of those wonderful days when the bluefin move in to gorge on the huge schools of baitfish around the Channel Islands, it's a day never to be forgotten. The party boat will actually reach the scene before daylight and immediately the captain will study the current and swing his craft in a wide circle while the bait tender tosses live anchovies or chum overboard. The first wild swirl out on the dark surface of the water means that the tuna are coming in!

Immediately the bait tender ladles out more chum, and everyone on board pitches a live anchovy bait in the path of the tuna. Then they wait, and the suspense is terrific.

Fishermen go down to the sea for many reasons. One of these is to enjoy nature's magnificent and changing spectacle. I remember standing aboard the party boat, *Sea Angler*, just as the sun came up over the mainland mountains, revealing a clear blue and calm Pacific Ocean. The whole scene was exquisite. But suddenly a school of tuna reached the first baits tossed overboard. Everyone could see the shadowy blue forms moving underneath them. Then came the first lightinglike strike, and somebody's rod bent nearly double.

Those bluefins were crazy and hungry. Several reels began to sing at once and line vanished from all of them. Although every fisherman is expecting a strike when tuna are feeding all about him, the strike always comes like a sudden electric shock. The rod tip is whipped downward and at once the reel is thrown into gear as a fast-moving fish strips off a hundred yards and maybe even two hundred yards of line on the first wild run. When he finally stops, you begin to pump, but not for long, because in a few seconds the big bluefin will be off again.

The more tired the tuna becomes, the deeper he goes, and that means the tougher it is to pump him upward to the boat and to the gaff. To catch just one 30-pounder on light tackle is a hard day's work; a full morning of this kind of action is enough to send an angler home sore and tired, but completely happy.

The Pacific or California bluefin tuna, *Thunnus saliens,* is one of three members of the tuna family which inhabit Pacific coastal waters. Although adult bluefins have been taken as far north as Shelikof Strait, Alaska, to Cape San Lucas at the tip of Baja California, they are seldom very numerous north of Los Angeles or south of Magdalena Bay. Strictly pelagic, their appearance along our west coast is seasonal, sporadic and not always predictable.

Although a close relative, the Atlantic bluefin, attains a weight of 1800 pounds and perhaps even more, the largest known Pacific bluefin was a 297-pounder measuring 6 feet 2½ inches in length. This jumbo was caught off Guadalupe Island, Baja California, and was displayed at the fish market in San Pedro on February 26, 1958. The largest California bluefin taken on sport fishing tackle was a 251-pounder caught in 1908 off Santa Catalina Island. Average-size tuna taken by sport fishermen nowadays would run between 10 and 45 pounds.

The bluefin is another species about which very little is known. No fish has ever been observed or caught in California waters with what could be considered ripe or developing gonads. Therefore, nothing is known about the size or age at which they reach maturity, about the number of eggs a female will carry, and so on.

Also, nothing is known about where a bluefin wanders or where it comes from when it is not visiting along our coastline. It is estimated, however, that tuna grow as much as 15 pounds annually during the first few years of life. No very small or larval tuna have ever been recognized or identified to date. Occasionally a hooked bluefin will be lost to sharks, but apart from these and killer whales and fishermen, bluefin tuna have no known natural enemies.

Although there are days when bluefins strike with complete abandon, they are really much more reluctant to take a baited hook than any of the other tuna or tunalike fishes found along the Pacific coast. Also they are seldom caught (relatively) on trolled lures or trolled baits. The truth is that nine days in ten, Pacific tuna are shy and selective to a point of exasperation when an angler's bait is offered to them.

A tuna foraging near the surface wants a large, live and lively anchovy in which the hook is not readily visible. No leader or swivels are used because it's believed that the tuna will not strike any baits thus rigged. There *are* times, however, when tuna lose almost all their wariness. These occur when the bluefin is in mixed company, say with albacore or skipjacks, and the competition for food is especially keen. Naturally an angler is lucky to find such a mixed school of fishes because either live anchovies or firecracker sardines will work very well.

Occasionally, bluefins are located at depths of about 100 to 150 feet. At these depths they aren't nearly as selective as they are in shallow water. A fisherman then can use a sinker weighing as much as 2 ounces and a much stronger and larger hook without alarming them.

The first Pacific tuna was taken off Santa Catalina in 1898 by Dr. Fredrick Holder. Although he was using only the most crude kind of tackle and a knuckle-buster reel without mechanical drag, he still managed to land a 183-pounder. And that remains one of the most remarkable bluefin catches of all time.

Holder surely started something. Shortly after his historic catch, the famous Catalina Tuna Club was formed, and among its earlier visitors were Zane Grey and Gifford Pinchot. Mostly these early pioneers trolled (rather than used live bait), and the tuna they hooked were usually of large size. No doubt they hooked and lost many fish that would exceed the existing world's record for the Pacific.

In 1909, George Farnsworth introduced a most unorthodox system of fishing by trolling flying a fish from a kite. This was moderately successful and has been copied in Atlantic waters, where it works much better.

But more and more the bluefin tuna is becoming a light-tackle fish in the Pacific. And a few of the most serious tuna anglers have made some astonishing catches. Glen Bracken of the Southern California Tuna Club set a world's record for spinning tackle with a 30-pounder taken on 12-pound test line, and Dr. E. A. Moore set another record with a 16-pounder on 4-pound line.

Bluefins are likely to show up along the California coast anytime from May through September. Some of the most consistently productive fishing areas are to be found in Santa Monica Bay near the kelp beds between San Clemente and Oceanside, around Santa Catalina Island, San Clemente Island and Los Coronados.

But it's possible that some of the very best bluefin grounds have not been located. As long ago as 1921, R. C. Grey tells of encountering tuna schools off Santa Catalina which were more than 3 or 4 miles long, and the smallest fish taken from the school weighed well over 100 pounds. Commercial boats that travel at sea far beyond the reach of the usual sport angler still report seeing schools of similar size. Also, they report schools traveling so fast that their boats are not able to overtake them.

Two other tuna are found in Pacific coast waters. These are the big-eyed tuna, *Parathunnus mebachi,* and the yellowfin tuna, *Neothunnus macropterus.* The yellowfin, which has been known to reach 256 pounds, occurs southward from Santa Barbara all along the coast of Baja California to Central America. It is present around the Hawaiian Islands but otherwise is not common north of the Mexican border. It is taken in a manner and on tackle similar to that to the bluefin tuna.

PACIFIC ALBACORE

Not long ago the Tohoku Fisheries Laboratories in Japan notified officials of the California Department of Fish and Game that an unusual albacore had been caught about 145 miles east of Tokyo. The albacore was unusual in that it carried a spaghetti-type plastic tag that had been affixed to the fish nine months before in California. The fish had traveled 4600 miles and had gained 4½ pounds. It had traveled more than 500 miles a month—almost 18 miles a day!

But that is no isolated example. In 1953 and 1955 two other albacore, tagged and released off California's coast about a year earlier, also were captured by Japanese fishermen. And in addition, two more California-tagged albacore have been recovered off Midway Island far out in the Pacific Ocean. Still others were captured around Hawaii.

These recoveries substantiate that the albacore, also called longfin or long-finned tuna and abrego, is one of the most widely traveled as well as one of the finest game fishes in the world. It's also one of the fastest traveling fishes. Scientifically it's known as *Germo alalunga.* It can be distinguished from other tuna and tuna-like fishes of the West coast by the extremely long pectoral fins, which reach two-thirds of the way back to the tail.

The life history of the albacore is just as mysterious as its strange, unpredictable wanderings across the face of the Pacific. Spawning probably does not take place near our coast, or at least if it does, no evidence of it has ever been found. No Pacific albacore larvae have ever been identified in our waters or elsewhere in the Pacific. They probably haven't been identified anywhere. There are some vague indications, however, that albacore do spawn somewhere in midocean, possibly north and west of the Hawaiian Islands, because large specimens caught in this area during late summer on very deep bait have had nearly ripe eggs in their ovaries. Each one of these eggs measures about $\frac{1}{25}$-inch in diameter.

Contrary to a belief that is often mentioned on party boats and around fishing docks, the albacore is not a hybrid or "mule." It is a distinct, far-ranging species.

The albacore's diet varies, depending on whether they have been feeding near the surface or in extremely deep waters. It also depends largely on which foods are most easily available. Mostly though, the stomach content of albacore caught have revealed small fishes mixed with squid, octopuses and shrimplike organisms.

In many cases the complicated research studies of fisheries biologists make it possible for fishermen to enjoy far better luck. And when speaking of albacore, we have an extremely good example of it. Recent studies have indicated that out of every 100 albacore caught, 51 are hooked in waters with temperatures ranging between 60° and 64° F. An additional 37 of these fish are taken in temperatures of between 65° and 70° F. In other words, 90 percent were taken in waters between 60° and 70°, a fact that has simplified the finding of schools of fish.

The actual technique of fishing for albacore is much the same as for catching tuna, except that they can be taken far more often on artificial lures. And they are not as selective of live baits. Usually the first albacore of the season are taken in mid-June, and a few of them remain in United States coastal waters until the last half of February. But year in and year out, the best action occurs during August and September.

Albacore are much like many other fishes in the sea in that when they are actively feeding or "hot," as fishermen say on the West coast, they will strike almost anything. At times they even seem to catch the bait in midair. On the other hand, when they are "cold" it doesn't seem that any kind of live bait or artificial will work.

Many charter-boat captains are especially good at finding and catching albacores when there isn't any sign of them on the surface. This means probing around with a long line in depths from 100 to 300 feet. It isn't nearly as sporting or action-filled as fishing on the surface, but it is most productive. And some years, unhappily,

most schools of albacore seem to migrate northward along the coast either deep enough so that the sport fishermen do not find them or too far out at sea to be in range of sport boats.

An angler's best bet is to watch the outdoor columns in his local newspaper to learn of the arrival of albacore in local waters. Their presence along our coast is strictly seasonal and they first appear in the southern part of their range, which is off Baja California. Although there are records of albacore from Clarión Island off the coast of Mexico, they are rarely caught south of Magdalena Bay. Gradually they move northward along the Pacific coast and in the late summer and fall months they reach the southern coast of Alaska. Fishing in-between is extremely good at points along the coasts of Oregon and Washington.

The largest known albacore is a 93-pounder taken by commercial fishermen on long line gear in the mid-Pacific. There is much evidence, however, that larger fish have been caught, though not completely authenticated. The largest fish taken on sport fishing tackle is a 66¼-pounder landed years ago off Santa Catalina Island. Another outstanding Catalina catch is the 35-pounder taken in 1951 on 12-pound test line by D. E. Hanlon.

WHITE SEA BASS

No less than 9 kinds of croakers are found in one area or another along the Pacific coast of North America and one of the most important of these is the white sea bass. These fish can be readily distinguished from all the other croakers by their greater size when mature, and by the 4 or 5 dark and vertical bars on their flanks when they are young. There is also a raised ridge on the midline of the belly at all ages of the fish. The white sea bass, which isn't a bass at all, is also called white croaker, king croaker, weakfish, and sea trout. Its scientific designation is *Cynoscion nobilis*. It is taken near kelp beds and over shallow submerged banks and on the edges of banks with such live bait as sardines, anchovies, small mackerel and strip bait. Sea bass will take lures trolled at a fairly slow speed.

The recommended hook size for this fish is from number 1 to 2/o. Although white sea bass are not ordinarily as wary and shy as some other Pacific offshore fishes, there are times when they can become quite selective. Occasionally, for example, sea bass will strike only fairly large, live Pacific mackerel. At still other times a live squid appears to be the only successful bait. It's good to have both available.

Once white sea bass were far more plentiful in many localities than they are today. Large numbers of them were taken years ago in the San Francisco Bay area, but now they are missing from that environment. Since very small, young white sea bass are often taken in quiet waters near the surf zone, spawning is presumed to take place in late spring and on into the summer months. The shore areas in Santa Monica Bay, Belmont Shore, Dana Point, Oceanside, Coronado and similar localities appear to be rather important nursery grounds for young white sea bass.

But many of these same areas are sufficiently polluted nowadays so that the white sea bass appear affected by some of the toxic materials. These effects are evident in many ways, including hemorrhaging of the eyes, which causes blindness. Fish caught in these areas often have parasitic pill bugs attached to their fins and other parts of their bodies. It would seem, then, that the future of white sea bass fishing depends on how well pollution is controlled in certain areas along the California coast.

Large white sea bass have been taken in the Pacific as far north as Juneau, Alaska, but ordinarily they do not range much beyond San Francisco. Southward they extend all along the coast of Baja California and into the Gulf of California. The larger fish frequently gather into large but loosely grouped schools, and these are most common over sandy bottoms and around the offshore margins of kelp beds on the mainland coast. They are numerous offshore around San Clemente and Santa Catalina.

An adult white sea bass is a good strong fighter and anything over 10 pounds will give all but the heaviest tackle a good test. The largest known individual is an 83¾-pound fish taken off San Felipe, Mexico, in 1953. That must have been an extremely old fish because 40-pounders that are taken occasionally—especially in Mexican waters—will average about twenty years old.

Many saltwater species of fish are vastly more active at night than they are in daylight, and the white sea bass is certainly one of these. Fishing for the big whites at night is one of the most dramatic experiences possible for an angler along the Pacific coast, but still it's a fishing technique that has not really been fully exploited or "discovered."

To angle at sea in the middle of the night, for white bass as well as for any other game species, is a unique and wonderfully exciting experience. Often, summer nights on the Pacific are calm and completely still except for the activity of fishes and other marine animals that suddenly surge to the surface. At times the activity is so great that the sea appears to be seething—or boiling. At such times white sea bass lose much of their caution. They not only venture closer to the boat in darkness, but they feed nearer to the surface. And they strike any sort of lure or live bait with far more abandon.

As soon as night falls, the mood of the unexpected strike and of sudden action is multiplied, as when a white sea bass follows the bait right to the boat and grabs it as it is about to be lifted from the water. Such experiences are not recommended for anglers with weak hearts, but they do keep any angler on his toes. And in any case, this after-dark angling is a marvelous change of pace from the usual fishing in bright sunlight.

Even on those rare nights when action is slow and fish do not seem to be striking, there is a restful fascination to sitting quietly on board and waiting for the unexpected to happen.

PACIFIC BONITO

Many fishermen consider the Pacific or California bonito, *Sarda chiliensis*, one of the finest fighting fish for its size in the entire ocean. They have good reason to do so because it is a fish with a voracious appetite—which at times will strike any conceivable bait or lure or object that is tossed in its path. Once a school is aroused, it doesn't make any difference if the angler is using a dead or a live anchovy, a sardine, squid, jig, or even a freshwater plug, because a bonito will attack any or all of these. One bonito has been known to take two different baits at once—trolled behind a boat.

The California bonito is a most handsome member of the mackerel family, which in Mexican waters includes such other prizes as the wahoo and sierra mackerel. The only other member of the family which is found off the United States coast is the Monterey Spanish mackerel, a very rare summer visitor during some years.

Bonito are the only tunalike fishes that have oblique dark stripes on their backs. These grand game fish appear in almost every section of the eastern Pacific Ocean. They range from Vancouver Island, British Columbia, to Panama and from there along the South American coast to Chile. They are definitely a schooling species and are usually observed within a few miles of shore along the mainland coast and around any islands. Only occasionally are they found very far out to sea.

Most bonito are taken while trolling, perhaps for other fish, with chrome jigs, plastic squids or feather jigs. Quite often when a single bonito is caught and hooked, it is possible to hook others by casting in the vicinity of the hooked fish. By keeping one fish hooked all the time, one after another bonito can be taken until a fisherman's arms become too tired to continue the sport. A bonito of about 4 or 5 pounds on light or medium spinning tackle is a game fish of tremendous potential and unbelievable endurance. Its strength is amazing to freshwater anglers who hook a bonito for the first time.

There are numerous reports, none of them verified, of bonito up to 40 and even 50 pounds. But the largest one completely verified is a 28-pounder taken off the coast of Baja California. Most bonito weigh between 3 and 12 pounds and anything over 12 pounds is an extraordinarily fine specimen. Bonito are extremely important along the Pacific coast because they are as valuable as baitfish as for sport fishing.

At odd intervals, spawning occurs all along the West coast. The bulk of it seems to occur between January and May. The free-floating eggs require about 3 days to hatch and the small fish resulting are usually first observed by the livebait haulers when they reach 6 or 8 inches in the early summer months. By the time they are a year old they may weigh as much as 6 or 7 pounds.

Young bonito from 6 inches to more than a foot long are extremely fine baitfish. Some of the larger sizes are especially desirable for marlin, tuna and black sea bass.

SHEEPSHEAD

The sheepshead of the Pacific, *Pimelometopon pulcher*, which is one of three members of the wrasse family that travels along the West Coast, is certainly one of the plug-uglies of the fish world. As if its caninelike teeth and its lantern jaw were not enough, the male sheepshead develops a hump on his forehead during the breeding season. His scientific name means "beautiful fat forehead."

Even the body colors of the sheepshead are weird. At all stages, ages and sexes, these colors serve to distinguish them from the other kinds of wrasses. Young sheepshead of both sexes are a solid orange-red in color except for roundish black blotches. Adult females are a dull red or rose color, and adult males have a bluish black head and tail with a red midsection. Both males and females have light or whitish chins when full grown.

Most abundant near the bottom, particularly around dense kelp forests, sheepshead are taken in depths of from 20 to 100 feet, but they are occasionally caught in shallower water. Besides the regions of kelp beds, they also congregate along rocky shores and especially near mussel beds. Never abundant north of Los Angeles, they nevertheless have been taken from Monterey Bay to the tip of Baja California and throughout most of the Gulf of California.

Male or dog sheepshead are said to reach a weight of greater than 30 pounds, but there are no authenticated records of these. Most sheepshead caught by fishermen are less than 15 pounds They are taken on 3/0 to 5/0 hooks baited with mussels, rock crabs, lobster, shrimp with the shell on, clams, abalone, fish strips and live bait.

Although they will seldom strike a trolled or a cast lure that is retrieved in a normal manner, sheepshead can often be tempted into striking even a shiny bare hook or a small metal jig that is jiggled up and down in an enticing manner within a few inches of the bottom. They are expert bait thieves and their large, solid jaw-teeth often cause the hook to slip out without ever having been set after an angler strikes.

Any fisherman who hooks a sheepshead is immediately in for a strong and tugging battle. It often ends in disaster when the fish runs through or around a kelp plant or perhaps ducks beneath a rocky ledge. It's possible in some rocky areas to hook sheepshead all day long but never to land a single one. The best fishing areas for sheepshead are around most of the kelp beds south of Point Conception, California, and anywhere around the offshore Pacific islands south of and including Santa Cruz Island.

Not too much of the sheepshead's life history is known, but skin divers off the California coast have been able to give biologists some fairly valuable information. These same skin divers have often reported seeing what they believed to be the same sheepshead frequenting a particular reef, rock outcropping or other underwater landmark over the course of several years. There are so many similar reports that it is almost safe to assume that sheepshead do not wander about very much. And this is especially true in the case of large, adult fish.

Commercial fishermen do not consider sheepshead as anything more than a nuisance because they believe these strange wrasses are destructive to lobsters, abalone and other kinds of shellfish. It is true, according to skin divers, that sheepshead spend a great deal of their time trying to live up to this bad reputation. On the other hand, while a sheepshead's stomach is usually filled with such shellfish as lobster and abalone, many a large black sea bass has been found to contain a good-size sheepshead in its innards.

Lobster fishermen frequently use sheepshead as bait in their lobster traps but sheepshead often reciprocate by entering the fisherman's trap and by eating all the lobsters they find inside.

Until recent years there has been a widespread belief that the flesh of the sheepshead was inedible and perhaps even poisonous. Of course, this meant that many fishermen didn't even bother to take home their catch. But this reputation is entirely false. Actually the flesh of a sheepshead is white, firm and rather mild in flavor. When it is fried in thin fillets, it is difficult to surpass on the table, and chunks of sheepshead meat can be used as the fish stock in an extremely delicious fish chowder or fish salad.

BOCACCIO
All together there are 52 members of the rockfish family native to Pacific Coast waters of North America. The bocaccio, *Sebastodes paucispinis,* is one of the most available and game members of the family. It reaches a length of 36 inches and a weight of 21 pounds but an extremely good fish would be one about half that size.

Almost any rocky or rubble bottom at from 250 to 750 feet in depth is likely to yield an extremely good catch of bocaccio. The secret to this fishing is entirely in finding the right type of bottom.

The usual fishing rig is made up of from 4 to 6 hooks, above a sinker that is heavy enough to take the whole business to the bottom on a fairly straight course. The rig can be fished from a large specially built reel attached to the rail of a boat, or from a reel of large capacity such as that used for fishing for the large billfishes and tunas. Because of the depths fished, it takes considerable time just to let the line down and then to haul up this rig again. And it requires muscles, too. Consequently the bait should be sufficiently tough to remain on the hook while being nibbled and chewed upon by bocaccios and other fishes which inhabit these deep places. Squid makes an ideal bait for this type of fish.

Once the angler finds the bottom with his bait, he should leave it there long enough to catch a fish on every hook. This is quite a trick because the impulse is to strike immediately when a nibble is felt.

Bottom fishermen have caught bocaccio from Queen Charlotte Sound in British Columbia to Ensenada, Baja California. Although adults are most commonly found at the depths we mentioned before, they sometimes go as deep as 1000 feet.

Other members of the rockfish family caught in great numbers include the olive rockfish, which is often confused with the kelp bass and which has been taken as deep as 480 feet. It reaches a weight of 7 or 8 pounds, and some kelp beds, such as those in the vicinity of Santa Barbara and San Nicolas Island, are almost paved with them.

Still another important rockfish is the blue, which ranges from the Bering Sea to Santo Tomás, Baja California. It never reaches more than a few pounds in size. But it can be caught in quantity near rocky shores, around breakwaters, sunken ships, piles of rubble and in similar localities along the entire California coastline and then northward along the Oregon and Washington coasts. The best baits usually are mussels, clams, crabs, shrimp or squid. For their size, blue rockfish put up an excellent battle when hooked on light tackle.

Vermilion rockfish have been caught from Vancouver Island south to Guadalupe Island, Baja California. They reach a length of 30 inches, a weight of about 15 pounds and commonly occur in water from 180 to 500 feet deep over irregular, rocky or rubble bottoms. In extreme cases they are caught in depths as great as 650 feet. Vermilion rockfish usually make up a majority of the bag of southern California anglers. The same rig, bait and technique can be used as it used for catching bocaccio.

Because a good rockfish hole often will yield a dozen or more kinds of rockfish on any given day, it can be said that rockfishing is colorful, interesting, productive and mysterious. It's also good exercise. And it produces unusual fish.

The strangest member of the rockfish family is the sculpin, which reaches a maximum weight of about 4 pounds and is an excellent fish for chowders and soups.

A curious thing about the sculpin is that its eggs are imbedded in the gelatinous walls of hollow, pear-shaped egg balloons. The balloons, each 5 to 10 inches long, are joined at the small ends. The walls of these balloons are about $\frac{1}{10}$-inch thick, transparent or greenish in color and contain a single layer of eggs. Few other fish bother to eat them. Although the balloons are spawned at the bottom of the sea, they rise rapidly to the surface, where the eggs hatch within 5 days.

Any fisherman should be extremely careful when handling sculpin because all of the sharp, fin spines—dorsal, anal and pelvic—are venomous or mildly poisonous and can cause an extremely painful wound if the skin is punctured by one of them. Immersion in hot water in which Epsom salts has been dissolved will do much to alleviate many of the discomforts from a sculpin wound. But if undue swelling, nausea, dizziness or fainting follow, a doctor should be called immediately.

OCEAN WHITEFISH

The ocean whitefish, *Caulolatilus princeps,* which is no relation to the freshwater whitefish, is the only member of the blanquillo fish family known to inhabit California waters. It reaches a weight of 20 pounds but seldom exceeds 10 pounds and is caught from just north of Point Conception southward to the tip of Baja California and then completely throughout the Gulf of California. The same or a very similar species is also found off the coast of Ecuador, Peru, Chile and offshore around the Galápagos Islands.

Whitefish live mostly at depths of from 30 to 300 feet where the bottom is rocky. They will eat just about anything they can get their mouths around, including crabs, shrimp, many crustaceans, small octopuses, squid and an assortment of bottom-feeding fishes. Evidently they consider shrimp or a piece of lobster as the most desirable because these are the baits that fisherman use with the greatest success.

Once the fish is hooked, any fisherman is in for a thrill he will not forget because even a small ocean whitefish wages one of the strongest battles of any of the Pacific fishes. When a good whitefish hole is found, an angler can use a rig with from 2 to 4 hooks and sometimes catch that many fish at one time. The very best spots are around the offshore islands south of the Santa Barbara County line. Cortez and Tanner banks are also extremely good. Spring, summer and fall months are excellent. The winter months provide good fishing, but in much deeper water.

PACIFIC OR CALIFORNIA HALIBUT

Living completely around the world is a family of flounders, soles and halibut, called the flatfish family, all of which are delicious on the table but extremely curious to see. Their compressed bodies with both eyes on one side make these adult flatfish easy to recognize immediately.

After flatfish or flounders spawn, their eggs develop into normal-looking small fish, but gradually one eye begins to "migrate" or shift to the other side of the head and the young fish settles to the bottom. There they spend their entire lives, lying on one side, with both eyes on top, while feeding on small fish and bottom-dwelling invertebrates. Usually the bottom side of the fish becomes white and the top side exactly matches the ocean floor. It can even change in color and pattern as the fish moves from one location to another and therefore is one of nature's finest examples of camouflage.

The largest member of this flatfish family, or rather of the left-eyed flounder family, is the California halibut which, strangely enough, has a habit of being right-eyed about 40 percent of the time. Being left-eyed or right-eyed means both eyes exist on either the left or right side after the fish grows from its larval stage.

But the left-eyed California halibut is the largest species of its entire genus known in North

American waters, both in the Atlantic and Pacific. There are numerous reports of 70- and 80-pounders, but the accepted record is a 61½-pound fish, which measured 5 feet in length.

Unlike many of their relatives which depend mostly on crustaceans for food, halibut feed largely upon anchovies and similar small fishes. And as impossible as it must seem, they have been observed jumping clear of the water to catch anchovies from schools traveling near the surface. In turn, halibut are preyed upon by such predacious animals as angel sharks, electric rays, sea lions and Pacific bottlenose dolphins.

In the years immediately before 1957 the California Department of Fish and Game tagged 7000 halibut, and in the period immediately following, 350 recoveries of these tags were made. Only one fish had traveled as far as 80 miles from the place it was tagged. On the other hand, more than 90 percent of the recaptured fish had traveled no more than one mile from the point of release.

California halibut are most abundant on sandy bottoms in water that is shallower than 10 fathoms. Some of the largest halibut seem to congregate around dense beds of sand dollars in the shallow water just outside a pounding surf. They are found south from the Klamath River in California to Magdalena Bay, Baja California. At times they reach great abundance in the fast-running channels of Morro and Mission bays and at other times they are caught in the strong surf along open, exposed beaches or in areas where rocky bottoms and rugged shoreline are broken up by small sandy areas.

The Pacific Coast waters of North America include two other game fishes of considerable importance to fishermen. One is the sablefish, *Anoplopoma fimbria*, which is the only member of the sablefish family that inhabits the coast. Adult sablefish live on the bottom and appear to prefer those localities where there is blue clay or hard mud near submarine canyons and depressions. They have been taken in such habitats as this almost everywhere between northwestern Alaska and the southern tip of Baja California. They are not abundant south of San Francisco except in a few localities of quite deep water like Newport Beach.

The record sablefish probably exceeded 50 pounds, but most specimens caught weigh less

Large halibut taken along the Oregon coast.

than 30 pounds. Tagging studies reveal that they do not travel very far.

Sablefish sometimes abound in inshore waters and smaller individuals are even caught in the surf, but most of the time they live in extremely deep water from 450 feet to about 1000 feet. They seem to migrate into deeper waters during the winter season and in the summer months are most likely to be found in shallower water. They will strike chunks of salted mackerel or fresh squid with equal abandon. Although not a very strong fighter, their heavy weight in some cases more than makes up for the lack of fighting ability.

Another Pacific coast species of importance is the lingcod, *Ophiodon elongatus*, which exists from northwestern Alaska to Central America. Ordinarily though, they are not abundant south of San Francisco.

They inhabit deep areas near the bottom, generally in close association with rock piles and kelp beds, especially where there is a strong tidal current. About 350 feet is an ideal depth to find lingcod, which are reported to reach lengths of 5 feet and 70 pounds in weight.

Chapter Fourteen

INSHORE ALONG THE PACIFIC COAST

CORBINA, SURFPERCH, GREENLING SEATROUT, MANY OTHERS

From Point Barrow, Alaska, down along the Pacific coast to Panama, including all the bays, the river estuaries and the Gulf of California, is a shoreline distance of approximately 4000 miles. Included in that distance are some 2500 miles of surf available to any saltwater angler who likes to stay close to or on the shore.

Most of this surf line, except in Mexico, is paralleled by excellent highways. Motorists using the highways can often scan this vast expanse of water and wonder how on earth the surf angler knows where and when to drop his bait. But it isn't as difficult as it seems and the rewards in fish are amazing.

Here's a quick partial list of fish available to the saltwater inshore fisherman along the Pacific coast: opaleye, surfperch (many varieties), bass, cod, cabezone, croakers, corbina, several kinds of rockfish, halibut, flounder, sole, sculpin, sheepshead, sand dabs, striped bass and salmon. These are only the major varieties. Elsewhere in localized areas other fish can be taken. A good example is the extremely game and spectacular roosterfish, which occurs in the Gulf of California and at certain other points southward.

For the man who hasn't much time for his fishing or who lacks knowledge of certain waters, there is one sure way to locate a productive hot spot and this happens to be true on the Pacific coast, the Atlantic coast, the Gulf Coast, the Florida Keys or anywhere else. Watch for the bait and tackle shops and the boat liveries located along the coastal highways. Wherever such an establishment appears, its fairly sure that good fishing exists nearby. At least, good fishing information is available.

Stop at any of these little stores and explain to the proprietor that you are new to the section and that you want to go fishing. Invariably he'll tell you where to fish, whether to concentrate on a rising or a falling tide, what bait to use and how to rig tackle. If you do not have your own tackle the chances are that you can rent whatever you need for a nominal sum.

But tackle and bait stores are not the only sources of information. There are other reliable ways to find productive waters in any given stretch of shoreline. Here is what you will want to look for:

On a shoreline that is mostly rocky, look for a short stretch that is smooth and sandy. Any fish in the vicinity which like a sand or open-type bottom will congregate there.

Or on a long, uninterrupted stretch of smooth sandy beach, look for a place where the breakers occur consistently 30 to 50 yards out and where there is one large breaker rather than a series of small ones. Many game fish will lie just outside that one big breaker to feed on the food released by an incoming tide.

When the shoreline is all rocky, unbroken by smooth stretches, look for a spot where you can get beyond the breakers into deeper water. Such a place might be a pier, a seawall, a breakwater or a natural ledge extending beyond the surf line. Many breakwaters enclose harbors and extend for many miles into deep water. They are always good fishing spots and the fact that they are rather rough going on foot keeps them from being overcrowded as are so many sport-fishing piers. Watch also for small estuaries where freshwater streams empty into the ocean. Fish where the water blends with saltwater.

On the Pacific coast, try all freshwater inlets north of central California for striped bass, steelhead and salmon. Try the surf on rocky, rough shores for rockfish and rock bass; the sandy shores from central California south for perch, halibut, sand dabs, smelt, sheepshead and certain bass. About 80 percent of the West coast surf fishing is concentrated in southern California and down into Mexico.

At many piers in or near towns on coastal highways you will find small boats and motors for rent. There is usually excellent fishing, which is not accessible from the shore, to be enjoyed nearby. These spots are mainly behind seawalls not connected with the main shoreline or perhaps they're kelp beds, reefs or sand flats farther out. If it's a seawall, fish close to the wall, using a medium weight to get the bait down. If it's a kelp bed, fish at its edge, dropping the bait straight to the bottom then raising it about a foot. Many favorite game species gather around these weed beds. At the seawalls there are many mussels, small crabs, rock worms and crustaceans which lure the larger game fish.

Here's another sure sign of fish. Always watch for gulls and terns wheeling and diving. Birds milling anywhere usually means bait fish close to the surface and that in turn means game fish will be attracted to the bait fish. So, fish where the birds are fishing. That's good advice anywhere.

Wherever you fish along the West coast, it's a good idea to seek advice about tackle and bait from local sources. In general, you want a rod with at least an 8-foot tip and a 30-inch two-handed butt, a free-spool reel with star drag and not less than 200 yards capacity of, say, 9-thread line or 20-pound monofilament line. You'll need sinkers from ½ to 8 ounces, wire leader material, swivels, and hooks from size 6 to 5/0, depending upon which fish you are trying to catch.

Your bait will be what local experts advise (at least to begin) or what is available. However, there is a way to discover the best bait for yourself. Attach 3 hooks to the line, each on an 18-inch leader and spaced about 3 feet apart. Put the weight beyond the hooks at the end of the line. Now put a different bait on each hook. Try mussels, cut fish, shrimp or sand crabs on alternating hooks. Whichever bait is most productive is the one to use eventually on all the hooks.

In the absence of advice to the contrary, you should fish on a rising or full tide, either early or late in the day.

Use pear-shaped weights on a rocky bottom, pyramid-shaped weights on a sandy or mud bottom. If you find the breakers are bringing your bait back, you need more weight. The best all-around bait for many kinds of fishing in the surf as well as in rocky areas—at least to try in the beginning—is a shrimp with its skin removed. Of course, certain local conditions make some other bait advisable, but shrimp is always a good bet to start with.

In any case, do not hesitate to seek advice. It would take too long to learn inshore coastal fishing on your own, and anyway, most fishermen are friendly and always happy to help you.

This is a good spot to talk about the inshore fishes and to describe how they have adapted to their chosen habitats. The shape of a fish's body is usually indicative of the kind of habitat he needs or in which he lives. For example, the typical open-ocean types of fishes, such as tuna, mackerel and bonito are streamlined and cigar-shaped because they rely on speed to capture food and to escape enemies.

Bottom dwellers, on the other hand, are of two different types. Either they are flattened out—such as the halibut, sole, flounder and ray—or they have short, bulky bodies with large pectoral fins for quick short movements—the sculpin, rockfish and greenling.

It has been pointed out before that most inshore areas are turbulent and under bombardment by breaking waves. A part of this inshore area is covered with water at high tide and is high and dry at low tide, with occasional tide pools along rocky coasts. Especially suited to this area are fishes with slender, elongated bodies able to entwine or to hide among seaweeds and rocks and to seek shelter in holes and crevices from both the force of the water and from their enemies.

Others, very small in size and with slender bodies, hide in holes, in cavities under ledges and among seaweeds. Because of their shape, deep-bodied fishes such as the surfperch, half-moon and California sargo are difficult for most predators to swallow. When these fish face head on into the force of the water, they offer little surface for resistance.

Now let's look at some of the game species an angler is likely to encounter along our Pacific coast.

CORBINA

It has often been stated that the surf caster is the aristocrat of all saltwater fishermen. His arena is usually a clean, soft beach scoured by the surf, where the noise of breakers is always present. There really isn't any other sport exactly like it, no matter whether the surf is on the Pacific or on the Atlantic coast. Just as many surf anglers go out to savor the inspiring beauty, to obtain a suntan or for the therapeutic value to mind and muscles as to catch a string of fish.

Also, the surf fisherman is a different personality than his gregarious cousin who enjoys fishing with many other people on a party boat. The surfer ordinarily likes solitude. He prefers to find his own fishing hole, to bait his own hook and to fight his fishes single-handed. And on the Pacific—at least from the vicinity of Point Conception on the California coast south into Central America and including the Gulf of California—one of the most abundant fishes he will find is the corbina.

The corbina or California corbina or California whiting or corvina or surf fish, *Menticirrhus undulatus,* is among the most difficult of the surf fishes to hook. There are times when an entire school of them will be actively feeding on soft-shell sand crabs all around a fisherman's bait, ignoring the sand crab with a hook in it. Some say that hooks too large keep the fish away. Others maintain that the corbina is spooked by

a leader that is too heavy and too stout. Possibly it's a combination of both, and perhaps also it's that the corbina is extremely selective.

Many members of the croaker family inhabit Pacific coast waters and the corbina is only one of them. A single, fleshy, chin whisker on the lower jaw distinguishes the corbina from all other croakers except the yellowfin, which frequently lives in the same waters. The yellowfin has two strong spines at the front of the anal fin, and its body is laterally compressed. The corbina has only one or occasionally two weak spines. Its body is more rounded. These are the main characteristics by which the two fishes can be separated.

The corbina is normally a bottom fish that lives along sandy beaches and in shallow bays. Occasionally it is found in muddy estuaries where freshwater rivers enter saltwater. This condition occurs most frequently in Central America rather than along the California Pacific coast. Corbina travel in small schools in the surf zone of the sea in from only a few inches of water to depths of around 50 feet. The average depth in which a fisherman can expect to find them is about 6 feet. Apparently they move offshore into deeper water during the winter and when they are spawning. But they tend to move closer inshore during high tides at night.

In August of 1945 a 7¼-pound corbina, which measured 28 inches, was taken at San Onofre and this remains the largest verified record in California. However, corbina of twice this size have been captured in the Gulf of California and along the coast of Costa Rica.

Male corbina mature at about two years of age and females at about three years of age. The spawning season extends from June through September, but always is the heaviest during late July and early August. This activity apparently takes place offshore as ripe females are seldom found in the surf zone by fishermen.

Although there are few better food fishes in the world, it has been forbidden to take corbina commercially in California since 1915. In this state they make up about 17 percent of the surf fisherman's total bag. And they are caught the year round on the state's sandy beaches.

About 90 percent of the corbina's diet consists of sand crabs and the other 10 percent is mostly composed of clams and other crustaceans. Nearly all the feeding on crabs is done in the surf, sometimes in water so shallow that their backs are exposed. They scoop up mouthfuls of sand and then separate the food from it by sending the sand through the gills.

Corbina are such extremely selective feeders that they apparently spit out bits of clamshell and other foreign matter and swallow only the meaty parts. This habit of delicately mouthing food probably explains why fishermen seldom are thrilled with a really hard strike. The angler must have a very good sense of touch or a highly developed intuition to detect the slow bite of a corbina.

Here's how an experienced surf fisherman goes about catching corbina and other croakers. His tackle includes a 6-ounce or smaller pyramid or triangle sinker, whichever size is heavy enough to hold against the undertow or current of the tide. This is tied to the end of a 48-inch 2-pound gut leader with two loops on the leader about a foot apart. Two shorter leaders, each about 8 inches are attached to the loops and to these are knotted No. 1 or No. 2 short shank hooks. While most fishermen bait with sand crabs, the corbina's favorite food, there are certain times and conditions when pileworms or rock worms are also extremely effective.

A surf caster always keeps a wary eye on the weather, but the only element that really hinders him is a strong and unfavorable onshore wind. Most surfers prefer to fish on an advancing or flooding tide, but if the man has not gathered his baits beforehand, he will arrange to arrive at an early-morning low tide. This gives him a chance to collect all the mussels or sandworms or softshell sand crabs that he needs.

An early low tide also gives an angler a chance to select his spots. These are the deep holes or depressions along any beach which will be under some depth of water at a later high tide. It is always extremely valuable, and this point cannot be stressed enough, to locate these hollows or depressions before actually fishing. If they are not discovered before the tide comes in, it will be necessary to do much extra casting and probing with a heavy sinker to discover such hot spots. Good surf fishing depends very much on finding the right holes.

This is a good place to mention that the times of tides are available in booklet or pamphlet form in many sporting goods stores, at Coast Guard offices and at most docks and marinas. No surf fisherman should be without such a table. Many newspapers and radios regularly publish this data. A telephone call to the local weatherman or weather station will predict expected wind conditions.

Once a good corbina or croaker hole is located, whether it be in the surf zone or when fishing in a bay, a unique method of baiting or chumming can be used. Open a dozen or so mussels and without removing the meat, toss them into likely holes or depressions. This will attract numerous smaller fishes and the resultant commotion will in turn attract corbina. A hook baited with a mussel is then dropped within a short distance down the tide from the bait.

What happens here is something experienced saltwater fishermen understand very well and which they have been able to use successfully on many game species. That, simply, is to arouse the competitive feeding instinct among fishes. Quite often if one fish in a school can be tempted to strike, others will become wildly excited and probably begin striking with abandon. Corbina are especially susceptible to this kind of maneuver.

During the warm period of midsummer it's an extremely wise corbina fisherman who goes to the surf to try his luck at night. Most surf

Lonely pier fisherman at daybreak along the central California coast. (*Photo by John Gartner*)

fish are very active night feeders and the corbina is no exception. Furthermore there is evidence that they are somehow attracted by a bright light, especially on a very dark night. A Coleman-type lantern is like a magnet and is likely to bring corbina close to the caster if any are feeding in the vicinity.

Corbina and all their close cousins, the croakers, become more daring and feed closer into the beach at night. Of course, an angler cannot see the fishes feeding as in daylight and therefore he must work by the touch system. But sometimes at night it's possible to hear fish noisily feeding close to shore. This fact alone has accounted for many extremely fine catches.

Besides the corbina and the yellowfin croaker, several other members of the croaker clan deserve mention here. Most important is the white croaker, which ranges from Vancouver Island southward to the tip of Baja California. Like the corbina it is a school fish that concentrates around sandy areas in the surf zone and in shallow bays and lagoons. Mostly it's found in depths of 10 to 100 feet. The largest individual on record in California weighed only 1½ pounds, but they are extremely numerous.

The spotfin croaker, which reaches a weight of 12 to 15 pounds in Central American waters, is a far more widely traveled and migrating fish than his cousins. They appear sporadically along the California and Mexican coasts in large runs, mostly in midsummer, and then they disappear as suddenly as they arrived. The schools of large spotfin which cruise off shore are seldom touched by sport fishermen.

SURFPERCH

Twenty different kinds of surfperch have been identified in California waters and possibly there are others along the Pacific coasts. The most common ones in California waters are the barred, calico and red tail, which are very similar in habit and often confused with one another. The barred surfperch is usually found in the surf along sandy beaches, where they congregate in certain holes or depressions along the bottom. They constitute about 50 percent of the surf angler's bag in southern California, but their range extends almost entirely from Vancouver Island southward to the tip of Baja California and perhaps beyond.

The barred surfperch also happens to be one of the few saltwater fishes whose life history has been fairly well explored in recent years. The largest fish taken in California waters weighed only 4¼ pounds and this fish was known to be nine years old. But any fish over 3 pounds is an extremely good one and the average catch will weigh a pound or less.

Barred surfperch as well as all other surfperches are viviparous, which means they give birth to living young. As many as 113 embryos and as few as 4 have been found in female surfperch, but the average is about 33 per individual. The fertilization of the eggs is entirely internal and these eggs hatch and the young develop in saclike portions of the oviduct. The young surfperches are usually born in springtime between April and July. They are about 2 to 3 inches long at birth. Some mature when they are only 6½ inches long and between one and two years old.

An analysis of stomach contents of barred surfperch caught by fishermen revealed that their diet, like the corbina, is 90 percent sand crab. However, they are known to feed heavily at times on other crustaceans and on bean clams.

Thousands of barred surfperch have been tagged by California Fish and Game Department biologists and the results have revealed that, like corbinas, they travel very little. Their average movements figure to be less than 2 miles and only one individual had traveled 30 miles from the place it was tagged.

The tasty, white-meated, barred surfperch can be taken any time of the year and any time of the day or night. But the largest and the most fish are usually taken in midwinter, January being the best month. Best baits are sand crabs (which have moulted only recently and which therefore have soft shells), bloodworms, mussels and pieces of mackerel. In some areas the entrails of freshly caught sardines are widely used.

In recent years it has been discovered that surfperches and especially the barred surfperch will readily strike certain artificial lures. Small jigs are very effective and so are small streamer and nymph-type flies, such as the Pink Shrimp. Fly casting for these fish on relatively calm days is an extremely sporting and lively proposition.

The areas for most consistently catching barred surfperch are the sandy beaches between Point Mugu and Pismo Beach, but there are other hot spots. Calico surfperch fishing is best along the beaches of Monterey Bay while red-tails are most abundant northward from San Francisco. Some especially good areas are along the Humboldt and Del Norte counties coastlines.

Other members of the surfperch family which are taken in considerable numbers along the Pacific coast are: the walleye, which is especially abundant around open rocky coasts and fishing piers; the black perch, which ranges from Bodega Bay to Abreojos Point, Baja California; and the shiner perch, which reaches a maximum length of 8 inches and which is taken in numerous places from shore, docks, piers, rocks and in fact almost anywhere.

Another fish, the opaleye, which superficially resembles the surfperches, is a year-round resident of the rocky shorelines and kelp beds between Monterey Bay and southern Baja California. Opaleye live in caves and among sea-weed-covered rocks in shallow water, but they are also sighted occasionally at mid-depths and in offshore kelp beds. In recent years spincasters and flycasters have found that they are extremely game, dogged, light tackle fish. They occasionally reach a length of 20 inches and 6 pounds. Probably skin divers take the most. Opaleye will bite on mussels, sand crabs and pieces of other fish.

Still another Pacific coast fish that resembles the surfperch but is not a member of that family is the half-moon. Half-moons have been caught as far north as Eureka, California, but they are most abundant on the southern California coast and in the Gulf of California.

Probably the greatest number of half-moons occur around the Channel Islands where they are year-round residents of the kelp beds and the shallow waters and rocky shorelines.

The largest known half-moon weighed under 5 pounds but 1- and 2-pounders are the sizes most commonly caught on such fresh-cut bait as anchovies, sardines or squid. Pier fishermen account for quite a number of them, but spincasters using artificial lures have very poor luck. Half-moons are excellent eating because their flesh is white and very mild in flavor. Frequently found in the same waters and caught by the same methods used for half-moons are kelp rockfish and grass rockfish, both members of the largest family of fishes found off the Pacific coast.

GREENLING SEATROUT

There are many extremely interesting and brightly colored fishes along the Pacific coast, but one of the most striking of all is the greenling seatrout, *Hexagrammos decagrammus*. It is one of those rare fishes in which the male and the female are marked and colored in an entirely different fashion. To make the matter of identification all the more confusing, there are two other closely related greenlings sharing the same waters. These are the rock greenling and the white-spotted greenling.

Very little scientific information is available on the greenling seatrout. It's known to live entirely on the bottom in very shallow water, especially along rocky coasts, around jetties and in kelp beds. It ranges from Kodiak Island, Alaska, and possibly farther north than that, to La Jolla, California. It is extremely rare south of Point Conception. The largest seatrout recorded in California measured only 21 inches long and weighed about 3½ pounds, but larger fish than this have been caught along the Washington and Vancouver Island coasts.

The diet of the species consists mainly of various sea worms, crustaceans and a wide assortment of smaller fishes.

An excellent food fish, the greenling seatrout can be an extremely difficult fish to land even though it does not grow to great size. Once hooked, it will immediately try to dive into crevices or caves or beds of seaweed and somehow snag the lure or cut the line on any of these obstacles. The successful landing of a greenling seatrout is worthy of mention because the catch is always as beautiful and unusual in appearance as it is good to eat.

Most greenling are taken on such bait as cut fish, clams, mussels, shrimp, squid, worms and crabs. Greenling themselves are an excellent bait for many other fishes and especially for the lingcod, which is taken in deeper water.

The best greenling hole in California is said to be the south jetty at Eureka.

MISCELLANEOUS PACIFIC COAST FISHES

Almost anyone who fishes the inshore waters of California and lower California eventually catches the California sargo, which is the only member of the grunt family found in these waters. It's also called the Chinese croaker.

California sargo are found close to shore and in virtually all the bays between Point Conception and Cape San Lucas, and in the Gulf of California. They have been observed in water from only a few feet to 130 feet deep. Sargo reach a maximum weight of only about 4 pounds. It's interesting to note that they were introduced into the Salton Sea in 1951 and since then they have reproduced and seem to be well established.

A weird resident of Pacific inshore waters is the shovelnose guitarfish, which lives on most sand or mud-sand bottoms from central California southward through the Gulf of California. They are gregarious, occur in large numbers in some areas and are found the year round throughout most of their range.

The largest known shovelnose guitarfish was a 5-footer that weighed 40½ pounds and was a female taken in San Quintín Bay, Baja California. Individuals over 3 feet long, however, are quite uncommon. Shovelnose guitarfish bear their young alive, with as many as 28 being carried by a single female parent. Little else, however, is known about their life history.

Although the creature seems entirely inoffensive, it has been known to attack men. Several years ago at La Jolla, a shovelnose guitarfish bit a skin diver on the leg while he was collecting sand dollars in about 18 feet of water. This particular fish, a male, was probably courting a female and apparently resented the intrusion of the diver.

Guitarfish ordinarily are caught by anglers who are seeking other fish. They will take either live or dead bait, clams, mussels, sand crabs, in fact just about anything that is edible.

Only one member of the eagle ray family is known to exist in Pacific waters and this is the bat ray, which is relatively abundant along the Oregon coast and southward to Central America. It can be distinguished from other California rays by the presence of a sting and a distinct head, which is elevated above the disklike wings. Bat rays reach a large size as attested by the 209-pound specimen taken recently at Newport Bay. There are many unconfirmed reports of larger bat rays and a picture was published several years ago of a ray taken along the Mexican coast which was said to weigh 340 pounds. Many bat rays are hooked but never landed because they are hooked on tackle that is much too light for them because the angler is concen-

trating on some other game fish. The big rays are most numerous in San Diego Bay, Newport Bay, Alamitos Bay, Morro Bay, Elkhorn Slough, San Francisco Bay and Humboldt Bay.

A few southern California fishermen specifically fish for bat rays because they are extremely strong and wage an interesting fight, but ordinarily they have no value. Commercial fishermen despise them because of the damage they cause to nets, and oyster growers would like to see them completely exterminated. One ray can almost completely destroy a whole oyster bed overnight.

An extremely common fish in the quiet coastal waters, bays and sloughs with muddy or sandy bottoms from Cape Mendocino southward to the Gulf of California is the diamond turbot, a right-eyed, porcelainlike flounder. They live in water depths that range from only a few inches to almost 100 feet, but they are most common in water between 4 and 10 feet deep.

Diamond turbot rarely reach a weight of 3 or 4 pounds and 1 pound is the average size. They're easy to catch on small pieces of clams or shrimp impaled on extremely small hooks—their mouths are quite small. Mission Bay and Newport Bay in California are especially good for this species. They can be taken the year round. Considering their size and shape, they put up a very good fight on light tackle.

A close relative of the diamond turbot is the starry flounder, which exists on sand, mud and gravel bottoms from central California northward to Alaska and into the Bering Sea, then eastward along the north Alaskan coast as far as Coronation Gulf in northern Canada. It is also found in the Aleutians and in the western Pacific from Kamchatka to Japan and Korea. It even enters freshwaters at times and has been taken as far as seventy-five miles upstream in the Columbia River.

Like diamond turbot, starry flounder have been caught in water from only a few inches deep to 150 fathoms (900 feet). Although they sometimes reach 20 pounds in weight, the average starry flounder will measure 16 inches and average about 2 pounds. Like other flatfishes, the young flounder is born with an eye on each side of the head but by the time it is about half an inch long, both eyes are on the same side and it resembles the parent in all respects. A check of stomach contents of starry flounder taken by fishermen reveals that most of them live exclusively on sea worms and such small crustaceans as copepods and amphipods. As they grow larger in size, they are able to eat crabs, clams, sand dollars, and similar marine life. The largest individuals also will eat such fish as sardines, sand dabs and perch.

Some of the best fishing for starry flounder occurs on the Oregon and Washington beaches. They can be taken there the year round but are most readily caught between January and March on a vast variety of baits which includes sardines, clams, shrimp and squid.

Our Pacific coastal waters contain more than a normal share of strange fish and one of the most curious-looking of all is the cabezon. It belongs to the large family of sculpins. Sometimes it reaches a length of 3 feet and a weight of 25 pounds. Females grow much faster than males and therefore attain a much larger size.

Cabezon are caught from northern Mexico to Puget Sound with most of them being taken in the northern half of that range. They are among the most sought-after of the fishes that inhabit the rough and rocky shorelines. The best bait for them includes abalone trimmings, mussels, clams, squid, shrimp, sea worms and cut or strip bait. They will also take live, swimming bait when it is available.

Here is another rock dweller which is much more difficult to land than to hook. Every cabezon as soon as it is hooked will try to retreat into the shelter of a rock or cave or seaweed bed. And once he's inside it's virtually impossible to pry him loose on sport fishing tackle.

These unique fish with the oversize fins, stout bodies and wide heads are found the year round on rocky bottoms in every depth from shallow tidal pools to more than 250 feet. Their favorite average depth off Oregon is about 35 feet. They normally lie motionless right on the bottom and never stir except to grab something to eat.

Although their flesh is often a bluish green in color when fresh, cabezon are excellent food fish after they are filleted, skinned and fried in deep fat. But one important word of caution: *Never eat the roe!* The eggs are poisonous and will make anyone violently ill.

The monkey-faced eel is not a true eel, but it is certainly one of the strangest fishes along the Pacific coast, or anywhere else, for that matter. The shape of its body and the absence of pelvic fins distinguish it from all common inshore fishes except the rock eel. It varies in color from a dingy black to a brownish green and normally has one or more reddish spots on the flanks or on the belly. This color combination makes the fish seem all the more weird in appearance.

Monkey-faced eels as long as 3 feet have been taken and they are reported to reach 4 or even 5 feet, although the usual catch in California and Oregon waters is much smaller. They are found from the Oregon-California border southward to San Quintín Bay, Baja California. They inhabit rock-pool areas between the tide lines and seek cover in crevices, caves and other secluded places. Even skin divers rarely see them moving about in open waters.

These strange fish can be taken wherever rocky areas rim the ocean, either in bays or along the outer coast of central and northern California. Some of the favorite spots are the rocks north of Crescent City, California, between Bodega Bay and Dillon Beach, between Stinson Beach and Muir Beach, around the Golden Gate and Shell Beach and near Pismo Beach. Low tide seems to be the best time to fish for them, and although the fish will strike all year the best weather for them probably occurs during the summer months.

Even the method used to fish for monkey-faced eels is as unique as the fish itself. The typical angler uses a bamboo pole about 10 feet long. At the small end of the pole is a wire leader about 6 inches long with a No. 4 hook fastened to the end of it. The end of the pole with the baited hook is then inserted into likely crevices and cracks in a process called "poke-poling." The usual bait is shrimp, but mussels, clams, marine worms and sardines work very well. As soon as the fish is hooked, it is jerked immediately from its hiding place.

Monkey-faced eels are cleaned exactly the same as our freshwater catfish—by skinning them first. They're excellent eating.

Chapter Fifteen

THE COMMUTERS
SALMON

Five kinds of salmon are found along the Pacific coast of North America. These are the king, silver, sockeye, chum and pink. But 90 or 95 percent of all salmon taken on sport fishing tackle are either kings or silvers and our discussion of the salmon family will be limited to these two species.

King salmon, which have the almost unpronounceable scientific name of *Oncorhynchus tschawytscha*, are called chinook in the Columbia River system, tyee in British Columbia (if they weigh over 30 pounds, otherwise they're springs), or quinnat. They can be separated from silver salmon at a glance by checking the color of the fleshy lining over the crown of the gums where the jaw teeth come through. In king salmon the lining is always blackish while in silver salmon it is white. The rest of the inside of the mouth of both kings and silvers is dusky or blackish.

Kings have been caught in the Pacific from San Diego all the way north to Alaska and the Aleutian Islands, and south along the Asiatic coast to Japan. On our side of the ocean, however, they're only rarely taken south of San Luis Obispo County, California, or north of Bristol Bay, Alaska. The Sacramento-San Joaquin river system is the site of the southernmost salmon run of any consequence.

Nearly every fisherman knows the story of how salmon, after spending several years in the ocean, return to their home streams or rivers— where they were born—to spawn and then to die. But since the commonly accepted life history of the Pacific salmon is full of misconceptions, perhaps it's wise to go into more detail here.

Unlike silvers, which enter rivers only during the autumn, king salmon enter streams and rivers during two different periods annually. Those that enter during the spring run spend the summer months loitering in deep holes throughout the river system. They may even make a quick dash back to the ocean. In any case, they continue on to their spawning grounds in the fall. On the other hand, kings that enter during the fall run move directly to the inland spawning grounds.

Not all chinook return to their home river to spawn, although most of them apparently do. On many occasions adult fish have been captured during their spawning run many miles from the ocean, only to be recaptured again much farther downstream. In one case, an adult king salmon was caught 30 miles offshore from San Francisco almost a year after it had been netted and tagged 80 freshwater miles up the Sacramento River.

Most kings spawn when they are either three or four years old, but there are exceptions to this too. Males, especially, may spawn when they are only two years old, and some large females do not spawn until they are five or six. The average female king salmon will deposit from 3000 to 4000 eggs, but there have been instances in California where Sacramento salmon

This 25-pound king salmon was landed by charter-boat captain Bill Eslick near Westport, California.

have carried an average of 6000 eggs each. The time it takes for eggs to hatch depends on the temperature of the water and therefore it may vary from 15 to 20 days in various streams. Hatching occurs earlier in warm water than in cold rivers.

Young chinook salmon migrate downriver tail first—usually at night—within several months after hatching. During these migrations many are lost when they drift or are sucked into irrigation canals. Still others are consumed by the multitude of predators along the migratory route. Then there is evidence that on reaching the sea they disperse rapidly and travel for considerable distances. Not too much, however, is known about their travels after they reach saltwater.

Any chinook salmon is a savage striker with a stout heart and tremendous fighting ability. It would be a pleasure to report that they are as numerous as always, but that simply isn't true. The annual toll taken by gill-netters, commercial trawlers and numerous other factors including pollution leaves fewer salmon for sport fishermen every year. Salmon fishing is indeed a sporty proposition no matter how it's done. But

it does seem to be declining almost every year.

Most ocean fishing for king salmon is done primarily by trolling with dead bait or with quite a number of different artificials. Occasionally live bait will be used while still-fishing or drift fishing; this method is more popular than elsewhere in the ocean south of Monterey, California.

Kings normally stay very deep, usually in from 40 to 250 feet of water, except for certain unpredictable occasions when they rise to the surface while following schools of baitfish. It isn't a hard and fast rule, but generally salmon are taken in shallower waters the farther north they are found along the Pacific coast. Occasionally off Ketchikan, Alaska, and thereabouts, they are taken in water as shallow as 10 or 12 feet. Nearly always a heavy weight is necessary to keep the trolled bait at the desired depth, which is quite near the bottom.

The preferred trolling speed used by most salmon experts is around 2 knots and the most productive trolling depth along the California and Oregon coasts would seem to be between 100 and 150 feet. The areas where fishing is best off California are Monterey Bay and northward, but there is usually excellent sport at least for a limited period out of Avila, Port San Luis, Morro Bay and San Simeon.

Oregon's best salmon fishing occurs around Coos Bay and near Astoria. In Washington, the waters of Puget Sound and the Strait of Juan De Fuca are world famous. A super hot spot is the Hope Island "slot" near the mouth of the Skagit River, which has produced an astounding number of trophy-size salmon through the years. For one reason or another, the Skagit River breeds an unusually large race of kings that are bigger on the average than those hatched elsewhere, except at a few places to the north in British Columbia and Alaska.

One of the most successful fishermen in the Hope Island area and in fact in entire Puget Sound is Herb Mills of Seattle, a tackle salesman who has taken more salmon than any other four or five fisherman put together. It's interesting to investigate the tackle and techniques that Mills used (while serving as a professional guide) to boat 559 big salmon in one season at Hope Island.

It should be emphasized that the Hope Island "slot" is only about 200 yards wide and a

Landing a good king salmon along the northern California coast. (*Photo by John Gartner*)

quarter of a mile long. At low tide it's 24 feet deep and at high tide about 36 feet. The slot is studded with underwater rock piles and reefs among which salmon loiter close to the bottom, probably to escape the full pressure of a tidal current that sometimes races by as fast as seven knots.

Mills's method, which is deadly for king salmon anywhere, is to troll with precisely the correct amount of line to keep the spoon flashing or the plug darting through the water only a few feet above the rocks or underwater obstacles. Of course, that isn't an easy matter for a beginner, but it's a good target at which to aim.

The trolling outfit that Mills uses consists of a 7-foot 6-inch glass rod and a heavy-duty, star drag reel holding 100 to 150 yards of 72-pound test nylon backing, 500 feet of 54-pound wire line with a 20-foot Cuttyhunk tip. The business end of the line is a 4-ounce slip sinker set about 15 feet up the line, a swivel and then 6 feet of 68-pound piano-wire leader followed by a No. 7 Canadian Wonder spoon, half brass and half nickel with a 4/0 galvanized treble hook.

Normal action of the Canadian Wonder spoon is a side-to-side wobble, but at a slightly faster speed it will revolve about 3 or 4 turns in one direction and then dart off to one side and revolve 3 or 4 times in the reverse direction. This peculiar action seems to be more deadly than the normal action, but it requires constant manipulation and adjusting of the motor to assume the proper trolling speed. Even the tiniest piece of seaweed caught on the hook will destroy the entire action of the lure.

The biggest fish caught around Hope Island usually are taken between June 15 and the end of July, but fishing is good and at least the fish are present throughout June, July, August, and into the first part of September.

Chinooks taken on hook and line will range from 10 to 30 pounds, and perhaps the average will be about 20 pounds. However, 40-pounders are fairly common in Alaskan and British Columbian waters and they're not too rare in Puget Sound. Occasionally in Alaska, however, kings run to 60 and 70 pounds. On extremely rare occasions, 100-pounders have been captured by commercial fishermen. A 126½-pounder appears to be the all-time record for the species.

Although heavy-tackle trolling is as popular as ever, there is a trend among some fishermen to change to lighter tackle and different methods of fishing. The Tyee Club of Campbell River, British Columbia, has pioneered in this use of light tackle. Now it's spreading up and down the coast. The change, however, came as a result of a new technique that began in the Puget Sound region. A number of anonymous but experimental anglers decided to try something new.

Since the king salmon live principally on herring almost until they enter the rivers to spawn, these pioneer fishermen began by using this natural bait on a light line and a flexible rod. Two closely related techniques which developed have since been called "mooching" for salmon and "spinning" for salmon.

Both spinning and mooching are ideal for use in any of the fairly sheltered waters from Puget Sound to Juneau. It seldom gets too rough to fish from a small boat, which is the ideal craft for a moocher. The method is simplicity itself. It relies upon the way in which salmon attack a school of herring, slashing into it and crippling as many as possible. Then at leisure they return to pick up the wounded, which are moving in a slow, uncertain manner. The idea in mooching and spinning is to make a herring perform in this same uncertain manner. If these baits are properly manipulated by the flexing of the rod tip and by movements of the tide, they're extremely deadly.

The typical salmon spinner or moocher uses a rod that is fairly long, say from 8 feet 6 inches to 10 feet, quite flexible and with a fairly long two-handed grip. His reel can be either conventional design or a spinning reel, as long as it's capable of holding at least 200 yards of 10- or 12-pound monofilament line. To this line should be added 8 or 10 feet of slightly heavier monofilament material.

A crescent sinker with a swivel on the leader end is attached to the line with a long loop and the leader is looped to the other end. This type of sinker offers little resistance to tidal current and has a keel effect that prevents twisting of the line when the bait spins.

The herring bait should be prepared or cut to imitate the action of the wooden plug baits with beveled or grooved heads. The way to do it is to cut off the herring head at an angle of about 60° to the backbone, cutting diagonally downward to produce a beveled front. The herring's body then is rigged with 2 hooks as shown in the bait section of this book.

Spinning or mooching is successful wherever salmon can be found. In the inland passages of the Pacific Northwest coast, kings seem to move back and forth constantly in search of schools of herring or candlefish. Occasionally they work near the shoreline or at least off points or peninsulas of land that jut out into fairly deep water. Sometimes where the sweep of the tide isn't too great, it's most advantageous to anchor the boat, and elsewhere it's far better to drift with the tide. The best time for mooching appears to be just before flood tide and just after, when salmon are normally most active and when there is enough movement of the tide to keep the bait acting "alive."

It is done something like this. The whole rig, herring bait and keel sinker, is cast out and allowed to settle to the bottom. Then, a yard at a time, the angler retrieves the bait upward at an angle, trying to imitate the fluttering helpless action of a wounded fish. Obviously different weights of sinkers are needed to cope with various tide movements and with different depths.

These crescent-shaped sinkers (most commonly used) come in sizes of from 1½ to more than 6 ounces, but ordinarily the 2- to 3-ounce sizes will be most valuable.

During periods when the tide is slack or very slight and when baits seem to go dead, it is possible to mooch with the boat set at its slowest idling speed. Only experience can give a salmon fisherman the right touch for mooching,

It was worth it! (*British Columbia Government photograph*)

but once this is learned it becomes almost involuntary.

Most of the time kings will hit a mooched bait like a freight train going at high speed. But there are times, however, when they are hesitant strikers, nibbling or teasing the bait for a long time before actually taking it. That, of course, is a good reason for using the lightest possible tackle.

If an unusually big fish *is* hooked on light tackle, it's often necessary to crank up the motor and follow the fish to keep all the line from being peeled from the reel, but that's all in a day's salmon fishing. And along our northwest Pacific coast there is no more exciting sport.

In some ways the silver salmon, which is also popularly known as the coho, is a more exciting game fish than it's larger cousin the chinook. More often it's found near the surface and therefore it can be taken on lighter tackle.

Silvers have been found in the Pacific Ocean from Los Coronados, Baja California, north to Alaska and south on the Asiatic side to Japan. Adults ascend almost all of the accessible streams from Santa Cruz north to Alaska to spawn. However, the most successful fishing is probably in the British Columbia area where the largest silver of which there is an authentic record was taken. This was a 31-pounder captured in 1947. The California record was a 22-pounder taken at Papermill Creek in 1959. The average landed by sportsmen on hook and line would be less than 24 inches long and run from 6 to 9 pounds.

Unlike chinooks, which sometimes enter streams in springtime, silvers always move upstream to spawn in the fall or winter, beginning in September and continuing through March. The bulk of the spawning actually occurs from November to January. Adult males enter the streams when they are either two or three years old, but females seldom return to spawn until they are at least three years old. All silvers, male or female, spend the first year of their lives in the stream or river in which they hatch and all adults die after spawning. This means, of course, that silvers spend a much shorter time in saltwater than do the larger chinooks. But during the time they are at sea, their growth is extremely rapid and, in fact, borders on the phenomenal when compared to their growth while still in the home stream.

Food study findings indicate that in the ocean, cohos feed mostly on many kinds of small fishes, on a few crustaceans and squid. In saltwater, silvers are caught primarily by trolling with shiny spoons or the old favorite, beveled plugs. Less often they're taken by trolling with whole dead herring. They're usually found within 30 feet of the surface and therefore are within "range" of medium spinning tackle. The best trolling speed appears to be about 2 knots per hour.

Coho fishing is extraordinary sport off the Canadian Pacific coast, where it's often possible to catch them on standard bait casting, spinning, or fly casting tackle amid magnificent mountain scenery. The fish are very acrobatic and they fight with the same abandon, the same long runs, and with the violent leaps of the Atlantic salmon. In fall on the Tlell River in Queen Charlotte Islands, the cohos gather in schools and there it is possible to take them by trolling large streamer flies—as used for large freshwater trout and Atlantic salmon—or small spoons or spinners. They also provide great sport in the bays of Vancouver Island, where the common technique is to drift-cast for them near the surface with light tackle and large bucktail flies or darting spoons.

Chapter Sixteen

THE FISH
NOBODY LOVES

SHARK

Perhaps because of their completely sinister appearance and even more sinister reputation, almost nobody has any affection for sharks. But in recent years, a few anglers have come to recognize their value as a genuine sport fish, and in some cases as a fairly high quality food fish. Some sharks are actually good to eat, so good in fact that the meat has been sold as swordfish by some commercial fishermen. And a few of the sharks, such as the mako, are crazy enough jumpers to be ranked with the finest game fish in the sea.

There are about 100 species or subspecies of sharks in this international family of fishes; 47 of these have been taken in the Atlantic coastal waters of North America, 29 species on the Pacific coast. Some live in deep water, some in shallow water. Some are pelagic. Some travel in schools. A number of species are dangerous while others are quite harmless. Some even venture into brackish or shallow water.

The largest shark in the world is the whale shark, which is found everywhere in warm waters and is known to reach 25,000 pounds in weight. It is probably completely harmless. On the other hand, there are small sand sharks that weigh no more than a pound or two when full grown.

Sharks differ from other fishes in that their skeletal structure is composed of cartilage rather than bone. None of the sharks are scaled, and most of them are equipped with sets of formidable, oversize teeth unlike those of any of the bony fishes.

Many fishermen believe that all sharks constitute a menace and should be destroyed. They have been known to attack human beings, of course, but so have swordfish, barracuda, groupers and even triggerfish. And sharks do consume a vast quantity of game fishes, but this is only a phase in nature's savage and relentless balancing act. The truth is that sharks are valuable and perhaps indispensable residents of the sea.

Occasionally American prejudice against sharks reaches the point of absurdity. Throughout other parts of the world, these fish are prized as delicacies and cooked in the same manner as other fishes. Even in the United States, during World War II, thousands of pounds of shark were colored and sold as salmon. Nobody knew the difference. Still others were marketed as fillet of sole, halibut, and as we've pointed out, as swordfish.

But no matter how a saltwater angler feels about sharks, much more fishing for them is done today than ten years ago. On a warm June morning every year, for example, one of California's most unusual sporting events occurs at Elkhorn Slough, a winding channel of salt which joins the ocean at Moss Landing on the beauti-

Landing a small shark in the Shark River region of southern Florida. (*Photo by Florida State News Bureau*)

ful Monterey coast. This event, which has been approved by state fish and game authorities, is called the Elkhorn Slough Shark Derby. Hundreds of fishermen participate every year to fish especially for leopard and shovelnose sharks.

Actually, shark fishing can be the answer to man's yen for catching big fish—for the biggest fish of all, in fact. Consider how all world's records were decisively smashed on April 21, 1959, when fisherman Alfred Dean of Mildura, Australia, landed a white pointer shark weighing 2664 pounds. He was using 130-pound test line. This giant remains the biggest fish ever caught on rod, reel and line anywhere in the world. It establishes for Dean a new all-tackle world's record and wins him the 130-pound-class world's record previously held by Australian radio star, Bob Dyer, of Sidney, New South Wales.

This was the fourth time that Dean had broken the all-tackle record for the biggest shark. His previous record was a 2536 pounder taken on 54-thread line. Bob Dyer had held the 39-thread record (that's a 130-pound test) with a 2350-pounder.

Dean's new world's record was taken off Bird Rocks near Thevenard, South Australia. It measured 16 feet 10 inches in length and had a girth of 9 feet 6 inches. Twice in its desperate fight to free itself the big fish leaped completely out of the water. According to Dean it was an unbelievable, almost terrifying sight to see such

a monster lurch out of the water and stand on its tail.

Perhaps because sharks are so extremely numerous in Australia, shark fishing there is very popular and very highly regarded. In North America it's more popular on the California coast than on the eastern seaboard. Although California sportsmen are likely to catch any of twenty different species, two are more actively sought than all the rest. These are the common thresher and the blue shark.

The common thresher is one of 5 members of the thresher family, which is so named because of a tail that is almost one half the total length of the shark. The common thresher runs from bluish gray to brownish gray on the back, shading to white on the belly. It has a small mouth and relatively small, weak teeth for a shark, but there are about 40 teeth in a row in each jaw.

The common thresher isn't limited to California offshore waters. Instead, it's found in nearly all temperate and tropic waters around the globe. It's a pelagic species living in clear blue water, sometimes far offshore, and it's often observed on or near the surface of extremely deep water. It is taken, however, both on the surface and as deep as several hundred feet.

All sharks are very interesting critters and the common thresher is no exception. It is also no exception to the rule that very little of a factual nature is known about sharks. It is believed that the thresher reaches a length of from 20 to 25 feet and a weight far exceeding 1000 pounds. There is evidence that it doesn't become mature and capable of spawning or breeding until it is at least 14 feet long. The young are born alive and usually about 2 to 4 at a time. An 18-footer which was caught off Newport Beach in 1954 contained 4 young sharks that weighed from 11 to 13½ pounds apiece and which measured from 4 feet to 4 feet 6 inches long.

The average thresher taken in California waters will measure from 5 to 8 feet long and will average less than 100 pounds. However, commercial fisherman reported catching two fish in 1948 which weighed 1094 pounds and 968 pounds.

The best places to find threshers along the California coast include the San Francisco Bay area, the inshore coastal waters between Point Conception and Hueneme, Santa Monica Bay, especially around Malibu and Paradise Cove, and in Los Angeles Harbor. They seem to be most abundant during the summer months when they are observed swimming slowly on the surface or even jumping clear of the water.

When hooked on light or medium tackle, some thresher sharks will often put on a display of aerial jumping that isn't too unlike that of a marlin of the same size. Others, however, do not jump, and they depend on a subsurface, brute-strength type of fight which can tow a fishing skiff for many miles.

The best baits for threshers have proven to be live sardines, anchovies, and mackerel, but there are a few examples of the fish taking artificial lures or salmon plugs. No matter what the bait, it's important to use a stout wire leader of 10 to 20 feet. But such leaders are a necessity in every type of shark fishing—to cope with the teeth of the shark and because an ordinary nylon line will wear through after long rubbing against the abrasive hide of a shark.

There is no known record of an unprovoked attack by a common thresher shark upon a human being. Because of its habit of sometimes swimming on the surface and waving its large tail above the water, it has been mistaken for some strange kind of sea serpent.

Another shark familiar to California sportsmen is the blue, which belongs to the requiem or requin shark family and which is a close relative of soupfin and tiger sharks. It's readily iden-

tified by its brilliant blue topside, which shades to white below. It is found in all the temperate and tropic seas of the world. The blue shark is occasionally common off southern California but it rarely appears north of Point Conception unless currents of abnormally warm water bathe that area. Often it is observed swimming on the surface some distance from shore.

The blue shark is not considered a dangerous maneater, but no doubt it is responsible for some attacks on injured swimmers and skin divers. It should be considered with suspicion because of its great abundance and because it is so quickly attracted to blood.

A 11½-footer is the largest blue shark of authentic record, but no doubt the species grows to much larger size. Most of the blues taken in California waters are shorter than 6 feet and weigh less than 50 pounds.

It's interesting to note that during a recent southern California shark derby, every one of the 100 blue sharks taken was a male. This would indicate that there is geographical dis-

Landing a dusky shark off the Isle of Pines, Cuba. It was hooked while fishing over an offshore reef.

tribution or segregation of the species by sex, at least during part of the year.

From March through October, blue sharks are easy to capture off the southern California coast. They are not nearly as exciting and difficult to land as the thresher sharks, and it's possible to handle even the largest ones on light tackle. But once a blue is brought to the surface it twists and rolls in such an ugly manner that wire leaders are twisted and tangled almost beyond further use.

In natural surroundings, blues feed on crustaceans, fish, squid and octopuses. They will also take flying fish and pelagic crabs so that any of these items are also good when used as bait by fishermen. Blues also have the reputation for being readily attracted to garbage from ships and they will gorge themselves on anything small enough to swallow.

Along our Atlantic coast, the mako shark is considered the most desirable member of its family. The mako is found in abundance in such widely separated parts of the earth as off New Zealand, Ceylon, Cuba, Puerto Rico and northward along the Altantic coast to about New Jersey. Perhaps it is the only shark usually fished for by North American charter boats.

A large mako is certainly a formidable adversary. It reaches a weight of 800 pounds, and perhaps more, and is difficult to land because it mixes a deep, dogged fight with sudden and spectacular jumps. And there have been cases where it made a last ditch attempt to turn upon the man who was trying to gaff it alongside a boat.

You have to use heavy tackle for makos. The best recommended outfit is a 6-foot overall boat rod with a 36-ounce tip, 18- to 20-inch butt and a reel with a capacity for from 800 to 1200 yards of 130-pound or heavier test line. Use such whole live baits as menhaden, mackerel, whiting or herring on 10/0 to 14/0 Sobey hooks. A stainless steel cable or piano-wire leader should be at least 15 or 20 feet long.

The largest mako shark of which there is a record was a 1000-pounder measuring 12 feet which was caught near Mayor Island, New Zealand, in 1943, on 130-pound test line. A far more remarkable catch, however, was the 261-pounder taken in 1953 by Chuck Meyer off Montauk, New York. Meyer's line tested only 12 pounds!

Another shark familiar to Atlantic fishermen is the strange and awesome hammerhead, named for the elongated nostrils that give its head the general shape of a hammer. It is possible that this unique head formation enables the fish to use its head as a rudder and to make sharper turns in pursuit of its prey than any of the other sharks.

The hammerhead is often seen swimming with its dorsal and caudal fins above the surface of the water and it can be found almost anywhere in warm waters on the high seas. I have also found and hooked hammerheads, and big ones too, far inshore around the Isle of Pines while fishing for tarpon and bonefish.

It seems that few fishes have as remarkable a sense of smell as the hammerhead, which is able to scent blood at a great distance. Because of this ability it is generally the first shark to arrive when a hooked fish is badly hurt and begins to bleed. And the chances are that most of the game fish lost to sharks are lost to hammerheads.

The average hammerhead spotted or caught offshore will average from 10 to 12 or 13 feet in length, but they are known to reach almost 18 feet. No completely accurate weights for the largest fish are available, but it's assumed that they will reach 1500 pounds. Ordinarily the food of a hammerhead consists of sea clams, fish and barnacles, but it's easy to hook a hammerhead simply by tossing or trolling a large chunk of fish or meat close to its mouth.

Hammerhead females produce extremely large families alive. Thirty-nine young were found in one hammerhead caught off the Texas coast several years ago.

The white pointer shark that furnished Alf Dean with the current record for the largest rod and reel fish also occurs in the warm temperate waters along the Atlantic coast. Occasionally it is found as far north as eastern Nova Scotia. Its main food consists of sea turtles and large fish and it has been known to attack man on many occasions.

The stomach contents of the great whites have also included the following: a Newfoundland dog (in Australia); two 6- to 7-foot sharks inside a 15½-foot female (Florida); and a 100-pound-plus sea lion (California).

A close relative of the white pointer is the porbeagle. This heavy-shouldered fish reaches a length of about 12 feet and occasionally ventures as far north as Nova Scotia. It is mostly known as a nuisance to commercial fishermen because it gets into their nets when following schools of menhaden, herring or shad. The largest porbeagle of record is a 366½-pounder taken in 1960 near Montauk, N.Y.

Tiger sharks are most plentiful in Australian and New Zealand waters where the world's record, a 1422-pounder was taken in 1958. But occasionally the large brutes with the sickle-shaped teeth wander north along our Atlantic coast as far as Maine. Tigers will average about 12 feet in length but there are vague reports of individuals that reach 30 feet. They feed mostly on sea turtles, on large fishes and on other sharks. They're greatly feared as man-eaters around the world, especially in certain parts of the West Indies.

A most familiar shark along our entire Atlantic coast is the sand shark, a sluggish fish that swims leisurely with tail and dorsal fin above the surface of the water and sometimes reaches a length of 6 feet and weight of 300 to 400 pounds. It's gray in color, spotted with brown or olive, with a fin occasionally edged in black. It's found as far north as the Bay of Fundy, but during the warm summer months it swims close to shore and into the mouths of rivers. As soon as cold weather sets in, it departs and is found in numbers farther south along the Atlantic seaboard.

The sand shark is really a poor man's big game fish. When hooked and fought from shore, a 200-pounder can provide all the thrills of hooking a fish of equal size offshore in a boat. This fish is not particularly fast, but it is strong enough to strip several hundred yards of line from the reel before it can be stopped.

Some coast sportsmen fish especially for sand sharks, and the tackle they use is quite heavy. A heavy surf or boat rod with a 400- to 600-yard capacity reel full of 45-pound test line is suitable. The hook should be no smaller than from 9/0 to 12/0 and the leader should be a 15-footer. A whole fish such as menhaden or mackerel is extremely good bait.

Most sand shark specialists chum with menhaden, which can be either fresh or frozen. Although almost any chummed fish will attract sharks, menhaden seem to be far more effective. To prepare the menhaden for chum, use a meat

Hammerhead shark taken near Bermuda. Notice the strange head. (*Bermuda News Bureau photo*)

grinder, small hand ax or sharp knife. Cut it into tiny bits. Chum with the outgoing tide in deep water off a beach near an inlet or off a rocky formation or jetty.

Sand sharks will strike readily both day and night but probably night fishing is by far the best. And if you're lucky enough to land one of the critters, be extremely careful when handling it. A blow from the tail of a 100-pound sand shark threshing about can easily break a man's leg or smash his fingers.

Several years ago the Sayers brothers, Frank and Homer, and I pioneered in a new and exciting way to capture sharks. Significantly it worked equally well with manta rays, eagle rays and sawfish. And it all began during a fishing trip in the vicinity of Marathon, Florida, which was only a mild success.

For several days we cruised and fished the waters about Marathon aboard the *Fiesta* with skipper Johnny Brantner. We were fishing for tarpon mostly and saw quite a number of them but noticed that both sharks and rays were extremely numerous in most of the bays, lagoons and even on some of the shallow flats. None seemed to be easily spooked.

"You know what I'm thinking?" Frank asked

Capturing a ray with bow and arrow near Marathon, Florida, aboard John Brantner's boat *Fiesta*. That's Frank Sayers in blocked shirt, Brantner in shorts, Homer Sayers in light hat and long-sleeved khaki shirt. This is also a good way to hunt sharks.

one evening at the Plantation Yacht Basin. "I'm thinking that if we had a bow and arrow . . . and some harpoon points for our arrows . . . that we could have a whale of a time with those sharks."

Johnny sat for a minute in deep thought. Finally he said, "Say, I think you've got something there."

Brantner continued, "And I just happen to have one of Fred Bear's fine Kodiak bows and maybe even a harpoon tip."

At daybreak the next morning we embarked on what must have been one of the strangest fishing trips in that area in many a moon. As

soon as it was light enough we were cruising slowly across the flats. Frank stood on the foredeck leaning against the pulpit rail with a harpoon arrow nocked in the bowstring. A line from the harpoon point led to a heavy boat rod and reel, which Homer held at the ready nearby. We hadn't traveled very far when Johnny spotted a shark and eased up close behind it. But this shark was suspicious and Frank's hurried shot missed the mark.

It was only a few minutes more, however, before Johnny moved up close to our second target—a leopard ray—and Frank plunked an arrow right into one of the critter's wings. That was like pushing the button to fire an underground rocket because the ray zoomed off across the flat with a powerful burst of speed, leaving a thick muddy wake behind it.

Line vanished from Homer's reel at an alarming rate, and even when he tightened the drag, the ray kept traveling. The next few minutes we had a lively time on our hands. Brantner maneuvered the boat so that Homer would be in a better position to play the ray. At the same time he had to keep an eye peeled so that he wouldn't run aground on the shallow mud flats all around. Finally Homer was able to turn the ray. After that it was a slow and difficult tug-of-war working it close to the boat.

As soon as the ray was within range, Frank began to take potshots with regular hunting arrows. We were amazed to see how easily the ray would break the arrows into slivers simply by moving its wings. Eventually, when it began to look like a pincushion, we landed the ray and estimated that it would weigh about 125 pounds.

For the rest of that day, and for several days, in fact, we had the time of our lives chasing sharks and rays across the flats. We also left a trail of broken arrows drifting toward the Gulf Stream, but that didn't make any difference when the action was as wild and as fast as we found it.

The moral of this incident is simply that sharks can provide a world of fun for sportsmen. If catching them with hook and line and live bait seems dull, or if sharks are plentiful and other species are on a hunger strike, I can only suggest that hunting them Indian style is a great change of pace.

There's absolutely no limit to the thrills and excitement, as long as your supply of arrows holds out.

Chapter Seventeen

SOME SALTWATER HOT SPOTS

BRITISH HONDURAS, BERMUDA, THE FLORIDA KEYS, ACAPULCO, CAPE HATTERAS REGION, THE BAHAMAS, SAN DIEGO REGION, SURINAM, CAPE COD, SHARK RIVER (FLORIDA) REGION, PADRE ISLAND (TEXAS) REGION, SEA OF CORTÉS (CALIFORNIA)

No group of sportsmen in history were ever so lucky as the saltwater anglers of this golden day day and age. The whole world of saltwater is available to them and much of it is still unexplored and unexploited. There are countless new places to try, new species of fish to discover, new tackle and new techniques to be invented.

Nowadays, with modern transportation being as fast and efficient as it is, most of the new promised lands are in reach of every angler. And they are also in reach of his pocketbook. A man in Chicago or Cleveland, for example, can catch a jetliner in the morning and by afternoon be catching fish somewhere in Central America.

The modern fisherman doesn't even have to make his own plans. Some travel agencies specialize in sending fishermen to the hottest spots at the times they're hottest. It's a wise fisher-

man, in fact, who contacts such an agency. For example there's Medina County Travel Service, 124 W. Washington, Medina, Ohio, an organization that sends fishermen to such places the year round. This agency has constant contact with the best fishing areas, with fishing conditions and with the most capable outfitters in all these areas. They can arrange a trip from beginning to end for any sportsman. All the sportsman needs to do is to enjoy the fishing.

With brief descriptions, here are some of the best saltwater fishing holes in North America today:

BRITISH HONDURAS

North America is full of great fishing spots, and one of the greatest of all is British Honduras, the tiny British colony in Central America,

Exploring mangrove channels of British Honduras for snook, tarpon, snappers, while living aboard a houseboat.

tucked in between Mexico's Quintana Roo Territory and Guatemala on the Caribbean Sea. But the truth is that no one knows just how good the fishing really is because most of it is still unexplored and unknown.

The entire eighty-mile coastline is irregular and laced with tidal channels and river estuaries, but virtually every bit of it is perfect environment for such fish as tarpon, snook, ladyfish, barracudas and snappers. About twenty-five miles offshore is an archipelago or system of cays called the Turneffe Islands. This region is also the natural environment for tarpon, snook and other inshore species, and all around the islands are extensive lukewarm flats that contain bonefish in amazing numbers. Beyond the Turneffe Islands is the second largest barrier reef in the world. Only the Australian barrier reef is longer. But unlike the Australian reef only a few isolated scattered sections of the Honduras reef have ever been fished by sport fishermen. The reef is literally working alive with giant groupers, snappers, barracudas, amberjack, mackerel, rockfish and all the other species that live around Caribbean coral reefs. There is absolutely no limit to the number of fish an angler can catch in British Honduras waters except his own endurance. All of it except the reef fishing is superlight tackle fishing. It isn't impossible to jump as many as fifty medium size tarpon in a days fishing.

Although Belize, the capital of British Honduras, is not equipped with luxury accommodations for fishermen, an American outfitter offers packaged trips, which are high adventure. Visiting fishermen live on comfortable houseboats while traveling the endless number of picturesque lagoons along the coast. Meanwhile they fish with light tackle from small skiffs, while using the houseboat only as a headquarters and a clubhouse. In this way, fishermen can reach the best fishing holes with the least inconvenience and the least time wasted. It's really an idyllic arrangement.

British Honduras is only two and a half hours from New Orleans by TACA International Airlines nonstop flights. There are other flights from Miami via Mexico City and Mérida which are just a little longer.

BERMUDA

It was still early morning when Bill Backus strolled down to the bridge at The Flatts to make a cast or two beneath the narrow span. Nobody stirred on this typically quiet Bermuda morning. Backus had the place to himself.

The tide was changing and soon it began to flow under the bridge with a current as strong as a wild wilderness river, which it resembled. Backus made a couple of casts to the edge of the current, but nothing happened. Then he made a longer cast, allowing his bait to settle and . . . his rod almost jumped out of his grasp.

For the next half hour Backus could have used an extra pair of hands to compete with a heavy fish that kept boring down and down and down. Even in the cool of early morning, he soon was sweating like a stevedore. And he was weak in the knees when he finally gaffed a 16-pound grouper. But the morning had only begun.

Just as no poker player leaves the table after the first winning hand, so did Backus make another cast—and lightning struck again in the same spot. For thirty minutes, maybe more, he lost line and gained a little of it back until all his muscles complained. This time he'd hooked a gwelly, *caranx guara*, a little-known member of the jack family which lives up to the jack's reputation for playing fishermen rather than vice versa. Somehow he gaffed that fish, too. But still there's more.

Backus made one more idle cast and had another strike, which he could feel all the way down to his heels. This time it was a big gray snapper that didn't give him much of a fight.

It broke his line before the fight could begin.

"I feel I was lucky," he told me. "I couldn't stand another five minutes of that kind of fishing . . . without any breakfast."

Backus' experience wasn't unusual. On the other hand, it's quite ordinary for Bermuda, an Atlantic midocean atoll completely surrounded by more than 300 species of fish. There are few places around the globe where an angler can find grab-bag fishing of this high quality.

The reefs around Bermuda are especially productive. In a single afternoon, and fishing from one spot called Snapper Rocks (which lies in water of 100 fathoms), I caught 10 separate species of fish. The catch included red, princess, salmon, tiger and monkey rockfish; red and Nassau groupers; a dusky shark; an 18-pound porgy; a rock hind; a triggerfish; a small amberjack; a senet; several red and yellow coneys.

Fishing around the outer reefs, or just beyond them, is a great spot to catch amberjacks, which are the strongest game fish in any ocean. They're plentiful here and they run to unusually large size, but you're never certain what other grab-bag species will intercept your bait in exactly the same waters. It might be a school of swiftly moving false albacore or bonito or Spanish mackerel. You never know.

Trolling out on the open Atlantic is most

Joe Brooks landed this 55½-pound wahoo off Bermuda on a 10-pound test line. He battled the fish for thirty-five minutes. (*Bermuda News Bureau photo*)

likely to produce a big wahoo, but these same deep blue waters contain blue marlin, dolphin, Allison tuna and blackfin tuna. Some of these come in record and near-record sizes.

But potential record fish are also common in the scattered shallows and flats close to shore because many trophy bonefish are taken here every year. Pete Perinchief, who is an addicted bonefish-on-light-tackle fan, believes it is only a matter of time before someone breaks the existing world's record with a bone from this picturesque island. He did it himself several years ago.

Bermuda has its share of exclusives, too. One is the Bermuda chub, a small but incredibly strong battler that isn't found anywhere else. It's about as selective in taking a bait as the most sophisticated brown trout. Another offbeat fish is the gaff-topsail pompano, which is taken along the pink sand beaches by chumming with slices of bread! Perhaps there are still others yet to be found by pioneering sportsmen.

Today Bermuda is only a couple of hours from New York. And in few other places on earth is it so easy to enjoy spectacular fishing while living the luxurious, abundant life.

THE FLORIDA KEYS

It has been said that the Florida Keys are a way of life rather than a location on a map of Florida. Perhaps that's true because the Keys have a flavor or an atmosphere that goes far beyond the splendid year-round fishing.

There is good fishing all the way from Jewfish Creek to the tip of Key West, but I have always found it best to begin in the areas of Marathon or Key West for the greatest fishing. Near to both of these places are the celebrated bonefish flats. And in the deep channels nearby are plenty of tarpon. Throughout the maze of shallow reefs, flats and channels, there are as many species of saltwater fish as a fisherman can find anywhere else on the continent.

Although it would seem that the number of fish caught is phenomenal, Florida conservation officials believe that this fishing pressure is not enough to match the natural production of game species. The record seems to prove they're right because year in and year out new records are broken and the fishing continues of the same high quality.

Although there is good trolling offshore for marlin and sailfish, this is really light-tackle country. Either fly-casting tackle or spinning tackle capable of holding plenty of line is sufficient. In recent years anglers from all over America have trailered their own boats to the Keys and this is well and good because it's hard to match the thrills and adventure in cruising this maze of islands in one's own boat. Just the same, all types of craft are available for rent.

Skiffs rent from $3 to $5 a day, charter boats from $25 to $150 a day including the guide. For bottom fishing, fishermen can go on party boats for as little as $5 per person with bait included. Or they can charter boats for big game fishing for from $65 to $150 a day. Outboard motors rent, depending on the size, for from $4 to $12 a day. Boat rentals and bait shops are located at intervals all along U.S. 1, the overseas highway that terminates at Key West.

Few areas have more or more varied accommodations for fishermen. They range from economy housekeeping cottages to American resorts complete with cocktail lounges and swimming pools. It should be mentioned, however, that in some parts of the Keys the demand for accommodations often exceeds the supply and in midwinter especially it's advisable to make reservations far in advance.

For additional information on Key fishing write to Jim Sumpter, Executive Secretary, Chamber of Commerce, Key West, Florida, or to the Chamber of Commerce in Marathon, Florida.

ACAPULCO, MEXICO

Acapulco is perched high on the Pacific coast about 280 miles south of Mexico City. It's world famous for its sailfish but the fertile waters all about also contain marlin, barracudas, dolphin, yellow tails, tuna, bonito, jewfish and roosterfish. Fishing with light tackle is always emphasized here even when fishing for sailfish and marlin. However, the type of tackle to be used is determined by the fisherman.

The city is within reach of any point in the United States via Mexico City. There is a good four-lane highway from Mexico City to Acapulco

Typical day's catch of large Pacific sailfish and striped marlin by only three cruisers at Mazatlán, Mexico.

Sailfishing at Acapulco, Mexico. Angler is George Laycock and the sail is a 115-pounder.

and driving time is only about 6 hours. Regular flights from Mexico City are only one hour by Aeronaves de Mexico.

Boats and guides can be chartered at most of the hotels in Acapulco or they can be arranged for at the main fishing pier. Prices per charter average about $40 or $50 per 6-hour trip. Licenses and equipment are usually included. Fishing is good the year round but the best months are January, February, and March. There are excellent accommodations in all price ranges but it's best to have a reservation in advance of making the trip.

Similar excellent fishing exists at Mazatlán and at Manzanillo, both farther north along Mexico's Pacific coast.

CAPE HATTERAS REGION, NORTH CAROLINA

Hatteras Island as described elsewhere in this book is a thread of surf and sand which stretches 60 miles southward from Oregon Inlet off the coast of North Carolina. It's separated from the mainland by Pamlico Sound. It is one of an almost unbroken chain of islands called the Outer Bank and at Cape Hatteras extends 30 miles into the Atlantic Ocean, at which point it's only 12 miles from the edge of the Gulf Stream.

All of Hatteras Island except for the land within its villages is within America's only National seashore park to date. It's called the Cape Hatteras National Sea Shore Recreational Area and extends from the intersection of highways 64 and 264 and 158 near the Roanoke Island Sound Bridge to Ocracoke Inlet.

Because the sport fishing is so consistently good, this is the most important recreational function in the area. There are outstanding surf-casting spots, all now accessible by paved motor road, at Oregon Inlet, Cape Hatteras and on the southern tip of the island near the village of Hatteras. Channel Bass are taken in the surf from April until December. May and June are great for bluefish, kingfish and Spanish mackerel. June, July and August see a mixture of everything. Dolphin, amberjack and snapper are taken the year round while August marks the beginning of sailfish and marlin runs.

Besides the surf casting, there are three piers for bait fishermen in the Nags Head and Kitty Hawk areas. Also there are about 55 charter boats available for offshore fishing based at Hatteras, Oregon Inlet, Wanchese and Manteo. These charter boats, which range out as far as the Gulfstream, can be rented at from $65 to $100 a day. Boats for sound, harbor and bay fishing are priced from $20 to $40 a day, depending upon the crew and the size of the boat. Charter prices for Gulfstream and offshore generally include tackle and ice. Bait and lunch is always provided by the fisherman. Autumn fishing boats to Pamlico Sound charge $2.50 per person for a half day's fishing. Bait and tackle is not provided.

There are a number of motels, inns and guest homes on Hatteras Island which are open the year round.

Here is an Outer Banks fishing calendar compiled from a consensus of the best local anglers and charter captains:

JANUARY

Best chances for striped bass (rockfish) in fresh or brackish waters of Wilmington-Southport area and for small channel bass (puppy drum) on beaches; Belhaven area reports stripers throughout winter. Gray trout, Topsail to Southport.

FEBRUARY

Striped bass fishing improves from Belhaven south. Gray trout, Topsail to Southport.

MARCH

Sportsmen await start of channel-bass run, which sometimes begins at Bald Head Island latter part of month; it's a better bet to plan trying for them in April.

APRIL

Channel bass on big run at Oregon Inlet, and also appear at Ocracoke, Hatteras, Buxton, Drum Inlet, Topsail, Bald Head Island, Rich's and Elmore's, and other points; bluefish schools show up off Frying Pan Shoals (Southport); at Morehead City, sheepshead, trout, spot, mullet, largemouth bass fishing usually at peak in coastal waters.

MAY

Channel bass good at Oregon Inlet, Hatteras Inlet, Ocracoke, and southeastern beaches; Spanish mackerel show up from Morehead City to Swansboro; good bluefish catches off Frying Pan, Hatteras, Oregon Inlet, Topsail and Morehead City, blues also good in surf and from piers; Gulf Stream fishing begins; largemouth-bass fishing good generally.

JUNE

Channel bass from beaches or inlets, notably at Nags Head, Hatteras, Ocracoke, Topsail; dolphin off Hatteras, Morehead City, Beaufort, Topsail and Southport, and with them come amberjack in large numbers; bluefish caught all along coast; cobia appear at Atlantic Beach, Hatteras, and Oregon Inlet, and bonito off Southport and Wrightsville Beach; Spanish mackerel and king mackerel off Morehead City, Southport, and Hatteras; barracuda in southeast.

JULY

Like June, except that channel-bass fishing falls off and is scattered, although usually good in southeast; bluefish and mackerel caught in good numbers at most points; large king mackerel begin showing up off Morehead City, Topsail and Wrightsville Beach; red snappers off Cape Lookout and Wrightsville Beach.

AUGUST

Sailfish appear off coast; good Gulf Stream fishing month also for amberjack, bonito, dolphin, king mackerel, and barracuda, which are caught from Cape Hatteras to Cape Fear; many reports of large catches of trout, mackerel, blues.

SEPTEMBER

Offshore fishing good from now through November from Hatteras to Southport, and amberjack, dolphin, and sailfish are recorded; channel-bass fishing resumed at Oregon Inlet; puppy drum show up at beaches; fishing for blues and mackerel picks up in southeast.

OCTOBER

Prime surf casting for channel bass and bluefish at Ocracoke, Hatteras, Drum Inlet, Portsmouth, Smith (Baldhead) Island, Topsail and other points; striped bass begin schooling up in sounds to the north, in Croatan Sound and in rivers flowing into Albemarle and the Pamlico sounds; large king mackerel taken off the Capes, along with amberjack and dolphin; largemouth-bass fishing improves generally as weather turns cooler. Speckled-trout fishing in surf with artificial baits good from now through November at Topsail Island.

NOVEMBER

Surf casting for channel bass fine at Hatteras, Ocracoke, Drum Inlet, Smith Island and Topsail; striped bass fishing often at its best in northeast—Albemarle and Croatan sounds and adjacent waters; deep-sea fishing continues in the Cape Fear section, with good catches when weather permits boats to go offshore.

DECEMBER

Striped bass fishing continues good in fresh waters of the coast—in the Neuse, Pamlico, Pungo, Alligator, White Oak, and similar rivers; puppy drum appear in salt, brackish, and almost fresh waters from Ocracoke to Cape Fear. Gray trout, Topsail to Southport.

THE BAHAMAS

East and southeast of Florida are some 70,000 square miles of topflight fertile fishing grounds around the Bahama Islands. From northwest to southeast, this string of 30,000 cays extends for a distance of 700 miles. Many of the world's record fish have been caught here and there is good reason to believe that still others are waiting to be taken in these most productive waters. Some of the most important Bahama fish are groupers, bonitos, kingfish, Spanish mackerels, barracudas, dolphin, bonefish, blue and white marlin, sailfish, all three species of tuna, wahoo, permit, mako sharks and amberjacks. Every conceivable method of fishing from trolling to fly casting is used and, depending upon the species of fish, is productive.

A party of four can charter a boat in Nassau for fishing and living and then spend one or two weeks wandering among the uninhabited islands for as little as from $20 to $25 per day per person. This price includes a comfortable seaworthy boat, a crew of two, bait and tackle, food, fuel and ice.

For the budget fisherman this hotel by night and fishing boat by day cuts down costs considerably. Elsewhere skiffs can be rented for from $18 to $20 a day. A Bahama guide with a dingy or skiff for bonefishing costs about $20 to $30 a day for two people.

Nassau and other destinations in the Bahamas are only minutes away by plane from Miami or West Palm Beach. There are accommodations for fishermen on the following islands and perhaps on still others: Grand Bahama, Great Abaco, Bimini, Andros, Eleuthera, New Providence and Great Exuma.

SAN DIEGO REGION, CALIFORNIA

Although the fishing pressure is extremely heavy, the warm ocean currents off San Diego make the coastal waters one of the outstanding saltwater fishing holes in North America. Many towns about San Diego depend to a large degree on sport fishing for part of their income. They furnish baits, boats, and guides for the thousands of anglers who fish San Diego Bay, Mission Bay, the beach, the bluffs and the kelp beds along with Los Coronados. Yellowtail and albacore are the most popular fish in this region, but tuna, bonito, barracuda and black sea bass are extremely important. And in deeper water beyond Point Loma, fishermen find striped marlin almost the year round.

Boats and motors are available in San Diego, but there are no guides in the usual sense of the word. Competent skippers, however, will give good sound advice and information if you charter a boat to do your fishing. Prices vary according to the type of fishing that the angler wishes to do. Charter party boats carry up to about 20 persons. Bait is usually provided by the skipper of the boat.

CALIFORNIA OCEAN FISHING SCHEDULE

Place (south to north)	Kinds of Fish	Best Months	Fishing Methods & Facilities
BOAT FISHING			
San Diego (fishing principally at Coronado Island, Mexico)	Yellowtail, bluefin tuna, marlin, swordfish, white seabass, bonito, barracuda, kelp bass, halibut, black seabass	April–Sept.	Trolling for marlin and swordfish, live bait for others. Party boats, charter boats, barge.
Oceanside	Yellowtail, barracuda, kelp bass, white seabass, halibut, bonito, mackerel, albacore	April–Sept.	Live bait fishing. Party boats, barge, and charter boats.
San Clemente	Yellowtail, barracuda, kelp bass, white seabass, halibut, bonito, mackerel, albacore	April–Sept.	Live bait fishing. Party boats, barge, and charter boats.
Capistrano Beach	Yellowtail, barracuda, kelp bass, white seabass, halibut, bonito, mackerel, albacore	April–Sept.	Live bait fishing. Party boats and barge.

Place (south to north)	Kinds of Fish	Best Months	Fishing Methods & Facilities
BOAT FISHING			
Newport-Balboa (*some boats run to Santa Catalina Island*)	Barracuda, yellowtail, tuna, albacore, marlin, white seabass, black seabass, bonito, kelp bass, halibut, mackerel, albacore	April–Oct.	Live bait fishing and trolling. Party boats, charter boats, barge.
Huntington Beach	Barracuda, white seabass, black seabass, halibut, bonito, mackerel, kelp bass, albacore	April–Sept.	Live bait fishing. Party boats and barge.
Santa Catalina Island	Yellowtail, barracuda, albacore, bluefin tuna, marlin, swordfish	Barracuda & Yellowtail: May–Sept. Other species: Aug.–Sept.	Charter boats, trolling.
Seal Beach	Barracuda, white seabass, black seabass, halibut, bonito, mackerel, kelp bass, albacore	April–Sept.	Live bait fishing. Party boats, charter boats.
Long Beach, Wilmington, San Pedro (*some boats run to Santa Catalina and San Clemente islands*)	Barracuda, yellowtail, tuna, albacore marlin, white seabass, black seabass, bonito, kelp bass, halibut, mackerel	April–Oct.	Live bait fishing, trolling. Party boats, charter boats, barges, skiffs.
		Oct.–March	Bottom fishing. Cut bait.
Santa Monica Bay towns: Redondo Beach, Ocean Park, Santa Monica, Malibu	Barracuda, white seabass, bonito, kelp bass, halibut, mackerel, albacore	April–Oct.	Live bait fishing. Party boats, charter boats, barges.
Port Hueneme (*Santa Cruz and Anacapa islands fishing*)	Halibut, white seabass, kelp bass, rockfish	May–Sept.	Live bait fishing. Party boats, charter boats.
Santa Barbara	Barracuda, white seabass, halibut, kelp bass	April–Sept.	Live bait fishing. Charter boats, party boats.
Avila	Rockfish, lingcod, flatfish, cabezon	Feb.–Sept.	Artificial lures. Party boats, charter boats.
Morro Bay	Rockfish, lingcod, flatfish, cabezon	Feb.–Sept.	Artificial lures. Party boats, charter boats.
Cayucos	Rockfish, lingcod, flatfish, cabezon	Feb.–Sept.	Artificial lures. Party boats, charter boats.

Place (south to north)	Kinds of Fish	Best Months	Fishing Methods & Facilities
BOAT FISHING			
Monterey	Rockfish, salmon, lingcod, cabezon	Feb.–Sept.	Trolling for salmon, cut bait for others. Party boats, charter boats, skiffs.
Santa Cruz and Capitola	Rockfish, salmon, lingcod, cabezon	Feb.–Sept.	Trolling for salmon, cut bait for others. Party boats, charter boats, skiffs.
Princeton	Rockfish, lingcod, flatfish, cabezon	Feb.–Oct.	Trolling and cut bait. Party boats and skiffs.
San Francisco, Berkeley	Salmon, rockfish	Feb.–Nov.	Trolling. Charter boats, party boats.
Sausalito	Salmon, rockfish	Feb.–Nov.	Trolling. Charter boats, party boats.
Bodega Bay	Rockfish, lingcod, flatfish, cabezon, salmon	Summer	Trolling, artificial lures. Charter boats, party boats, skiffs.
North to Oregon Noyo, Eureka, Trinidad, Crescent City	Salmon	June–Sept.	Trolling. Charter boats, party boats, skiffs.
SHORE FISHING			
(including surf, piers and rocks) From Mexican border to Santa Barbara	Corbina, spotfin croaker, yellowfin croaker, surfperch, sharks and rays, halibut	April–Oct. some fishing all year	Casting with bait: mussels, sand crabs, pile worms. Also live bait from piers. Piers are located at: Pacific Beach, La Jolla, Del Mar, Oceanside, San Clemente, Balboa, Seal Beach, Long Beach, San Pedro (breakwater), Redondo Beach, Hermosa Beach, Manhattan Beach, Ocean Park, Santa Monica, Malibu, Port Hueneme, Ventura, Santa Barbara, Goleta.
Pismo Beach to Santa Cruz	Rockfish, surfperch, halibut, greenling sea trout	All Year	Bait: mussels, clams, sardines. Piers are located at: Pismo Beach, Avila, Cayucas, Monterey, Moss Landing, Aptos, Capitola, Santa Cruz.
Princeton to Bolinas	Striped bass, rockfish, surfperch, greenling sea trout	All year	Bait: mussels, clams, sardines. Piers are located at: Princeton, Bolinas.
Point Reyes to Oregon	Rockfish, surfperch, greenling sea trout	All year	Bait: mussels, clams, sardines, Piers are located at: Pt. Reyes, Trinidad, Crescent City.

SURINAM

One region that is of great interest to tarpon fishermen, and especially to sportsmen looking for a new world's record tarpon, is Surinam, formerly called Dutch Guiana. The jungle rivers of this small country on the north coast of South America are full of big tarpon—especially the Tibiti and Coesiwijne rivers. Access to these rivers, which also contain many other game species, is from Paramaribo, the capital.

Once Paramaribo was difficult to reach, but now KLM has three weekly flights from New York, via Curaçao (where there is other good saltwater fishing). Other KLM connections are possible from Miami. There are excellent accommodations in Paramaribo and the potential of the fishing there is absolutely unlimited.

CAPE COD

Cape Cod, a 70-mile arm of land off southeastern Massachusetts, encircles the comparatively quiet inshore waters of Cape Cod Bay while the "outside" is washed by the wild, gray Atlantic. The Cape itself is narrow: far out at the tip it's no more than a spit of windswept sand. But Nature might have created it for fishermen alone.

Historic, picturesque Cape Cod is best known for its fine fishing for tuna, striped bass and bluefish. Between May and October, one of the greatest concentrations of saltwater fish in North American waters exists hereabouts. Besides the tuna, stripers and blues, a fisherman can expect to find pollock, swordfish, fluke, tautog, cod, mackerel, white marlin and weakfish. That's an impressive lineup.

Many kinds of fishing are possible in the Cape Cod region. There are charter boats available for trips offshore and of course it's possible to cast from the surf or from a skiff. Boats and guides are available at Provincetown, Wellfleet, Orleans, Barnstable, Buzzards Bay, Chatham, Cotuit, Falmouth, Harwich, Hyannis, Osterville, Sandwich and Eastham. Normally the rates for any boats are reasonable but they depend on the size and the quality of the boat.

Except perhaps in August when the Cape area is crowded (unhappily!) with nonfishing summer visitors, Cape Cod is an ideal place for a family fishing vacation. There is a wide range of accommodations everywhere, plus limited facilities for camping. No license is required to fish in saltwater but there are definite size limits on such saltwater species as striped bass, pollack, weakfish and shad. A nonresident fisherman should be certain to check these limits before he begins to fish.

SHARK RIVER REGION, FLORIDA

The Shark River is a winding, fairly shallow waterway, very wide at its mouth, narrowing and twisting more and more as it meanders inland. Solid, dry ground is nearly nonexistent for the entire navigable length of the Shark because it's more of a vast, saltwater swamp than a river. Its upper reaches are slightly higher and have tropical vegetation resembling the true Everglades while the lower reaches are an impenetrable tangle of mangroves.

Although fishing in the Shark River is extremely good today, it probably doesn't compare to what the first sport fisherman found there some twenty to thirty years ago. Still, the country is completely wild, lonely and virtually uninhabited. It's too remote to fish satisfactorily on a one-day trip, and on any trip it's advisable to hire a guide. Entrance to the Shark River region can be made from Everglades National Park, from Everglades City or from the vicinity of Marco Island.

Tarpon, snook, channel bass, jacks and mangrove snappers are numerous in the period from early June through October. There are many other fish abounding in the Shark River and there is good angling the year round.

The best tarpon fishing in the Shark occurs in July and August. The poorest month for fishing is May. Since this is saltwater, no fishing license is necessary.

The most feasible and frequently used method of fishing the Shark River is from a charter houseboat, living aboard and then traveling or fishing from skiffs. Any length of trip is possible. The cost ranges from $65 a day upward.

Individual anglers or perhaps two anglers can hire a boat and a guide for shorter trips into the Shark River. Such trips will cost from $50 a day upward for guide, boat and motor. The guide will also furnish any heavy tackle that is necessary but generally this is strictly light-tackle fishing country.

PADRE ISLAND VICINITY, TEXAS

Beginning at Corpus Christi, Padre Island parallels the Texas coast for 120 unbroken miles southward to the Brazos de Santiago, the pass through which ocean freighters enter Brownsville harbor. At no place is the island more than 5 miles wide but still it contains one of the most unspoiled wilderness-beaches within United States boundaries.

Padre is a strip of sand and surf and sea oats. You can drive out on the island from either end (from Corpus Christi or from Port Isabel) and motor across the sand to the opposite end. For almost 100 miles in the center there is little habitation of any kind. You simply pick a lonely spot, set up a handy camp and fish. Surf casting doesn't run much better anywhere in the world, especially in autumn.

A Padre surf caster is apt to run into almost anything: pompano, blues, whiting, spotted weakfish, Spanish mackerel, sharks and even kingfish when they wander in close to shore, but mostly this is channel-bass country. Big bull reds congregate here wholesale beginning in September, and depending upon the tide and the weather, they often stay for several months.

Fishing at Padre is completely uncomplicated. The weather is bad only a few days in an entire year so a sheet of canvas decked out for shade is sufficient shelter. Charcoal or driftwood embers in a pit of sand will do the cooking. Just dig straight down for a few feet and you find water for washing and cooking. The subsurface water is just barely palatable so it's best to bring your own drinking water.

Many Padre regulars use jeeps or pickups with oversize tires and in these they patrol the beaches looking for schools of feeding fish or for telltale flocks of birds. When the birds are spotted, the anglers just slip into swimming trunks, wade out and cast. Nothing complicated there.

As this is written, numerous developments are under way on the lower or south end of Padre Island. Already this portion has been subdivided and some accommodations have been built there. On the extreme south end, just over the causeway from Port Isabel is Isla Blanca Park, a development of the local county government. It's a natural for visiting fishermen with its trailer camping sites and permanent shelters, all for rent at extremely nominal rates. Such other facilities as bait shops, tackle shops and restaurants are also available nearby.

Brazos Island is a smaller replica of Padre Island. It's about 5 miles long and 2 miles wide and except for the weathered shacks of beachcombers and bait collectors, it's uninhabited at this writing. In the center of the island is Boca Chica Inn, a crumbling deserted beach resort that once saw lively times but now only emphasizes the solitude a fisherman can find anywhere on Brazos.

Brazos Island, which is as perfect for a camping-fishing trip as Padre, is accessible over the Boca Chica highway from Brownsville. Construction of the highway was only possible after the hurricane of 1933 closed Boca Chica Pass from the Gulf of Mexico to the Laguna Madre.

Padre and Brazos islands are divided by Brazos de Santiago Pass, which has been

Jumbo grouper boated in the Midriff section of the Gulf of California. (*Photo by Don Sandusky*)

Typical bluewater fishing boat with outriggers set, going out at sunrise to troll for big fish—anywhere.

widened and deepened to accommodate ocean vessels. On both the Padre and Brazos sides a mile-long concrete jetty extends out into the Gulf and serves as an entrance for the ships. It also serves as a funnel through which fish must migrate from the Gulf to inshore waters. The day rarely passes when anglers are not numerous on both jetties. On weekends they gather here by the hundreds and almost always everyone has action.

The pass is a natural spot for big tarpon. In fact, the Texas record tarpon was taken here. But for the average jetty angler it's a grab-bag affair. They catch everything from snook and saltwater catfish to mackerel and groupers. Jewfish weighing several hundred pounds have been taken in quantity just off the outer tips of the jetty.

Inside the pass and covering hundreds of square miles of clear shallow flats behind Padre and Brazos islands is the Laguna Madre. There are no records or scientific data to prove it but surely this must be among the most productive bodies of water in America. On good days you can drift for miles and miles casting with light tackle and it's no trick to catch spotted weakfish every foot of the way. Even on the worst days it's possible to fill an icebox with them.

Ladyfish are also superabundant in the Laguna and so are flounders. In certain areas channel bass seem to gather and to find such a place (as Redfish Bay east of Raymondville and the mouth of the Arroyo Colorado east of Rio Hondo) is one of fishing's busiest experiences. And more than one sportsman has been leisurely fishing for weakfish only to find, suddenly, that he has a wild-eyed tarpon on his hands.

For a change of pace many local fishermen look for oyster beds in the Laguna Madre and when they find one it's a beach party for sure.

Port Isabel, a bleached and picturesque fishing village that has seen better days, is the jumping-off place for Laguna Madre fishing. Headquarters for the Texas International Fishing Tournament, which is held every August, it's also the starting point for fishing trips out into the Gulf of Mexico.

Fishing in the Gulf hereabout is still in its infancy and much pioneering needs to be done, but the number of sailfish taken each year increases. And both white and blue marlin are showing up more regularly on the docks. Anglers have also returned to port with fine catches of kingfish and barracuda; a few tuna are beginning to appear in the catch. Cobia are plentiful offshore and the big boats never fail to troll for them around channel buoys as they pass them en route to the deep blue waters. Known locally as ling, no doubt there are record-book cobia still swimming in these waters. Charter-boat rates in the Port Isabel area run somewhat below those in Florida waters. Other facilities are also less expensive.

Some weather statistics on the Padre Island area are especially revealing to saltwater anglers. For example, the sun shines 69 percent of all daylight hours, and this is one of the highest averages in the United States. Fog and smog just do not exist here. The average temperature for twelve months day and night is 73.1°. It's hot in summer, warm in winter and there's seldom the wilting humidity that often exists at similar latitudes elsewhere.

THE SEA OF CORTÉS
The Sea of Cortés, or rather the Gulf of California, is a body of water so fertile and with such a great potential for saltwater angling that it is difficult to describe in less than a volume.

From Cabo de San Lucas and Puerto Chileno at the southern tip of Baja California, all the way northward to the point where the Colorado River enters the Gulf, are incredible numbers of many species of fish. In a thousand bays along both the east and west coast, shore anglers can tie into a hundred different species of fish. In brackish lagoons are snappers, spotted bass and groupers. Along white sandy beaches are croakers, corbina, jack, yellowtail and roosterfish have been known to chase baitfish right out onto the beach.

The submerged rock formations that extend at intervals all around the Gulf shores are loaded with strange new critters as well as better-known, large game species. Among these are the groupers and cabrillas. Another, is the sierra, an acrobatic favorite of light-tackle fans which is abundant both along beaches and along the rocks. Just offshore in the Gulf, especially around the Enchanted Islands, come the huge totuava, white sea bass, yellowtails, big jacks, dog snappers, bonito and at certain times of the year, sailfish in great numbers.

Time was when only a few fishermen could sample the Sea of Cortés, but new roads and new facilities have opened it up considerably. Now it's possible to drive from the border town of Calexico southward 130 miles to San Felipe and beyond over a good road to Puerto Cito. This makes it possible to fish the fantastic region of the Gulf known as the Midriff. The Midriff is about 1000 square miles of blue water dotted with numerous islands, the largest of which are Tiburón and Ángel de la Guarda. Here in water 200 feet deep, black sea bass gather as thick as rock cod and they run up to 600 pounds apiece.

It isn't possible to catalog all the fishing that is possible in the Sea of Cortés, but some of the very best is the marlin- and sailfishing which exists around the southern tip of Baja California in the Cabo de San Lucas area. Now there is regular airline service to La Paz, which is near the Cabo, via Trans Mar De Cortés Airlines. Taxicabs are available for charter from La Paz to the various fishing ports on the Gulf. There is good fishing the year round for inshore fishes as well as for the big billfish, but the best season is from October 1 to July 1.

It's wise to make advance reservations for accommodations and boats when traveling to La Paz. Be sure to take light fishing tackle and favorite lures as well as heavy tackle. Carry also a face mask and flippers for skin diving. To enter Mexico it is necessary to have a birth certificate or other proof of nationality and to secure a tourist permit card for three dollars.

Marlin charter boats in the La Paz area rent for from $45 to $65 per day. Small skiffs rent for about $1.00 an hour, or $2.00 or $3.00 an hour with guide and motor.

Chapter Eighteen

NATURAL BAITS FOR SALTWATER FISHING

ALBACORE Principally a fine game fish, but used whole or as cut bait for marlin, sailfish, and other large game fish.

ALEWIFE Adult alewives measure about one foot in length, are caught in large numbers in the nets of commercial fishermen. Also called spring herring.

ANCHOVY The anchovy is considered one of the best baits along the Pacific Coast for yellowtail, halibut, barracuda, and other fish. Difficult to keep alive on a hook, but the oils which they give off make them extremely attractive. Anchovies caught along the Atlantic Coast are used for striped bass, weakfish, and others.

BAITFISH There are many baitfish that are used in saltwater fishing. SILVERSIDE MINNOWS or SPEARING, KILLIFISH, HERRING, SARDINE and SAND LAUNCE are all used at times. Many large fish, such as mackerel, bonitos, dolphin, flying fish, butterfish, and silver hake, are used in big game fishing. Most baitfish can be bought in fish markets, from commercial fishermen or bait dealers. They can also be caught in seines, drop nets, cast nets, minnow traps, or on hook and line and kept alive in large tanks or bait cans, or frozen, kept on ice or pickled in heavy brine. Live baitfish can be hooked through the lips, back, belly, or sides. Dead ones are hooked by running the hook either through the eyes or

This is the method most frequently used to gather such baitfish as mullet, balao. Net is a cast net. Photo was taken in Puerto Rico.

mouth and gill opening, then into the body near the tail.

BALAO or BALLYHOO A member of the halfbeak family, resembling the needlefish, and used as a bait for tarpon, barracuda, amberjack, and especially sailfish. Found in southeastern United States.

BARRACUDA Small barracudas are sometimes used whole in fishing for large game fish, or as cut bait for smaller fish.

BASS KILLY Another name for the striped KILLIFISH.

BEAK THROWER Common name for BLOODWORM.

BILLFISH Common name for NEEDLEFISH.

BLACKBELLY A common name for glut herring, common along the Atlantic Coast. See HERRING.

BLACK-TAILED SHRIMP A bait shrimp found along the Pacific coast.

BLOODWORM Found in mud flats along the Atlantic and Pacific coasts. Sometimes measures more than 8 or 10 inches in length. Their name refers to their having red-hued bodies. When handled, they shoot out a long proboscis with four tiny black jaws. Both bloodworms and clam worms can be found along rocks and sandy bottoms, at low tide on flats or sandy basins. They can be kept in a cool bed of rock moss or on ice. For hooking fish such as rockfish, bass, and weakfish, use a single worm or cut in pieces. Two or three get best results for blackfish, croakers, and nippers. See CLAM WORM

BLUE CRAB Also called blue-claw crab and edible crab, the blue crab is large, dark, and white-bellied. It gets its name from its long bluish claws, which are red at the tip. Its hind legs are paddlelike to propel it through the water. Blue crabs are found in bays, inlets, and rivers and have a preference for mud bottoms. They can be caught in nets and will live for several days out of the water if kept in a cool spot. Hook the hard crabs in the underside of the top shell. Soft-shell crabs can be tied to hook. Crabs make the best bait for bluefish, weakfish, tautog, and many other varieties.

BLUEBACK Another name for glut herring, used as bait along the Atlantic Coast. See HERRING.

BONITO A common sport fish, sometimes cut in strips and used as bait for sailfish and marlin, or used whole for swordfish, blue marlin, sailfish, tuna, and other big game fish.

BRAZILIAN SHRIMP Common shrimp caught commercially in the Atlantic from Massachusetts to Florida.

BUCKRAM Term for a crab which is past the soft-shell stage but not hard; shell caves in when pressed; sometimes called leatherback, paperback, or peeler crab.

Typical bait shop in the Florida Keys. This one is at Marathon.

BUNKER Another name for MENHADEN.

BUTTERFISH A bait fish sometimes used for weakfish, tuna, and other saltwater game fish.

CALICO CRAB See LADY CRAB.

CATFISH Saltwater catfish are sometimes used as bait for black sea bass, marlin, tarpon, jewfish.

CHERRYSTONE CLAM Local name for the East coast commercial hard-shell clam.

CHUM Various shellfish and baitfish crushed or ground up, either placed in a chum pot or thrown overboard to lure fish.

CLAM Includes CALIFORNIA RAZOR CLAM, CHERRYSTONE, LONG CLAM, NANNYNOSE, OCEAN CLAM PISMO. Among saltwater baits, these bivalve mollusks are among the most popular baits. Many kinds are used, but the big SURF CLAM, or sea clam, and the hard-shell clams are the most common. The surf clams are found along the ocean and surf in shallow and fairly deep water. The hard-shell clams are found in the more protected bays and sounds. They can be dug with clam hoes or forks on tidal flats. Clams can also be bought from bait dealers and in fish markets. You can keep clams for several days in a cool spot or on ice. For longer periods, they should be submerged in saltwater in a sack or other container. Open them with a knife or hit them against a hard object to get at the soft, meaty parts. For big fish such as cod, rockfish, and channel bass, put the meat from a whole clam or even two clams on a hook. For tautog, scup or porgies, sea bass, flounders, and other small fish, cut the muscular foot of the clams into sections.

CLAM WORM These marine worms are widely used and appeal to most saltwater fish. The clam worms (sandworms) and BLOODWORMS are the two kinds usually used. Clam worms have a brown, bluish, or greenish iridescence, rounded backs, and flat, pink or red undersides, with two rows of "legs" along the sides. Bloodworms have a pink or reddish round body tapering on both ends. When handled, they shoot out a long proboscis armed with four tiny, black jaws. Both clam worms and bloodworms can be dug with clam hoes or garden forks at low tide on tidal flats of bays in shelly sand or mud. They are also sold by most bait dealers. These worms can be kept in moist rockweed in a cool spot, preferably on ice. For large fish, such as rockfish (striped bass) and weakfish, hook a single worm, or even two or three for best results. For smaller fish, such as tautog, scup or porgies, flounders, and croakers, a worm can be cut in half or quarters.

CONCH These are univalve mollusks, most prevalent in tropical waters where the soft bodies are removed and used as bait for saltwater fish, including bonefish, groupers, grunts and snappers. They live in a spiral or coiled shell.

CRAB Although there are many crabs that make good bait, most popular are BLUE CRAB, LADY CRAB, SAND CRAB, FIDDLER CRAB, HERMIT CRAB, RED-JONTED FIDDLER and HAIRY HERMIT. They live in the ocean and bays among rocks and weeds, in burrows or empty snail shells. You can catch most by hand in shallow water or with crab nets and traps. Soft-shell crabs make the best bait. Crabs usually can be kept alive for several days out of the water if kept in a cool spot. For longer periods, they can be kept in cages submerged in saltwater. Hook the hard crabs through the back or side with the hook entering the underside and coming out on top. Soft-shell crabs can be tied to a hook with fine thread. Crabs will take striped bass, channel bass, bluefish, weakfish, flounders, tautog, and many other saltwater fish.

CUT BAIT Bait made by cutting large fish into strips.

DOLPHIN or DORADO A large fish frequently used for cut bait.

EARTHWORM Sometimes used for striped bass, flounders, eels, and other saltwater fish.

EEL Favorite bait for the striped bass. Found along the Atlantic Coast in basins, tidal drainage rivers, freshwater ponds and lakes. The female may reach 1½ feet in length; males, 2 feet. They are slim and snakelike, with color varying from gray to yellow on the back and white on the belly. Live eels are used for striped bass but are generally fished dead or cut in sections. The eel is tied onto an eel rig with one hook coming from the underside, the other from the topside, or more frequently, with both hooks coming from the underside. Eel skins are frequently attached to metal or rubber rings and used as casting or trolling baits. Either the whole eel or the eel skins can be kept in brine solution. Jewfish, weakfish, and a great variety of saltwater species will take this bait.

FAN MUSSEL Common mussel used for bait. See MUSSEL.

FIDDLER CRAB Common crab used for bait.

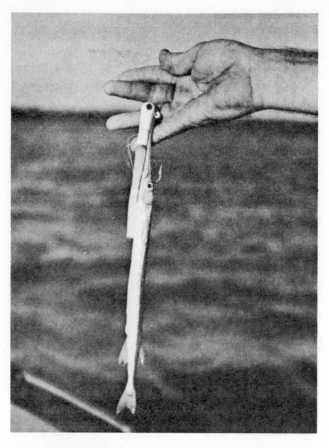

Nylon jig—needlefish combination, which is a great casting and trolling bait for many species.

FLYING FISH A common baitfish used for large game fish such as tuna, sailfish, swordfish; frequently skittered along the surface. See BAIT-FISH.

FLYING SQUID Another name for the short-tailed squid found along the East coast from Cape Cod to Florida. See SQUID.

FROST FISH Another name for common smelt. See SMELT.

GHOST CRAB Crab found along the East coast from Long Island south. See CRAB.

GHOST SHRIMP Burrowing shrimp that lives on sand beaches and mud flats. See SHRIMP.

GREEN CRAB Common name for sand crab. See CRAB.

HALFBEAK Another name for BALAO, which resembles the needlefish and is used for tarpon, sailfish, and other game fish.

HERMIT CRAB Crab that lives in abandoned shells of snails, moving from a smaller shell to a larger shell as it needs more space. Bait for bonefish, sheepshead, blackfish, permit, and snappers. Heat or cracks shell to get the crab and remove claws. See CRAB.

HERRING One of most common food fish in Atlantic and Pacific. Young are canned as sardines. Generally less than 12 inches. Herring are used either dead or alive, for many game fish. Are difficult to keep alive on a hook or in tanks. Can be hooked through the lips, through belly, or attached to special herring rigs, which hold them securely but do not kill quickly. Used dead, they are hooked through the lips and if trolled the hook may be spooned into the body cavity. Strips, chunks, or ground-up herring make good chum.

HICKORY SHAD Large herring often used as bait.

HOG-MOUTHED FRY Small minnow used for chumming and bait for many species in Bermuda.

ICEFISH Another name for SMELT.

INKFISH Another name for SQUID. Name is derived from habit of squirting an inky screening fluid from a siphon in the head.

JACKNIFE CLAM West coast clam generally difficult to collect since they burrow deep and fast. See CLAM.

JUMPING MULLET Another common name for striped mullet found abundantly along both coasts. See MULLET.

KILLIFISH Favorite baitfish for fishermen along the Atlantic coast. Seldom greater than 6 inches. They travel in large schools, can be caught in bays, tidal creeks, rivers. Fishermen like them because they live a long time out of water and on the hook. Often they can be carried in damp seaweed, but it is best to keep them in water or on ice. Good for bass, weakfish, bluefish, sea bass, and especially summer flounder or fluke. See BAITFISH.

KING MACKEREL Sport fish used as cut bait or whole for larger fish such as sailfish or marlin.

LABRADOR HERRING Common name for most abundant herring along the East coast. See HERRING.

LADY CRAB Also called calico crab; a swimming crab found along the East coast and Gulf of Mexico. See CRAB.

LEATHERBACK Another name for BUCKRAM CRAB.

LIMPET A small univalve mollusk found along both coasts, attached to rocks and other underwater objects. Soft body is removed from shell and used as bait.

LOBSTER Good for striped bass, black fish, and many saltwater species. Expensive to purchase as bait.

LUGWORM Abundant sea worm used as bait. See SEA WORM.

MACKEREL Commonly caught for sport, but commercial fishermen catch small ones to be sold as bait. They average several pounds in weight and are fished alive for large game fish such as tuna; the large ones are cut in strips and used for striped bass, bluefish, weakfish, flounder, or other species. Can also be fished whole. See BAITFISH.

MARSH FIDDLER Another name for mud fiddler crab found along the East coast, most commonly in mud flats. See CRAB.

MENHADEN Also called bony fish, bugfish, chebog, bunker, greentail, hardhead, porgy, razor-belly shad. The menhaden, or mossbunker, is one of best baitfish that can be used along the Atlantic and Gulf coasts. It is a flat, oily fish that often reaches more than a foot in length. Most menhaden are caught in purse seines by commercial fishermen and can be bought. When close to shore, they can often be caught with haul seines. Menhaden are used whole when small, or cut into steaks or filleted when large.

Also ground up and used in chumming. Menhaden will catch bluefish, striped bass, weakfish, channel bass, mackerel, sharks, and many other fish.

MOON SNAIL Large snails found on both coasts. Many have a shell diameter approaching 6 inches. Meat is removed from the shell and used as bait for bottom feeders. See SNAIL.

MOSSBUNKER Another name for MENHADEN.

Chumming as it's done in Bermuda. Gene Ray mixes hog-mouthed fry with sand, rolls it into a ball, then tosses it out to settle to the bottom. (Bermuda News Bureau photos by Gene Ray)

MULLET Includes jumping mullet, silver mullet, another popular fish along the Atlantic coast. Can be found in most bays, inlets, and surf, where they are caught in seines or cast nets. Commercial fishermen catch most of the mullet. Small mullet are used whole for bottom fishing; larger ones are rigged and used in trolling for sailfish. Big ones can be cut up and used for bait. Mullet are especially good for striped bass, blue fish, channel bass, weakfish, and tarpon.

MUSSEL Includes bay mussel, fan mussel, mud-bank mussel. These black, blue, brown, or olive-colored bivalves are well known and can be seen clinging to rocks, pilings, or the bottom of the saltwater bays and out in the ocean. They can be gathered at low tide in deep water. The larger mussels are best for bait, but even these are soft and difficult to keep on a hook. For some fish, such as tautog, the shell of a small mussel can be cracked, but not removed, to make it stay on the hook better and to keep other fish from stealing the bait. When removed from the shell, mussel meat can be tied around the hook with fine thread. Mussels will catch flounder, croakers, corbina, and many other fish.

NEEDLEFISH Also called longjaw or sea pike, these elongated, slim fish look like freshwater gar. They swim rapidly, close to the surface, and often can be caught in a dip net. Are fished alive for marlin, tuna, sailfish.

OCTOPUS Closely resembling squid. See SQUID.

OYSTERS Used for bottom feeders—sheepshead, flounder, etc.

PACIFIC SARDINE Also called California sardine, pilchard; frequently used like herring, for striped bass, yellowtail, and other game fish. See BAITFISH.

PACIFIC SMELT Known as whitebait, these are good for salmon, white sea bass, barracuda, yellowtail, halibut, bonito, and smaller tuna.

PERIWINKLE Small snails found clinging to piling, seaweeds, and other underwater objects. Most are too small to be used as bait, but since they are so prevalent, periwinkles serve in a pinch.

PILCHARD Another name for PACIFIC SARDINE.

PINFISH Small sunfishlike panfish used alive for tarpon, black sea bass, tuna, and other fish.

PINHEAD Small anchovy; usually hooked through mouth.

PISMO CLAM Collecting Pismo clams is sport in itself along the Pacific coast but they also make good bait. See CLAM.

PRAWN A prawn is a shrimp, also called mud shrimp, pin shrimp. Prawns can be netted with a small dip net. Chum for weakfish, bass, bluefish, blackfish, and scup. Hook through tail to keep alive to take white perch, mackerel, flounders.

RAZOR CLAM A clam with elongated shell, resembling a straight razor. See CLAM.

SALT WATER CRAYFISH   See SPINY LOBSTER.

SAND BUG Called sand fleas, beach bugs, sand crabs, mole crabs and mole shrimp. They look like small, tan eggs with several hairy legs on the underside and may reach 1½ inches in length. At ocean beaches from Cape Cod to Florida and along the Pacific Coast, you find them burrowing in sand where waves break. They leave the sand when a wave comes in but quickly burrow again when the wave recedes. Dig for them with your hands or scoop them up with a special, long-handled, wire-mesh trap. Sand bugs can be kept alive in a container filled with damp sand. To hook a sand bug, run the hook into the underside and out through the top shell. One bug is enough for small fish, while several lined up on a hook are best for larger fish. Sand bugs will take striped bass, channel bass, bonefish, sheepshead, tautog, pompano, corbina, croakers.

SAND LAUNCE Look like eels, are found in great abundance on both East and West coasts. Are so called because of their habit of burying themselves in the sand, sometimes getting caught above the tidewater mark, where they can be dug. Congregate in schools and are generally seined. They are hardy baitfish, can be kept alive for considerable periods of time. Small ones are fished whole; large ones are cut in pieces. Excellent for bluefish, striped bass and other sport fish. Also called SAND EEL.

SARDINE A common name for Atlantic herring—see HERRING—and for PACIFIC SARDINE.

SCALLOP Soft part of scallop makes good bait. Good trick for anglers is to crack shellfish, trim meat, and salt down in airtight container to preserve and toughen bait for later fishing trip. See MUSSEL.

SEA PIKE Another name for NEEDLEFISH.

SEA WORM Also called mussel worm, pileworm, ribbon worm, rock worm, and tapeworm. See

CLAM WORMS and BLOODWORMS.

SHAD Another name for MENHADEN.

SHEDDER CRAB A day or so before crab sheds its shell, the old shell becomes loose and can be peeled off easily. At this stage, the crab is called a shedder or a peeler. You can test this by breaking off the movable part of a pincer; if the shell breaks away leaving a soft inner portion exposed, this crab is a shedder.

SHINER Another name used for MENHADEN, and also for SILVERSIDE MINNOW.

SHORT-TAILED SQUID East coast squid generally inhabiting deeper water than the common squid. See SQUID.

SHRIMP Includes BRAZILIAN SHRIMP. In most species and numbers, shrimp are numerous. The big, edible shrimp found in fish markets are used for bait. And smaller sand shrimp and prawns are often sold by bait dealers. Catch your own with seines in shallow water of bays, sounds, and inlets. Keep them alive in bait cans in saltwater or on ice in rockweed or sawdust. Shrimp and prawns should be hooked through the tail for best results. Use for striped bass, channel bass, weakfish, bluefish, bonefish, sheepshead, snappers, groupers, and most saltwater fish.

SILVERSIDE MINNOW Saltwater minnows abundant along the East Coast; so called because of silver bands along their green bodies. They are caught in nets or traps.

SKIMMER CLAM Another name for surf clam, most common clam along East Coast. See CLAM.

SMELT Includes icefish. Occur in tidal creeks, inlets, and up in the freshwater streams, where they spawn. Sometimes reach a foot in length, but mostly less than 6 inches. Good cod bait.

SNAIL Includes the sand-collar snail: MOON SHELL or SNAIL. Many large and small snails in saltwater can be used for bait. There are the moon snails or sand-collar snails found along the Atlantic and Pacific coasts. They are often left high and dry on shore or can be picked up in shallow water. The periwinkles that are found along the Atlantic Coast clinging to rocks, piles, and seaweed are small but also make good bait.

SOFT-SHELL CLAM An extremely good bait found along the East coast south to North Carolina but most numerous north of Massachusetts. Also occur along West coast as far south as Monterey, California. See CLAM.

SOFT-SHELL CRAB Immediately after they shed their shells, crabs are referred to as soft-shell, and are most highly prized as bait at this time. See CRAB.

SPEARING Common name for SILVERSIDE MINNOW.

SPINNERS Strips cut from sides of sardines or herring in pennant or triangular shape.

SPINY LOBSTER Common in warmer waters along both coasts, sometimes called saltwater crayfish. Caught in baited traps or seined, but in many areas there are restrictions as to seasons, size, and number. Can be kept alive in cages suspended in saltwater. The hard head and body parts are frequently kept and used as chum, and the tail as a bait.

SQUID Includes blunt-tailed squid, inkfish, sea arrow. Among best all-round saltwater baits. Are usually found in the deeper ocean waters but are sometimes close to shore. Usually caught in pound nets, traps, trawls, and seines, they can be caught by hand or in dip nets when they come close to shore. Or you can buy squid, fresh or frozen, from most fish and bait dealers. Squid are difficult to keep alive, so they are usually preserved on ice, are frozen, or are pickled in brine. The whole squid is used for big fish such as striped bass and hooked with one or two hooks through the body and head. Small portions and strips cut into various lengths and shapes are used for sea bass, cod, bluefish, and other small fish.

STONE CRAB Formerly used for bait but now scarce, due to commercial demand. See CRAB.

TOP SMELT Pacific coast silverside minnow. See SIVERSIDE MINNOW.

WHELK Includes channeled whelk, waved whelk, knobbed whelk; all are large, 2- to 4-inch univalve shells. May be trapped or picked up in shallow water. Good, tough bait for codfishing; sometimes combined with softer bait like clam. May be cut up for bait for tautog, porgy, sea bass, and other bottom fish.

WORM See CLAM WORM.

YELLOWTAIL JACK When alive, it is great for barracuda, sharks.

HOW TO RIG LIVE BAIT

A most important skill of saltwater angling is properly preparing a natural bait. And that can mean much more than simply impaling it on a hook.

Hook is baited with fry, then tossed out to mingle with chum.

Quite often a fisherman must cut, clean, or even sew baits onto a hook to obtain the kind of action that will tempt the fish he is seeking. Just for example, a minnow impaled for still-fishing or drifting is almost worthless for trolling because the fisherman is trying to achieve an entirely different effect when he trails the bait behind a moving boat.

Naturally the terminal gear—the leader, sinkers, swivels and whatever—must also be rigged properly no matter whether the bait is being fished on the bottom or being trolled on the surface. Obviously no single rig or hookup will meet all these conditions. And in fact no single rig will serve very well for more than the one purpose for which it was intended.

I will attempt to describe and illustrate here a few of the basic, terminal tackle rigs that are popular on both the Atlantic and the Pacific coasts for a wide variety of fishes. Obviously

there are many more, but an angler with ingenuity can begin with these and vary them to suit his own specific fishing conditions.

Let's start with the common eel, which is known by many names, but which by any name is a great bait for surf casting and for trolling.

The easiest way to obtain eels is to buy them from commercial fishermen who trap them during annual spawning migrations. However, if you have to catch them for yourself, the best method is to use an eel pot. This is only a large, wire-mesh, minnow trap with a small opening. It should be set in a bay or inlet in the evening and then baited with chopped fish, clams, crabs, or even pieces of beef neck. It's a good idea to attach a float to the trap so that you can locate it easily the next morning.

An eel is a favorite bait for striped bass, blue-fish, school tuna, bluefish, cobia and quite a number of other big game species. And of course, there are many ways to rig and to fish eels. For surf casting from a beach or for shallow-water trolling, a good method is to hook the eel both in the head and about two-thirds of the way back toward the tail. The two hooks are connected by using a long wire needle to pull the leader entirely through the eel as shown in the diagram.

For deeper trolling, the head of the eel is skinned out and an egg sinker is slid over the wire leader and substituted. Then the skin is pulled back over the sinker and sewed shut. Eels are almost always used dead since a live eel will only twist and turn enough to tangle tackle into a hopeless mess.

It's quite a problem to cast a whole eel with surf-casting gear, so many beach fishermen use only the skin, which is rigged with weighted sinker head. This eel-skin rig is also deadly for trolling, as it has far more wiggle than a whole eel. The skins are used in sizes from 6 to 20 inches long, depending upon the species of fish.

Whenever fishing the bottom of the sea, whether it be in a bay or above the reefs, the use of two hooks will often help the angler to land more fish during the period when they're biting well and fast. It will also double the opportunity for fish to find the bait.

The most popular device for multiple bait fishing is called a spreader rig. This is only a section of spring steel or heavy wire with a loop at each end through which leaders and hooks are attached. The spreader bar itself is attached to the line at the center, much in the manner of a scales and to sink it rapidly to the proper depth a heavy sinker is tied just below the point where the main line ties on to the spreader bar. All kinds of spreader-rig variations are possible, depending upon the type of bottom to be fished and whether the fish be flounder, sea bass, porgie, blackfish or whatever.

Tuna fishermen have devised a method to rig herring for bait. It's called the "Wedgeport Teaser," and it's valuable because it can be applied to many other baitfishes to catch many other game fish.

This lure is made up by stringing several whole herrings together on a heavy line to imitate a small school of them surfacing. With backbones removed the herring are threaded through the lips and each one is knotted so that it will

NATURAL BAIT RIGS

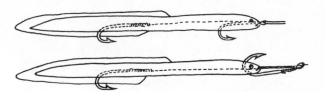

Alternate eel rigs for trolling or casting. A long wire needle pulls the leader through the eel's body.

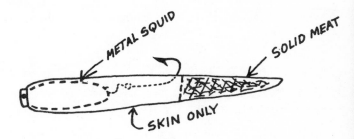

Eel tail made by slipping eel skin (with a bit of meat left in the tail) over a metal squid or an egg sinker and hook.

Eel skin slipped over a metal squid or lead-head jig.

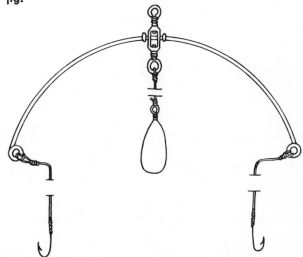

Spreader rig for bottom fishing. Makes it possible to fish two hooks at once. It is best over a soft bottom.

maintain a separate position on the line, about 6 or 8 inches from the other herrings.

Since frozen herrings are normally used for the teasers, they are rather stiff and wooden until the backbone is removed and the fish is completely thawed out. Of course, it's necessary to resew the back after removing the backbone to keep the herring from falling apart. The "Teaser" is trolled behind a boat.

THE EXPERTS' FAVORITE BAITS AND METHODS

Following is a list of favorite saltwater baits obtained by interviewing 200 fishing guides, pier operators, charter-boat captains and well-known sport fishermen in North Carolina. Many of these men operate seasonally both in Florida and North Carolina waters.

The total number of years of experience of the group is 4207! Baits, lures, and methods recommended here are considered best by the majority of these men, who live by catching or helping others to catch fish. But generally speaking, any charter-boat captain, guide or pier operator will recommend the best baits for his particular area and will probably have plenty on hand to supply you.

Here are the popular game fishes and the experts' consensus:

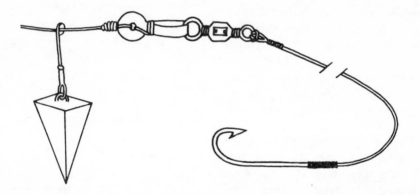

Fish-finder rig—a standard rig among surf casters. With this it's possible to feel softly biting fish, without drag of sinker.

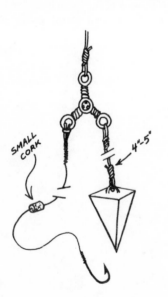

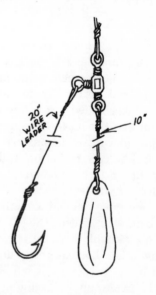

Three-way swivel rig—another favorite of surf casters which permits fishing bait just off the bottom.

Three-way swivel rig, this one with wire leader for such toothed fish as sharks and bluefish. Bank sinker is better for rocky bottoms.

ALBACORE Split mullets, whole mullets, strip squid and cut fish are preferred, in that order. Among artificials recommended, the No. 3½ Drone spoon is tops with a No. 4 Hopkins lure next, followed by the Reflecto spoon and white or yellow feathers.

Method: Skip bait on top of water; if no luck, troll slower, letting bait go deeper; if still no luck, let it sink to bottom. When albacore move inshore to feed, fly fishing, bait casting and spinning from pier, boat or surf present a real challenge.

AMBERJACK Live pinfish are best, live mullet next and squid third. Drone spoons top the artificials with white and yellow feathers next.

BARRACUDA Whole squid, whole mullets and strip mullets. (Live mullets are best.) The ½-ounce feather first among artificials, with several swearing by the Loon Bone.

Method: Trolling on an incoming tide; use 7/o or 8/o hook. Troll near bottom. Sometimes large spoons or jigs prove effective.

BLACK DRUM Shrimp leads the list. Squid and cut mullet are next, trailed by sand fiddlers and clams. Pier fishermen recommend Sea Hawk plugs and Clark spoons.

BLUEFISH Bait for blues varies with the size of the fish. Wilmington and Southport areas

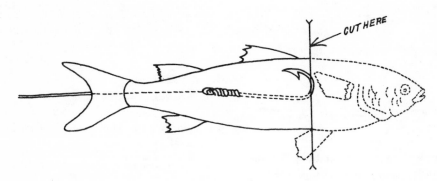

Mullet or grunt rigged for bottom fishing. This can be cast without dead fish coming off hook. It's a good hooker, too. Mullet is cut in half in front of dorsal fin and a wire leader with hook attached is threaded through. Thus the hook point is exposed and the hook bend supports the weight of the bait.

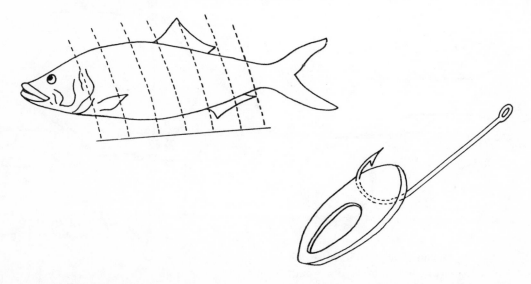

Top cut bait is the menhaden. Here's how to cut it and use it on hook. Use the head and entrails for chumming.

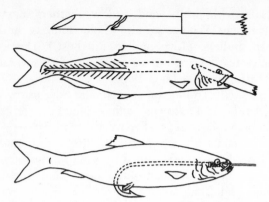

How to debone a herring, using a hollow steel tube sharpened at an angle. Technique is like coring an apple. With backbone removed—to make bait more flexible, lifelike—insert hook and sew mouth to eye as shown.

Mooching rig permits use of natural bait, but keel sinker prevents line twist, even though the bait spins behind.

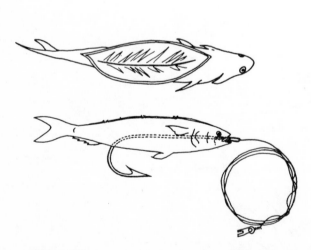

Mullet prepared for trolling. Fish is split down the back, backbone removed and entrails discarded. Hook is placed as shown, back is sewed up and eye of hook sewed to mouth.

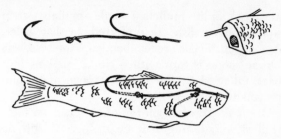

Plug-cut baitfish. When cut and rigged as shown, a herring or mullet can be cast and manipulated like a plug. Great rig for tarpon, big snook.

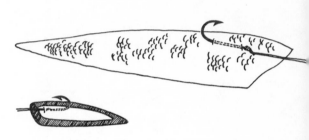

Cut spinner bait, which can be used in conjunction with keel sinker.

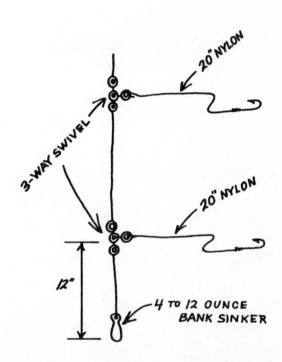

Codfish rig. Use 7 or 8 Sproat hooks, line of about 40-pound test and squid or skimmer clams for bait.

Two shrimp on a hook.

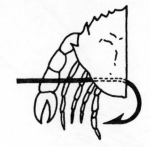

How to hook a live fiddler (or similar) crab.

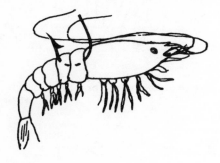

Edible shrimp hooked through back. Keep barb up.

How to hook a green crab near the base of the tail.

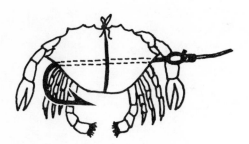

How to hook dead soft-shell crab.

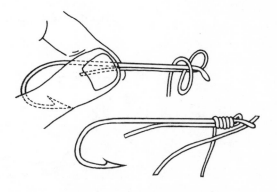

Sand shrimp hooked near tail.   Rigging two hooks.

Head of squid hooked for bottom fishing.

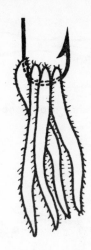

How to hook a squid for bottom fishing.

How to hook sand- or bloodworms.

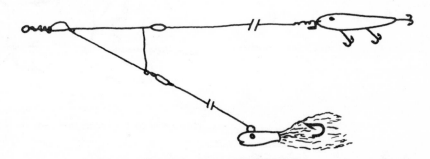

Striped-bass dual rig, with jig and plug, for trolling.

Another striped-bass rig, also good when trolling for other fishes.

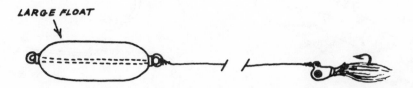

Surface-splasher rig, for stripers or weakfish.

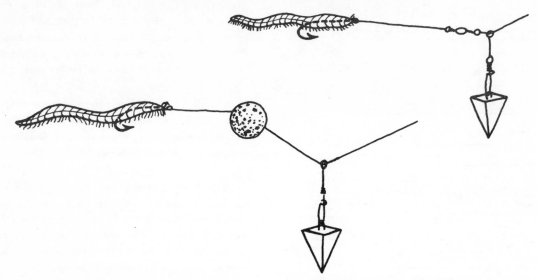

Fish-finder rigs using sea worms for bait. Good in both Atlantic and Pacific.

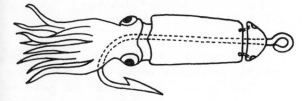

Lead-head jig in combination with squid.

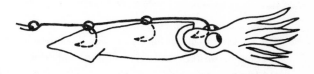

Three-hook squid rig. Will take a great variety of fish.

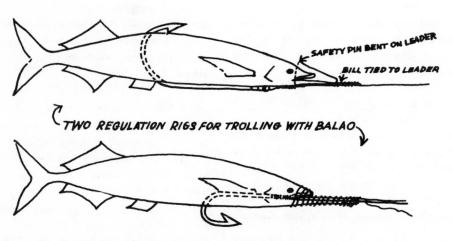

Techniques of rigging balao for trolling.

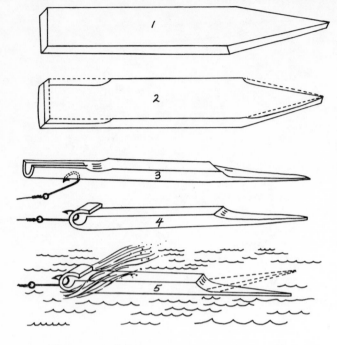

"Fig. 1. A 7½-inch strip. This fillet is cut from the freshest fish possible. Start at tail of fish, cut forward, place the slab skin down and tailor it to an inch wide and slightly over ¼ inch thick. This thickness can be varied according to weight desired —thin for slow troll, thick for faster movement.

"Fig. 2. Dotted lines show where fish is cut from 'head' end and 'tail'. Thus half of the thickness is removed. The front cut is 1¾ inches long, the tail end about 2 inches.

"Fig. 3. The edges of the 'head' end are pinched up into a fold so that the hook can be inserted completely through the lower part of the fold and about 1 inch back of the front end. The position of the hook is important in establishing balance and to produce 'rooster-tail' sprays.

"Fig. 4. The completed sled-shaped 'Skip-strip' with front end folded upward from hook.

"Fig. 5. Illustrates the bait being trolled or retrieved on surface. The 'rooster-tail' sprays shooting up from front end are indicated. This gives the illusion of flying-fish wings. The dotted lines suggest the flipping up-and-down of the 'tail'.

"After bait has been trolled for some time, or has been hit by fish repeatedly, some of the flesh may get stripped off and throw it out of balance, causing it to revolve or lose the 'rooster-tail' spray action.

"A fast troll against a strong current will often cause the bait to dive. A smooth sledding on the surface is desirable. If the water is very smooth, the bait will function a greater distance from the boat than when water is rough. For billfish, a slow-trolled bait 40 feet back of the stern is best. For dolphin the distance may vary from 50 to 150 feet, and speeds from 3 to 8 knots. For yellowfin tuna, 100 yards at 6 to 8 knots; for bluefin and yellowtail, 4 to 7 knots; for needlefish, 3 to 5. (These trolling speeds are not specific.) Fish will take this bait at a much slower pace than a lure. When a fish makes a pass and misses, pay out line at once, allowing the bait to remain near the spot of the strike. In all cases allow the fish time for one long run with free spool and added time for it to swallow the bait. This can not be over-stressed for billfish."

The Cannon Skip-strip bait designed to look like a flying fish about to fly. It was invented by Ray Cannon, western saltwater fishing authority of Los Angeles, and author of *How to Fish The Pacific Coast*.

Although the "Skip-strip" has already proven an electrifying bait for a dozen species in the Gulf of California, its full potential is yet to be learned in southern California waters. Some game fishes, on seeing this bait, rise to the surface and dash as much as 200 or 300 feet to nail it. It could be great in the Atlantic, too.

Although the drawings suggest a number of complicated operations, the whole business can be done in thirty seconds or less, with a sharp knife and a little practice. After large slab is cut from fish (mackerel, ocean whitefish, black skipjack, sierra or bonito are preferred), the work is done with the skin side down; the flesh is left flat enough on top to maintain balance. Here's how Cannon describes the rig:

"In order to give a simple, clear picture of the design and proportions, I am describing a 7½-inch strip, as for a dolphin-fish, rooster-fish, or large yellowfin tuna. A 12-to-14-inch strip would, in some areas, be better for billfish—on down to a 4-inch strip for needlefish. Again, different sizes should be tried out according to locality and the size of baitfish being pursued at the time by the game fish.

(North Carolina) preferred cut mullet for 3- to 6-pounders, while around Morehead City, Harkers Island and Atlantic, where 10- to 14-inchers are landed, shrimp predominates; ¼- to ½-ounce feathers and Sea Hawk plugs prove excellent in artificials. Also the Limper spoon.

Method: Troll fast with a spoon. Bounce Bomber Red Head Jig off the bottom from a pier or drifting boat. Latter has proved most satisfactory where Shackleford Banks drops off into the channel.

BONITO Cut squid, cut mullet, Drone spoon, generally same as for albacore.

CHANNEL BASS Surf casters prefer fresh mullet, salt mullet, crabs and fatback (pork). Puppy drum may be taken on shrimp. Plugs and flies take small ones. Use swivel leader. Channel bass mouth their bait before taking. Always let the fish run about 4 yards before setting the hook. Pfleuger Record spoon is deadly.

COBIA Live pinfish on a free line. Live shrimp on a free line. Spoons, Mirrolure, Pfleuger Mustang, Bomber Jerk Plug. Monofilament best bet for landing these.

DOLPHIN Strip mullet, strip mackerel, shrimp from piers; jigs and feathers in artificials. Leaving one hooked and in the water until next dolphin is hooked while trolling, will usually take entire school.

KING MACKEREL (KINGFISH) Whole mullets won hands down. Squid next. Artificials in order: No. 3½ Drone spoon, Big Bomber jig, feathers.

MAKO SHARK Whole mullet, whole mackerel, whole squid . . . or anything you can troll. Live bait generally proves best.

MARLIN Spanish mackerel, 2 to 3 pounds. Small bonito next.

Method: Using a special piece of copper pipe, the mackerel's spine may be removed and the hook placed in the tail from inside without breaking the external skin except where the hook protrudes. Meat inside should be mutilated. Bait is very lively when trolled just beyond the boat's wake some 50 to 75 feet astern. Troll with skip motion. Do not split baitfish.

SHEEPSHEAD Sand fiddlers, always, then sand fleas, clams and shrimp.

Method: Put 5 quarts of oysters in a sack. Tie the top with one end of a long line then beat them up thoroughly, shells and all. Drop it over the side of the boat or pier and make your line fast. Sheepshead will suck sack when it is lowered to the proper depth. This "controlled chumming" will allow you to take them on sand fiddlers. Count ten when you feel him hit bait, then strike. Monofilament line is best here.

SAILFISH Six to seven-inch live mullet, but don't split them out. Troll skip. Use free-line drift with tail-out rig in bait. Monofilament leader.

SNAPPERS and GROUPERS Squid, cut mullet. Wire line and lead for control.

SPANISH MACKEREL Spoon, Reflecto oo up to No. 1. Same as for bluefish.

TARPON Live blue crab or stone crab. Pull off one claw, hook tail end, but don't kill. Use big popper-cork, fish about 4 feet deep.

WAHOO Live mullet, strip mullet and in the artificials, Bomber Jerk, Mirrolure, spoons and feathers. Monofilament line.

Method: Same as for King mackerel.

WEAKFISH (SPOTTED TROUT, GREY TROUT, ETC.) Shrimp, minnows, cut bait, Mirrolure, Sea Hawks, Pal-O-Mine plug.

WHITING (SEA MULLETS, VIRGINIA MULLETS) Shrimp, cut bait and Sea Hawk plugs and jigs.

HOW TO CHUM

Saltwater fishing is a completely unpredictable activity, but one point that can be made with some certainty is: when fishing from an anchored boat, you're almost certain to have better luck if you use chum.

If you've ever awakened on a cool morning to smell coffee brewing and bacon frying, you can understand the theory of chumming which has a similar effect on fish. Oil or blood or other scented matter seeps through the water and is carried along with the tide. Hungry fish become aroused and they follow the "stream" of chum to its source. Small fish dart in first, ordinarily, and then big fish follow. By chumming you can sometimes turn a seemingly dead spot into an area alive with fish.

Quite a number of chumming techniques are used. Party boats, for example, collect unwanted fish from the docks, or the entrails left from dressing fish, and grind them into a mush. They carry the mush with them in buckets and toss it over by the cupful to attact many species for their customers.

Occasionally, when a party boat anchors, the mate takes a burlap bag of ground fish and ties it to the anchor line. The liquor or chum then seeps out and keeps up an automatic stream as long as the boat is anchored in that place.

Another common method of chumming is to mix the ground-up fish with sand and to shape this mixture into balls. This is a good method for deep sea fishing, as over reefs. Plain chum would drift away on the surface, but the sand balls, which cling together for some time, have enough weight to get down where the fish are concentrated. The farther it falls, the more the sand falls apart, and the chum is released at a productive depth. This is especially effective on snappers, groupers and yellowtails.

A method of chumming I once saw used in Bermuda was as follows: Hog-mouthed fry—tiny minnows that measured no more than an inch or so in length—were seined when they came into shallow water in vast numbers. The hog-mouthed fry were then frozen in buckets until ready for use. Then they were placed aboard ship, to be thawed out en route to fishing grounds. There they were mixed with sand and tossed overboard to attract snappers, porgies and groupers.

All the methods named so far require con-siderable preparation, and most of them are very messy, especially for small-boat fishermen. But they can be reduced to a simpler level.

An angler, for example, can replace buckets of ground chum with a simple meat grinder, which he attaches to the gunwale of his boat. Whenever he wants to chum, he simply runs a mullet or two through the grinder. As he fishes he is bound to catch many undesirable species that give him still more material for the grinder.

Just as a party boat ties a chum bag to its anchor line so can a small-skiff fisherman punch some holes in a can of sardines and then tie this can to his own anchor line.

Another good idea goes like this. Canned fish for cats is available at fairly inexpensive prices on grocery shelves. You can dip out spoons of cat food and toss it overboard for chum or you can use a beer-can opener to puncture the can before dropping the whole can overboard.

In any case, the idea is to get the fish into a hungry, even a voracious mood. The more fish to appear and compete for the available food, the better the system will work. From there on it's up to you and your tackle.

Chapter Nineteen

THE SALTWATER ANGLER'S GALLEY

It is far more than a notion that the finest food in the world comes from the sea. And the truth is that sometimes the cooking and the eating of fish is more fun than catching them.

Here are some recipes—a few simple, and others complicated—which make high adventure of eating fish. Some of the recipes are well known and some are the recipes of celebrated fish chefs who spend their lives developing such inspired comestibles as these.

BAKED FISH

Place 3 flounders (or mackerel or weakfish) of about a pound apiece in a baking dish or pan. Pour sauce (instructions follow) over the fish. Sprinkle lightly with salt, pepper, flour. Cover, bake 15 minutes at 375° F. Uncover, baste with melted butter and dry white wine. Bake 10 minutes more or until tender and flaky. It serves 3 or 4.

For sauce: In 6 tablespoons of melted butter, brown 2 tablespoons chopped onion and 1 minced clove of garlic. Add 2 tablespoons parsley, ¼ cup dry white wine and the juice of 1 lemon. Blend all together.

FISH IN SOUR CREAM

Put one 3½- to 4-pound haddock, mackerel, whitefish, snapper or flounder in a baking dish or pan. Pour sour cream sauce (instructions follow) into and over the fish. Surround with 1 cucumber cut into 8 strips. Bake 40 minutes at 375° F. or until tender and flaky, basting 2 or 3 times. It serves 3 or 4.

For the sour cream sauce: To 5 tablespoons melted butter or margarine, add ¼ tablespoon thyme, 1 chopped bay leaf, 1 tablespoon minced onion, ¼ tablespoon dried dill, ¼ teaspoon each of salt and pepper, 1 cup sour cream, ¼ cup of light cream.

FISH CREOLE

This recipe is best when using snappers of 3 or 4 pounds. Brush fish with butter or margarine. Place in baking dish or pan and pour sauce over the fish. Bake for 35 minutes at 375° F. or until tender and flaky, basting 2 or 3 times. It serves 3 or 4.

For the Creole sauce: Mince and brown in ¼ cup oil, 1 clove of garlic, 1 onion, half a green pepper. Next add 1 tablespoon each of capers, chili powder, 1 teaspoon salt, ¼ teaspoon each of pepper, cloves, allspice, 10 pitted ripe olives and 3 chopped tomatoes.

BARBECUED SMALL WHOLE FISH

Clean and remove head if desired from such small fish as flounders, bluefish, snappers, weakfish, mackerel or bass. Wash the fish and dry them with a paper towel. Coat the fish with a thin paste of equal parts of flour and corn oil seasoned with salt, pepper and tabasco. Place the fish on a grill over medium heat about 3 inches from hot charcoal brickets. Barbecue 6 to 8 minutes, turning the fish once. Allow about 2 fish for each hungry person.

FISH STEAKS

Such fish as salmon, halibut, bluefish, pollack or haddock are prepared for grilling the same as for smaller whole fish above. Cut or buy the steaks about an inch thick. Allow 1 pound per person. Barbecue approximately 12 minutes—turning once—with the grill placed about 3 inches away from the charcoal.

For extra flavor, marinate the steaks for about 30 minutes before barbecuing. Delicious herb marinade can be made by combining 1 or 2 bay leaves, ½ teaspoon of thyme, and 1 cup of wine vinegar. Heat it in a saucepan to blend the flavors and cool before marinating. Drain the fish before barbecuing.

SUPER COLE SLAW

This type of super slaw is especially good when served with barbecued or grilled fish. First assemble the following ingredients: ¼ teaspoon pepper, ½ teaspoon dry mustard, 1 teaspoon celery seed, 2 tablespoons sugar, ¼ cup chopped green pepper, 1 teaspoon salt, 1 teaspoon chopped red pepper, ½ teaspoon grated onion, 3 tablespoons corn oil, ⅛ cup vinegar, 3 cups chopped cabbage. Now place all the ingredients in a large bowl in the order listed. Mix well, cover, and place in a refrigerator to chill thoroughly. Garnish with watercress.

SAUTÉED SALMON STEAK

For 4 persons you need 4 salmon, swordfish or halibut steaks, ¼ cup of butter, ¼ cup apple cider, 2 tablespoons of prepared mustard. Spread the steaks with mustard. Melt butter in a skillet. Add cider and sauté the steaks 10 minutes on each side in this mixture.

STUFFED BONEFISH

Bonefish have always been rated among the gamest fish in the world but they're seldom regarded very highly on the table. Here, however, is a Bimini, Bahamas, recipe for cooking a large bonefish which refutes the common belief that bonefish are not extremely good on the table.

Scale and clean a fish in the 7- to 9-pound class but do not remove the head or tail. To prepare stuffing, combine 1 cup finely chopped celery, 1 cup finely chopped onion, ½ cup chopped green pepper. Place this in a skillet with ½ pound butter. Cook on a slow fire, uncovered, until the vegetables are tender. This should require about 20 minutes. Meanwhile, grate stale bread (half white, half wheat, if possible), to make 2 cups bread crumbs. Combine the crumbs with the cooked vegetables; add 2 raw eggs, 2 tablespoons evaporated milk, and a dash of sherry. Mix thoroughly. Stuff the bonefish with this mixture and sew up the stomach cavity of the fish.

Place the fish on a large sheet of aluminum foil with ¼ pound butter cut in small pieces and placed all over and around the fish. Wrap the fish in the foil and place it in a shallow baking pan. Place the pan in a preheated 375° oven for 2 hours. Every 10 minutes throughout the cooking, undo the foil and baste the fish with accumulated juices. Pour 1 cup of water in the bottom of the pan and keep replenishing the water as it dries up so that the foil-wrapped fish rests continually in a small amount of liquid. After the fish has cooked 1 hour, sprinkle generously all over with paprika. After the second hour, it's ready to serve.

FISH AND CHIPS

This English dish is so delicious and tasty that American anglers surely should try it. Rinse firm fillets of any such whitefish as sole, haddock, cod or weakfish and roll them in flour seasoned with salt. Dip the fillets in batter, coating them well. Use a deep-fry thermometer and heat 2 or 3 pints of vegetable oil to 400° in a 2-quart saucepan. Fry the fish 4 minutes or until golden brown. Drain them and keep them hot in a low oven.

For the batter: Mix 1 cup milk, 3 beaten eggs and then stir in 1 cup flour sifted with ¼ teaspoon salt.

For the chips: Peel several firm, boiling potatoes and cut them into 1-inch cubes. Cover with cold water for an hour then drain. Dry them with a paper towel and add salt. After a few minutes, dry again. Using a deep-fry basket and the same oil used for the fish, fry the potatoes, a cup at a time, at 370° F. for about 7 minutes. Drain them, raise the oil heat to 400°, add all the chips and fry them shaking the basket until golden brown. Drain and sprinkle the fish and chips with salt and a very small amount of vinegar.

POMPANO EN PAPILLOTTE

To serve 4 and to duplicate this distinctive recipe used at the Boca Raton Hotel in Florida, you need the following ingredients: a 2-pound pompano, ½ cup tomato puree, 1 cup peeled chopped tomatoes, ½ cup chopped mushrooms, 1 tablespoon chopped shallots, ½ cup bread crumbs.

Cook the tomatoes, puree, mushrooms and shallots, seasoning to taste, for about 20 minutes, sautéeing the shallots and mushrooms first and then adding the tomato. Lightly sauté the pompano, which has been filleted in butter. Lay out parchment paper, sometimes called cooking paper and available at many grocery stores, grease it lightly with olive oil and arrange the fillets in the center. Now spread the sauce over the fillets, sprinkle on the bread crumbs, roll the paper until the fish are completely encased and as airtight as possible. Allow this to warm on top of the stove, then place it in a moderately hot oven for 7 minutes or until the paper is inflated. Serve the fish still in the paper.

SWORDFISH MIRABEAU

To serve 4, the following ingredients are necessary: four 1¼-inch-thick swordfish steaks, 2 tablespoons butter, 1 tablespoon anchovy paste, ½ cup of olive oil, 1 lemon, 4 anchovy fillets.

Roll the steaks in olive oil and broil 7 minutes on each side. Season with salt and freshly ground pepper while the fish is cooking. Mix butter and anchovy paste and spread on the hot steaks as they come from the broiler. Serve with a slice of lemon which has an anchovy fillet and an olive toothpicked into it.

SPANISH MACKEREL VÉNITIENNE

To serve 4, you need three 2-pound mackerel, 2 tablespoons butter, 1 tablespoon chopped shallots, ½ pint dry white wine, ½ cup hollandaise sauce, a sprig of parsley.

Fillet the mackerel, place it in a pan with butter and shallots, cover with wine and bring to a boil. Now, cook this slowly for 12 minutes in the oven. Remove the fillets, keeping them in a warm place. Reduce the liquid in the pan by boiling. Add the juice of the sprig of parsley, which has been boiled and strained. Add 1 tablespoon butter and the hollandaise sauce, stir until smooth, pour over the hot fillets and serve.

BROILED STRIPED BASS

To serve 4, you need a 6-pound striper, ½ cup shallots, ½ cup chopped mushrooms, 1 lemon, 1 cup chopped peeled tomatoes, 1 teaspoon chopped chives, 1 teaspoon chopped parsley.

Fillet and skin the bass, cook it in wine in a hot oven in the juice of a lemon and a tablespoon of butter, for 15 minutes. Remove the fillets, reduce cooking liquid by boiling, then add chopped tomatoes and cook the works until done. Finally add 1 cup of cream sauce, chopped parsley, chopped chives, and the yolks of 2 eggs. Cook, stirring until thick and creamy. Then pour it over the bass fillets and serve.

POACHED RED SNAPPER OR COBIA FILLET

This grand formula serves 4 and requires the following ingredients: 2 medium red snapper or cobia fillets, juice of 3 lemons, salt, pepper, 1 bay leaf, ½ pound butter, 1 tablespoon flour, 2 egg yolks, ½ pint cream, ½ cup dry white wine.

The fillets should be about ½ inch thick. Marinate them for 1 hour in the juice of 2 lemons and 1 bay leaf. Sprinkle well with salt and coarse black pepper. Now roll the fillets, fasten with a toothpick to hold the roll, and place them in a deep frying pan. Cover them with water and poach for 5 minutes.

Strain and save the water from the poached fish. Melt the half-pound of butter, carefully mixing in the flour until the whole thing is smooth and golden. Now add the strained fish stock from the poached snapper. Boil this for 15 minutes and strain the sauce. Season to taste with white wine and the remaining lemon juice. Keep the sauce hot and blend in the cream into which has been stirred the 2 well-beaten egg yolks. Remove the toothpicks from the poached fillets, spread them out, cover with sauce and serve piping hot.

SNAPPER SOUP

This soup can be made from any kind of snapper as well as grouper, mackerel, kingfish, cobia, weakfish, bass or snook. Ingredients required are: ½ pound diced bacon, 1 pint diced onions, ½ pint diced carrots, 4 pints diced fish, ½ pint diced parsnips, 1 pint diced potatoes, salt, pepper, thyme, bay leaf, garlic, 2 pints tomatoes, ½ cup sherry wine.

Sauté the bacon in a saucepan. Add onions, carrots, parsnips, and blend until golden. Add the potatoes, fish, season with herbs and spices, and stir in the tomatoes. Cook slowly until the potatoes are soft. Sprinkle lightly with cornstarch to thicken. Add the sherry and some chopped parsley and serve hot in bowls accompanied with thick crackers and frosty steins of cold beer or ale.

PLANKED RED SNAPPER

Serve 1 whole fillet of a medium-size snapper per person. Season with salt and pepper, lemon juice and a dash of paprika. Rub with olive oil and broil slowly for 10 minutes. Remove from the broiler, place on a plank board, decorate with onion rings, peas and fresh-boiled asparagus tips. Place the whole board with fish and vegetables under the broiler again for a short time. Serve sizzling.

PLANTATION SNAPPER OR COBIA

Cut small pieces of fish and marinate for 5 minutes in lemon juice, salt and pepper. Then brush them with oil and broil a golden brown. Meanwhile, cut eggplant into ¼-inch slices. Dip the slices into flour, egg and bread crumbs. Bake in a pan with butter then remove and place fish on top of the eggplant and put on a platter. Garnish with boiled eggs and stuffed tomatoes.

HUSH PUPPIES

A traditional and extremely delicious complement to many fish dinners is the hush puppy, a flavorful cornmeal concoction that was born in the Deep South.

There are almost as many ways to cook hush puppies as there are cooks, but for a basic hush-puppy recipe, you need the following ingredients: 2 cups cornmeal, 1 cup flour, 1 teaspoon baking powder, 1 teaspoon salt and ½ cup milk. From these ingredients make up a batter. If you like, add an egg or two to the batter and substitute buttermilk for milk.

Now, heat your grease to about 375° or 400°, using the same grease that has been used to deep-fry fish. Roll the batter into egg-sized balls or patties and drop them into the boiling grease. Cooking time is short, usually only 4 or 5 minutes. When cooked too slowly, the patties absorb grease and turn out soggy and strong. When cooked too long, the outside will be delicious and crusty while the inner portion will be gummy and only partly cooked.

ANGLER'S RÉMOULADE SAUCE

This sauce is as fine for dunking shrimp as it is for serving as a sauce on many bland species of fishes. The following ingredients are required: 1 pint mayonnaise, 1 pint mustard, 1 ounce anchovy paste, ½ ounce lemon juice, 1 ounce grated onion, 1 ounce sherry wine, ¼ ounce tabasco sauce, ½ ounce Worcestershire sauce.

Blend all the ingredients in an electric blender or hand-whip them into a smooth mixture. It makes a tart and tasty sauce for poached fish, oysters, shrimp, crab cocktail, scallops or lobster.

FISH CHOWDER

The word chowder is derived from the French, *chaudière*, which means the cauldron or iron kettle in which French fish stew was originally cooked. But as a dish, chowder probably originated in North America among Newfoundland or Nova Scotia fishermen. In any case it is a relative of the French bouillabaisse that became famous in Marseille but is enjoyed everywhere on earth nowadays.

The first fish chowders in this country were made by cooking fish, salt pork, onions, potatoes and hardtack in water. Hardtack was unleavened ship's bread, which was made into very large, waferlike biscuits. That's still a tasty formula, but today there are many variations of this original recipe. And nearly all of them are more complicated and vastly more delicious. Herewith follow a number of good examples.

SAVORY BLUEFISH CHOWDER

For 3 pounds of fresh bluefish, collect the following ingredients: 1 medium onion, 4 cups milk, 1 tablespoon flour, 1 tablespoon butter, 1 cup cracker crumbs, 1½ teaspoons salt, ¼ teaspoon pepper, ⅛ teaspoon summer savory, ¼ teaspoon thyme. Boil the fish and onion together in a small quantity of water. When finished, mash the onion and fish together in a baking dish. Cover liberally with cracker crumbs and pieces of butter. Bake to a golden brown, adding more milk if a softer mixture is desired.

FLOUNDER CHOWDER

For flounder chowder you need 1½ to 2 pounds flounder fillets, ¾ tablespoon salt, pepper, paprika, 1 small chopped onion, 1 teaspoon chopped parsley, ¼ teaspoon minced thyme, 1 cup cider, 2 tablespoons butter, 2 tablespoons flour, ¼ cup chopped mushrooms, 3 medium tomatoes chopped fine, ¼ cup cracker crumbs, 2 cups scalded milk, 1 cup of scalded evaporated milk.

Wash the fish and season with salt, pepper and paprika. Chop the onion, parsley and thyme and sprinkle on the bottom of the chowder kettle. Lay the fillets over the herbs and pour cider over all. Simmer for 20 minutes until the fish is soft. Now melt the butter and add the flour and when brown, add mushrooms and tomatoes. Simmer 10 minutes. Cover the fish with cracker crumbs, top with the remaining butter and simmer 10 minutes more. Pour the scalded milk into the mixture, bring to a boil, garnish with parsley and serve.

POACHED COBIA WITH HOLLANDAISE SAUCE

Cut the cobia into small portions and poach in water spiked with vinegar, salt, whole pepper, bay leaf and onion. Poach approximately 5 minutes, then remove and drain off. Place the fish in a casserole and cover with hollandaise sauce.

To make the sauce: Place the following ingredients in a mixing bowl: 6 egg yolks, the juice of 1 lemon, salt, pepper and approximately 3 tablespoons of the fish stock that has been drained off the cobia. Beat the yolks over a double boiler until a fluffy stiffness, then remove and gradually add 2 tablespoons of butter, stirring constantly. Season with lemon and salt if not spicy enough.

FILLETS OF BLUEFISH GENERAL PATTON

This is a recipe of Chef Antoine Gilly at La Crémaillère, an outstanding suburban New York restaurant. The following ingredients are necessary: 4 fresh bluefish fillets, 1 pint dry chablis wine, 1 cup finely chopped shallots, ½ cup finely chopped parsley, ½ pint heavy cream, 1 tablespoon lemon juice, 2 beaten egg yolks, salt and white pepper.

Place the fillets on a buttered baking dish and sprinkle the chopped shallots and parsley over the fish. Pour the wine on the fish, dust with salt and pepper and bring to a boil. Cover the baking dish with oiled, waxed paper (or foil) and place in a preheated 350° oven for 15 minutes. Now drain the juice from the baking dish into a saucepan, add the cream, the lemon juice, the beaten egg yolks, and continue to stir this over the flame until it has reduced to a thick consistency. Pour this over the fillets, which you have kept hot in a baking dish, and serve very hot. It serves 4.

BOUILLABAISSE

This recipe is substantial enough to feed 10 or 12 people. But it can be made in a smaller amount, of course. The ingredients necessary are 3 lobsters of a pound apiece, 4 sea bass of about 2 pounds apiece, 1 eel of about 2 pounds, 1 red snapper of about 6 pounds, 2 pounds of mussels, 4 cloves of garlic, 3 leeks, 2 onions, 2 stalks celery, 1 bunch parsley, 1 quart dry white wine, ¾ ounce saffron, 8 tomatoes, 2 quarts of fish stock, ½ pint olive oil, 1 quart tomato sauce, 1 loaf French bread.

Make a Bouquet Garni by tying together 2 stalks of celery, 1 leek, 3 bay or laurel leaves, a sprig of thyme and a sprig of parsley.

Cut the lobsters, sea bass, eel and red snapper into larger than bite-size chunks. Slice the celery, onions and leeks into thin strips. Boil 1 sea bass in salted water until a thick stock has resulted. Place olive oil in a deep frying pan and heat.

Plunge the lobster chunks into the hot oil until they turn reddish. Season with good shakes of salt and paprika. Now remove all but 1 tablespoon of the oil.

Sauté the garlic in the pan for about 3 minutes, then add the white wine. Cook about two-thirds of this away. Then add the tomatoes, which have been peeled and cut into quarters. Now mix the celery, onions, leeks and the leeks that have been cooked in butter. Let this mixture boil for 10 minutes. Then add the quart of tomato sauce, the Bouquet Garni, and the fish stock. Bring this to a boil and skim. Then cook slowly for 15 minutes.

Now add the eel, then the sea bass and finally the red snapper. Season to taste with salt and freshly ground black pepper. Add the saffron and half the bunch of chopped parsley. Cook until the fish are flaky to the touch, remove from the fire and allow the mixture to settle for at least 30 minutes before serving. This brings out the full flavor.

In the meantime, cook the mussels—still in their shells—in the white wine. Serve in the half shell, 4 per person, and place them on top of the fish. Slice a loaf of French bread and rub a clove of garlic against each slice. Dip lightly in olive oil and brown the bread slices in the oven until golden. Bring the whole bouillabaisse dish, surrounded with the bread, to the table and serve with crisply cold white wine.

TROUT WITH SEA FOOD

Put 4 drawn trout—about 1 pound each—in baking dish or pan. Sprinkle with salt, pepper; pour sauce over fish. Cover; bake 10 to 15 minutes at 375° F., basting 2 to 3 times. And ¾ cup light cream, 18 clams, ¾ pound shelled shrimp. Bake covered, 25 minutes or until clams open. Serves 4.

For sauce: Blend ½ pound melted sweet butter or margarine, 2 tablespoons flour; add 1½ cups dry white wine, 2 tablespoons lime juice. Heat.

BASS ITALIAN STYLE

Put 1 scalded, drawn, 3½- to 4-pound striped bass in baking dish or pan. Pour tomato sauce over fish. Bake 30 to 40 minutes at 375° F., or until tender and flaky, basting 2 or 3 times.

Garnish with pimento strips and watercress. Serves 3 to 4.

For tomato sauce: In 4 tablespoons melted butter or margarine, brown 1 small chopped onion, 1 minched clove garlic, 2 tablespoons chopped parsley, 1 can (6 ozs.) drained sliced mushrooms; add 2 cups canned tomatoes, 1 bottle (8 ozs.) clam juice, ½ teaspoon each oregano, salt, ¼ teaspoon pepper. Simmer 15 minutes; stir twice during cooking time. Add 12 sliced pimiento-stuffed green olives.

STUFFED FISH WITH CURRY SAUCE

Put 1 scaled, drawn 3-pound sea bass in baking dish or pan; sprinkle with salt, pepper. Stuff; skewer. Pour curry sauce over fish. Bake 30 minutes at 375° F., or until tender and flaky, basting 2 to 3 times. Serves 3 to 4.

For stuffing: To 3 tablespoons melted butter or margarine, add ½ cup dry bread cubes, 2 tablespoons each chopped onion, celery, 1 cup cut cooked shrimp.

For curry sauce: Brown 1 chopped onion in butter or margarine; add 2 cups chicken broth, 2 tablespoons curry powder (or to taste), ¼ teaspoon each ginger, turmeric, 2 tablespoons flour, ¾ teaspoon salt, ⅛ teaspoon pepper. Cover; simmer 15 minutes. Stir in ¼ cup yoghurt, 1 tablespoon light cream, pinch of cayenne, paprika.

FISH IN PARCHMENT

Brush a scaled, drawn 3- to 4-pound flounder with prepared mustard. Sprinkle with salt, pepper; wrap with bacon slices. Wrap in parchment or greased brown paper; fasten with skewers or string. Put in baking dish or pan. Bake 30 minutes at 375° F. Open paper; bake 10 minutes more, or until tender and flaky. Remove paper. Serves 3 to 4.

FISH IN HERBS

Mix together 2 chopped onions, 2 stalks celery, chopped, 1 cup sliced mushrooms, 2 tablespoons chopped parsley, ¼ teaspoon each dried (or 1 teaspoon each chopped fresh) thyme, tarragon, rosemary, 6 tablespoons melted butter or margarine. Spread half of mixture in a greased baking dish or pan; add 1 scaled, drawn 3- to 4-pound flounder, haddock, sea bass or mackerel (or 2 or 3 small fish). Sprinkle with Parmesan cheese; top with remaining vegetable mixture. Bake 35 to 45 minutes at 375° F., or until tender and flaky, basting 2 to 3 times with melted butter, chicken broth. Serves 3 to 5.

The following recipes for trout or weakfish are recommended by J. George Frederick, founder of New York's Gourmet Society.

POACHED TROUT (OR WEAKFISH) WITH MUSHROOMS AND HERBS

4 large trout
Fish stock (bouillon)
4 tbs. butter
2 tbs. chopped parsley
4 tbs. chopped mushrooms
2 tbs. chopped spring onion or shallots or Spanish onion
2 pieces of stale bread
Salt and pepper

Clean, wash, and dry trout and simmer for 15 to 18 minutes in sufficient fish stock to cover, or until fish is flaky. Lightly sauté the mushrooms, onion, parsley. Soak the stale bread in some fish stock, squeeze out, add it to ¼ cup of the fish stock, and blend with the mushrooms, onion, parsley. Season. Place the trout on a hot platter and spread the herb mixture over them. Serve very hot. Serves 4.

BROILED TROUT (OR WEAKFISH) ITALIENNE, WITH RAISIN SAUCE

6 trout fillets
½ cup olive oil (or corn or peanut or sesame or sunflower oil)
¼ cup champagne (or tart white wine or just plain vinegar)
1 clove garlic, split
Salt, pepper
½ cup white raisins

Clean, wash, and quickly dry the trout fillets. Rub a pyrex or other baking dish with the split half of a garlic clove. Cut the garlic into 2 or 3 pieces and leave in dish. Add the oil and liquid, also salt, pepper. Blend by stirring. Place the fillets in the dish, and let stand 15 minutes; then turn fillets and let stand 15 more minutes.

Meanwhile, preheat broiler to high heat. Lift the fillets out of the liquid and without drying, place them on a broiling grid, not less than 3 inches from the flame. Brown the fillets on both sides, but be careful not to broil too dry. Meantime, put the raisins in the liquid marinade and bring just to a boil. Serve the fillets on warm plates. Pour the marinade and raisins over them.

BROILED, FLAMED TROUT (OR WEAKFISH) KOALA

12 or 14 oz. brook trout
½ cup flour
1 cup milk
2 tbs. butter
2 cups rock salt
½ to ¾ tsp. rosemary
Salt, Pepper
2 oz. orange extract
Ginger Sauce:
   1 chopped onion
   ¼ to ½ tsp. powdered ginger
   ¼ lb. butter
   2 oz. white wine

Immerse the cleaned, washed and dried trout, heads and tails on, in the milk for 8 or 10 minutes. Dredge the trout in flour and sauté gently in the butter for 5½ to 6 minutes. Place trout carefully on a broiling rack over a platter containing rock salt, warmed and spread even. Sprinkle rosemary evenly over the rock salt and pour orange extract around edges of rock salt, taking care not to get any on the fish. Light a match to ignite the orange sauce, which will flame around the fish. Before flame dies, turn fish to expose other side.

As soon as flame is out, remove fish to a plate and bone it, from tail upward. To serve four if fish is large enough, cut each fillet in half. Serve hot on serving plates and pour the hot Ginger Sauce over it.

Make Ginger Sauce as follows: Sauté the onion in butter until golden, add all the other ingredients and simmer for 6 or 7 minutes.

BAKED PACIFIC NORTHWEST SALMON STEAKS

6 salmon steaks, 1 inch thick
⅓ cup butter or margarine
½ tsp. salt

¼ tsp. paprika
1 tsp. Worcestershire sauce
2 tbs. grated onion

Preheat oven to 350°. Place salmon steaks in a greased shallow baking pan. Melt the butter; add seasonings and Worcestershire sauce and spread this mixture over the fish. Sprinkle 1 teaspoon grated onion over each steak. Bake in a moderate oven for 25 to 30 minutes. Makes 6 servings.

BROILED STRIPED BASS

Large stripers can be cut up into steaks 1 inch thick. Smaller bass up to 10 pounds should be filleted. Place the pieces on a sheet of heavy aluminum foil in a broiler or on a grill. Sprinkle liberally with salt, pepper and lemon juice. Lay a couple of bacon strips across the fish and broil in a moderate oven (about 375°) for 20 to 30 minutes. Allow 1 pound of fish per person.

BAKED MACKEREL MAINE STYLE

2 mackerel, about 2 lbs. each
1 large onion, chopped fine
1 large carrot, diced fine
½ green pepper, chopped
1 bay leaf
¾ cup vinegar
½ tsp. salt
1 tbs. parsley, chopped
¼ tsp. thyme, minced

Preheat oven to 400°. Make up a sauce by cooking the onion, carrot, green pepper, vinegar, salt, parsley, thyme and bay leaf for about 20 minutes over low heat. Remove the bay leaf and pour the sauce over the fish. Bake for 30 to 40 minutes.

FLOUNDER (SOLE) AND FLUKE FILLETS

Allow about ¾ pound of fillet per person. Fillets should be between ½ and ¾ inch thick.

Dip the fillets into a mixture of 2 beaten eggs and ½ cup milk. Roll the pieces in cracker meal or bread crumbs seasoned with salt, pepper and a little paprika. Heat the cooking oil or shortening until it is very hot and just starting to smoke. Put in the fish and cook about 3 minutes on each side. After the fish turns golden brown remove it and place on absorbent paper to remove excess oil.

BAKED BLUEFISH

1 bluefish, 3 to 6 pounds, cleaned with head and tail removed
6-oz. can stewed tomatoes or tomato juice
1 can mushrooms
3 tbs. lemon juice.

Preheat oven to 350°. Butter the bottom of a baking dish so the fish won't stick. Sprinkle the fish with salt and pepper and place it in the dish. Mix the lemon juice with the stewed tomatoes or juice and pour over the fish. Add the mushrooms and sliced onions too if you like. Put the fish in the oven and bake, making sure to baste regularly with the tomatoes or juice. The fish will be done when a fork penetrates easily and the flesh turns flaky.

HOW TO SMOKE FISH

Nearly all saltwater fish and especially the more oily species are wonderfully adaptable to smoking. Smoking is a simple technique that any fisherman can perform at home. The idea is to cook the fish slowly in warm and fragrant smoke.

The first step is to clean the fish, leaving the small ones whole and cutting the larger fish into pieces of about 1 pound apiece. Next marinate them in a brine and/or herb solution overnight. After that, place the fish in a smoker and smoke for about 12 hours with a low to medium heat. Experience will teach a fisherman whether to smoke his fish for a longer or shorter period of time.

It's extremely easy to make a simple smoker for home use. One idea is to use a 50-gallon oil drum as a beginning and then to rig it out with baffles (a coarse screen will do), cooking screens and a fire door, as shown in the illustration. The fish are placed on the top screen.

An even easier idea is to obtain an old refrigerator or icebox and then to place an electric hot plate on the lowest level inside. Now obtain the sawdust or wood chips of hickory, oak, or apple and allow this to smolder and smoke on the hot plate. The fish, of course, is placed on the wire shelves above the smoke. It's also necessary to build a small vent near the top of the refrigerator to release the smoke.

HOW TO FREEZE FISH

One of the dividends of fishing in saltwater is that an angler frequently catches more fish than he can use immediately. Many of the saltwater species are also among the most delicious eating. The best solution is to freeze any extra fish for later use.

Successful freezing of fish begins the moment the fish is caught. The only parts of most fishes which spoil very rapidly are the gills and viscera. Therefore, if the gills and viscera are removed as soon as the fish is caught, there isn't any chance of an overripe or strong taste later on. The first rule, therefore, is to clean the catch immediately—or as soon as possible.

Never pack fish in direct contact with ice during the trip from fishing water toward home. The ice will melt, and while it will not spoil the fish, it will soak them and have a deteriorat-ing effect on the fish. Too long an exposure will soften the meat and make it mushy.

A far better way is to pack the fish in polyethylene bags such as a freezer supplier recommends for storing turkeys and other fowls. Fill the bag with cleaned or filleted fish, seal it and then pack the whole works in ice. The fish will remain cool but dry until you arrive home.

Now collect the following materials: a large shallow pan containing a heavy brine solution, a pastry brush, a supply of freezer wrap and masking tape.

Brush each piece of fish carefully and thoroughly with the brine. Package as many pieces as you feel will make a good meal for the entire family and then wrap this much carefully. Seal it and freeze it quickly at about −10° F. Handled in this manner, fish eaten in October will be as tasty as they were when caught in April.

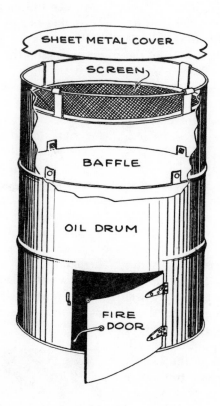

A simple fish smoker.

Chapter Twenty

SALTWATER TACKLE

Once upon a time saltwater tackle was a term used for a specific fishing outfit—a certain cumbersome Calcutta rod, a reel and a line. But nowadays a saltwater fishing rig can be anything from a medium fly rod to a 40-ounce big game tip and a 16/0 reel.

Rod, line, lures and other accessories are important in saltwater fishing, but the truth is that none of these are much better than the reel to which they are attached. Fishing in the salt can give any reel a terrible beating and that is the critical point in a man's tackle. The so-called "standard" saltwater reels for bay, big game and surf look pretty much alike as, indeed, they are. All have free-spool clutches, single over-size handle grips and a star or equivalent drag.

The star drag gets its name from the star shaped wheel located at the base of the handle where it can readily be adjusted while a fish is being played. In other words, tension can easily be increased or decreased.

The actual drag mechanism consists of a series of metal, composition or leather disks that slip with varying degrees of ease as the star wheel is tightened or loosened. Star drags have saved many an angler's thumb and knuckles through the years. It isn't necessary to apply the thumb to the spool when a fish runs and the handle cannot spin backward as on lighter freshwater models of casting reels.

The modern American multiplying-action star drag reel is an extremely efficient mechanism. Using a reel of the proper size and with other tackle in balance, an angler can subdue a fish ten times his own size. But still the saltwater reel as we know it was first developed for fishing in fresh water.

Until a watchmaker in Frankfort, Kentucky, built a multiplying reel to cast for bass, the single-action reels then in use made it virtually impossible to land a large fish. But quickly the principle of the multiplying reel was adapted to saltwater use and this, perhaps, was really the beginning of a whole new world of sport.

When a heavy fish ran in the old days of single-action reels, the reel handles revolved backward. And a speedy fish could convert the handles into a blur of motion as dangerous as a buzz saw. It's reasonable to believe that no modern angler would willingly tackle a marlin, for example, on such a reel.

The gear ratio in a modern saltwater reel runs from 2-to-1 to about 3½-to-1, in comparison with the freshwater bait casting reel's ratio of about 4-to-1. The lowering of the gear ratio makes cranking in the line easier than it is with a high ratio. With low ratios, you do not retrieve as much line per turn of the handle as with a high ratio, but as the leverage is greater with the low ratio, less effort is necessary.

The next great step forward in development of the saltwater reel was made by William Bos-

Pflueger Supreme

chen, who perfected the star drag pretty much as we know it today. This drag operates only when line is running out and this feature is the essence of the device. The fish must pull against the tension, but the angler can crank in line without it.

Basically, bay, surf and big game reels differ only in quality and in range of sizes available. Of course, the big game reels have smoother star drags and are built on heavier frames. They range upward in size to a line capacity of nearly a mile of 39-thread or 117-pound test line.

Surf casting reels are very much like other saltwater reels with wider, lighter spools and gear ratios of about 3 to 1. These features make for greater casting efficiency and more rapid retrieves than are possible with the big game reel that has a gear ratio of about 2 to 1.

There are three main types of saltwater rods: the big game or trolling rod, the boat rod and the surf rod. Big game rods generally are of very high quality split bamboo or glass construction. But nowadays very few split bamboo models remain in use. The better rods are equipped with low friction roller tip-tops and high bridge guides which minimize chafing by keeping the line above the rod when it is bent against a fish.

And they also allow the line to run in a straight line from the big reel spool through the guides. Big game tips are about 5 feet long, and they vary in weight from about 2 or 3 ounces up to 30 or 40 ounces, depending on the line used and the fish sought. Butt or handle lengths run from 14 to 24 inches depending upon the weight of the tip.

Boat rods, which are designed for use with bay reels, vary from 5-foot stiff action to the "whippy" live bait rod that may exceed 9 feet in length. Handles measure from 14 to 24 inches in length. Glass is by far the most popular and most practical material for boat-rod construction.

The classic or standard surf rod consists of a 6- to 7-foot one-piece tip weighing 9 to 14 ounces plus a 30-inch spring butt. These dimensions may vary slightly. Some split bamboo rods are still in use in the surf, but nowadays nearly all of the better rods are glass.

Now coming into great use with artificial lures are lighter surf rods with 6- to 7-ounce tips and spring butts of about 20 to 24 inches long.

Cuttyhunk line is still the favorite of many saltwater anglers, but nylon, dacron and other synthetic monfilaments are rapidly and almost completely replacing it. Cuttyhunk line is a twisted linen in which each thread tests 3

Pflueger Rocket

Pflueger Ohio

Pflueger Sea King

Pflueger Capitol

pounds when wet. Thus a 3-thread Cuttyhunk line tests 9 pounds while 9-thread tests 27 pounds.

Nylon first gained popularity as a squiding line. Although it wasn't completely adequate at first because of its stretch, this characteristic has been corrected.

Synthetic monofilaments have the following advantages for ocean fishing: (1) a finer diameter per pound test, (2) more stretch than found in linen, (3) a resistance to waterlogging or swelling, (4) they will not rot or mildew. Actually, these advantages mean that: (1) there is less line drag, which is important, especially in trolling, (2) there is more feel of the fish, (3) the line capacity of any reel is increased and (4) the synthetic line needs no care or frequent drying.

But more and more every year, fly casting, spinning and freshwater bait casting tackle is becoming more popular among saltwater anglers. Fly rods for saltwater use must have stainless steel guides and corrosion-proof ferrules and reel seats. And almost 99 percent of all saltwater fly rods in use are made of glass. A bass bug action in fly rods is probably best, as long casts with fairly large flies are sometimes necessary. In addition, the saltwater fly caster frequently must compete with stiff winds.

The saltwater fly reel should be a single-action model with a fairly large line capacity. To my thinking, at least, the automatic reel has no place in saltwater fishing. For snook, tarpon, striped bass and bonefish and such other rugged species, the automatic reel has too little capacity and therefore is only a liability. A single-action reel with adjustable drag, capable of holding at least 150 yards of 18- or 20-pound backing under the fly line, is necessary for the stronger saltwater species.

Fin-Nor Spinning Reels: No. 3, left; No. 4, right

Naturally fly lines for saltwater should be selected to match the rod just as they are in freshwater. Level or torpedo headlines are better than double tapers because of the long casts that are often necessary. Only the nylon or other synthetic fly lines will withstand the corrosion of saltwater. Never use a silk fly line. For backing, many experts use 18-pound nylon squiding line.

Except for the most rugged fishing, such as plugging for tarpon, the freshwater bass casting rod is a very good one to use in the salt. Although special casting reels with star drags and greater line capacity are made for saltwater fishing, the star drag is not entirely necessary on a bait casting reel. But without the star drag, a fisherman should use a knitted or leather thumb stall for thumbing the reel when he's after such lively species as the tarpon, snook, barracuda and bonefish. Eighteen-pound test nylon is good enough for all-around saltwater casting, but in such special cases as casting rocky shores or mangrove-lined creeks, slightly heavier line may be required.

Although some spinning tackle is made especially for saltwater use, it's sometimes heavier than necessary for much saltwater fishing. Ordinarily freshwater spinning gear is more enjoyable to use if the reel is made of corrosion-proof material and if it is of high quality construction to withstand extreme abuse.

Garcia Ambassadeur 5000

Garcia Mitchell 302

The rod should have stainless steel guides and what is ordinarily designated as a medium action in from 6½- to 7-foot lengths. Again, glass is the best spinning-rod material.

A spinning reel used in the salt should be able to hold a minimum of 150 yards of monofilament in either 8- or 10-pound test. Actually, it's better if the reel can hold 200 yards of line this size.

For nearly all saltwater fishing it is advisable to use a wire leader, the length and strength of which has been mentioned elsewhere in describing the various fishes and how to catch them. The most practical for general use is a stainless steel wire leader that is available in a large range of sizes from No. 2 (which tests 27 pounds) up to No. 19 (which will lift 360 pounds). For leader economy, carry a supply of stainless steel wire, some snaps and swivels and a pair of longnose pliers to roll your own.

For spinning and casting, use a No. 2 or 3 leader from 9 to 12 inches long. With a boat or bay outfit, figure on about 24 inches of No. 4 wire. For surf tackle, a good basis is a 36- to 48-inch leader of No. 5 or 6 wire.

Following is a list of reels that have been proven effective after long, hard use in the salt:

Pflueger Sea King: A high quality surf casting reel with extra-wide reel for large line capacity. The reel contains a mechanical thumber that prevents overrun of the reel spool during casting. This device is different from other automatic thumbers and from ordinary antibacklash devices in that it operates only when the line is going out. The Sea King can be field-stripped in less than 20 seconds, contains a free spool with throw-off button, star drag, a gear ratio of 3 1/13 to 1 and a line capacity of 300 yards of 30-pound monofilament. The reel weighs 18½ ounces and is inexpensive.

Pflueger Capitol: A deep-sea trolling reel of high quality with a deep spool for large line capacity. There are three models, varying in capacity from 250 yards to 450 yards of 30-pound monofilament. The reel contains a free spool with throw-off button, star drag and a gear ratio of 2⅓ to 1.

Pflueger Ohio: A lightweight trolling reel of excellent quality. Its two sizes have a line capacity of 250 yards and 320 yards of 30-pound test line. The reel is sturdily built and is very inexpensive.

Pflueger Rocket: A versatile casting or trolling rig on which a shift lever engages or disengages the star drag. It has a line capacity of 175 yards of 30-pound line, a gear ratio of 3⅝ to 1 and a weight of 14½ ounces.

Pflueger Bond: A versatile casting or trolling reel with a line capacity of 200 yards of 30-pound monofilament or 300 yards of 15-pound monofilament. Has a gear ration of 3¾ to 1.

Pflueger Sea Star: An all-around sturdy, but lightweight, heavy duty, open face spinning reel. The Sea Star weighs only 16 ounces yet can hold 200 yards of 12-pound monofilament. The gear ratio is 3¼ to 1. The drag is extremely smooth and dependable.

Pflueger Supreme: A bait casting reel of almost legendary accomplishments. More than two million of these reels have been sold through the years. The line capacity is 180 yards of 15-pound test line. The gear ratio is 4 to 1 and the reel weighs only 7½ ounces. This is the model which Jerry Coughlin used to break numerous tarpon bait-casting records in Miami's Metropolitan Fishing Tournament, even though the Supreme he used did not have a mechanical drag of any kind. Recently a new Pflueger freespool Supreme has been placed on the market. This is the same as the old Supreme except that it weighs 8 ounces and contains both a freespool and star-type drag.

Pflueger Summit: A sturdy bait-casting reel with a capacity of 175 yards of 15-pound test line. The gear ratio is 4 to 1 and the reel weighs 7¾ ounces. It's less expensive than the Supreme.

Fin-Nor Saltwater Reel

Fin-Nor Regal Reel

Garcia Ambassadeur 5000: An outstanding bait-casting reel that combines a free spool with level wind and centrifugal brake. Backlash is virtually impossible. It also has a mechanical brake to adjust for various casting weights, a soundless retrieve, a corrosion-proof red finish and it comes in a handsome leather case with tools.

Ambassadeur 6000: Similar to the 5000 but has a wider spool for larger line capacity and a single handle. It's excellent either for trolling or casting.

Shakespeare Wondereel: There are a number of models of Wondereels which vary mostly in price. All are extremely serviceable and if the antibacklash mechanism is adjusted correctly, no thumbing is necessary in casting. These reels have been thoroughly tested in saltwater.

Pflueger Pelican: Reliable spinning reel with die-cast aluminum frame, a drag that is easy to adjust while playing a fish, and a bale that snaps into position on only ⅛ turn of the reel handle. This reel has an extremely fine dependable drag and it comes in right- and left-handed models.

Garcia Mitchell 300: A well-known and extremely popular reel that is rugged and has given much outstanding service. It comes in left- and right-handed models, has a smooth and dependable drag, and a fast retrieve is possible.

Mitchell 302: Another sturdy and excellent spinning reel designed for saltwater. It can be used either for casting or for light trolling.

Garcia Mitchell 306: Sturdy, completely dependable and durable reel that can be used both for casting and trolling.

Orvis 100 & 101: Popular and dependable reels with smooth drag and simple, sturdy construction. The reel weighs only 10 ounces and is proven for light and medium saltwater spinning.

Garcia Mitchell 314: A serviceable spinning reel with push-button spool release, antireverse con-

trol and extra spool which would be suitable for light saltwater casting.

Orvis 300: A medium spinning reel with a line capacity for 200 yards of 8-pound test or 150 yards of 10-pound test. Has a 4.2-to-1 gear ratio and weighs only 8 ounces. In left- and right-hand models.

Orvis 200: A heavy duty saltwater spinning and surf casting reel with a line capacity of 560 yards of 8-pound test or 400 yards of 10-pound test or 300 yards of 12-pound test monofilament. It's sturdily built to stand punishment and the pressure of big fish. It weighs 18 ounces.

Fin-Nor Spinning Reels: A product of precise craftsmanship. Has a pickup arm, a full-circle disk brake drag with positive adjustment, is finished in a deep golden anodized finish and all parts are selected for durability and resistance to saltwater. The main reel spool is turned from solid aluminum bar stock. It comes in two sizes: No. 3, which holds 300 yards of 8-pound line, and No. 4, which holds 350 yards of 12-pound line.

Fin-Nor Saltwater Reels: The finest saltwater reels ever manufactured for the market. The reel frames and spools are made from solid aluminum bar stock, are fully anodized. The reel contains ball bearings throughout and internal parts are of Monel metal. The free-spool and brake adjustment is accomplished by a positioning lever that operates on a quadrant through approximately half a circle. The Fin-Nor comes in six models or sizes. The 2½/o holds about 400 yards of 20-pound test line. The 4/o holds about 550 yards of 20-pound test line. The 6/o holds about 600 yards of 30-pound test line. The 7½/o holds about 700 yards of 40-pound test line. The 9/o holds about 900 yards of 24-thread or 70-pound test line. The 12/o holds about 750 yards of 39-thread or 117-pound test line. Of course, all these reels are extremely expensive,

Fin-Nor Fly Reels

running about $250 for the 2½/0 to $595 for the 12/0.

Fin-Nor Regal Reel: Features a new principle in braking on saltwater reels. It's of extremely high quality and precision workmanship. Made from high-tension aluminum alloy bar stock with an anodized finish. In three sizes from 2½/0 to 6/0. The 2½/0 has a capacity of 800 yards of 20-pound monofilament line. The 4/0, which weighs only 36 ounces, can hold 800 yards of 30-pound monofilament. The 6/0 has a capacity of 800 yards of 50-pound monofilament.

Pflueger Medalist: Probably the most popular single-action fly reel ever built. Its construction is sturdy. It's easy to take apart and it has a lightweight aluminum frame. It comes in a number of size capacities, has a positive drag, and is very moderately priced. The best Medalist model for saltwater fishing is No. 1498, which has a 4-inch diameter with 1 inch between spool plates and it weighs 8¾ ounces. It also is equipped with an extra-heavy drag, a reinforced frame and spool.

Fin-Nor Fly Reel: A precision-made reel with all the qualities of strength, balance, and lightness required by serious fly fishermen. It also incorporates Fin-Nor's full circle disk drag. It comes in four sizes, but only three of these are suitable for saltwater fishing. The No. 2 fly reel has a line capacity of 200 yards of 15-pound test line, plus 40 yards of GAF fly line. The No. 3 has a line capacity of 250 yards of 20-pound test braided nylon plus 40 yards of GAF fly line. No. 4 has a line capacity of 300 yards of 27-pound test braided nylon plus 40 yards of F2AE fly line.

Garcia Landex: A high quality fly reel with ad-

Orvis 300

justable drag. The handle remains stationary when a fish pulls out line. It has a heavy duty, one-piece frame and ventilated spool. There are two models of Landex: one holding 100 yards of 15-pound backing, plus a GAF fly line; and the other holding 200 yards of 15-pound backing, plus a GAF fly line. Other Garcia fly reels of high quality and sturdy construction are the Beaudex and the Pridex.

Horrocks-Ibbotson Big Sea: A rugged boat reel with star drag and capacity of 300 yards of 20-pound line. Weighs 14 ounces. Moderately priced.

H-I Dolphin: A precision crafted reel for rough work. Has star drag, counterweighted handle, Bakelite side plates. Holds 250 yards of 9-thread line. Moderately priced.

H-I Sea Master: Similar to Big Sea and Dolphin, is sturdily built. Moderate in price.

H-I Sea Horse: A large capacity spinning reel of durable construction and high quality. Precision-manufactured to smallest detail. Holds 360 yards of 12-pound monofilament.

H-I Delfino: Open-face spinning reel with large line capacity. Holds 520 yards of 10-pound line, 390 yards of 15-pound line, or 300 yards of 300-pound line.

Horrocks-Ibbotson Big Sea

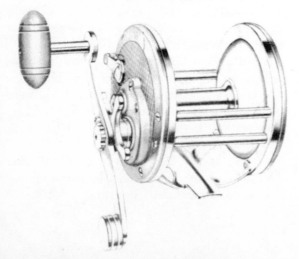

Horrocks-Ibbotson Sea Horse

Chapter Twenty-one

SALTWATER LINES, LURES AND ACCESSORIES

LINES

Someone once said that the cheapest part of the fishing rig is the line. Therefore, as a matter of fish insurance it pays to replace the line frequently.

Maybe the man who made the suggestion had a stake in the tackle business. Still, it makes sense to be rash about line expenditures when one considers how much he has invested in the big fish that someday takes his hook.

At the moment the thrifty fisherman sweats out his prize, he would gladly give a dozen times the cost of a new line to know that it was under his thumb. Big fish don't come very often. And line failure is one reason why many trophy fish never reach the gaff.

Nearly all fishing lines are made either of monofilament or dacron. This is true for so-called "big game" lines. Stretchy nylon has its place in shallow-water casting and in flounder and fluke fishing.

Now monofilament is standard for deep-water trolling for small and medium fish. But inelastic dacron is prescribed for the various species of fish that don't know their own strength.

Dacron is reasonably costly in the best grades. But even if we go by what the tackle experts say, dacron is good for at least two years. The line should be used one season, then reversed for the second season. After this, caution dictates that the line be replaced, the tackle men say.

Even if the line is kept only two seasons, the cost is not much when one apportions the dollars and cents over the number of times the reel was put into play. In our way of thinking, however, the average fisherman can get a third year out of his line unless he has beat it to death by catching vast quantities of tuna, marlin and such.

Dacron doesn't rot out. But it *is* subject to wear and tear from friction and strain.

The biggest problem with dacron is the knot. Inherent qualities of the synthetic fiber result in easy breakage at the knot. At one time, this weakness restricted sales. The problem was finally surmounted, first by use of the "twist" or "overhand whip knot" and second by eliminating knots altogether and splicing the line instead.

This latter was the great boon to dacron. With a simple splicing needle, the loop of double line—essential in big game fishing—is neatly woven into the line. Splicing two pieces of line is also done simply with the needle.

The Cortland Line Company, which probably sells more big game synthetics than any other line company, went so far as to inclose a splicing needle with each package of higher test line. This feature, begun last year, added further to the popularity of Cortland.

We might note here that some hard-woven dacron lines can't be spliced. The fisherman had best know his brands if he's going to splice.

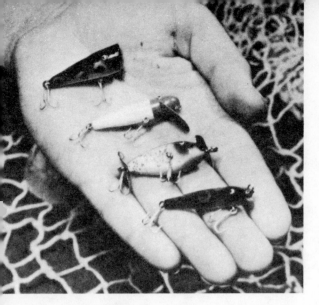

Creek Chub Darters

Pflueger Mustang

Pflueger Ballerina

Pflueger Record

Pflueger Lastword

Dacron comes in sizes as low as 20-pound test, but the larger sizes create the demand for the nonstretching fiber. Most of the line sold is in 50-, 80- and 130-pound test grades. These are the big game lines.

What are the recommended lines for the various size reels?

Starting with the 4/0 reel, which is about as small as one would care to use for school tuna, the angler will have a choice between 30-pound test and 50-pound test dacron—the latter preferred. A 6/0 reel might take either 50- or 80-pound test line. The 9/0 reel, which serves its purpose for over-size school tuna, is best fitted with 80-pound test.

The 10/0 reel is often used by light tackle fans for swordfish. It will hold 800 yards of 80-pound test dacron line such as Cortland "Greenspot." In the 12/0 and 14/0 reel class, 130-pound test is fairly standard.

It is worth nothing that though dacron is fine for big game, the line is not good for surf casting. Casting spools filled with dacron will scorch the fingers. The synthetic material holds no water at all. In addition, the fiber does not seem to stand up under the whip and strain of casting. Nylon still makes the best squidding line of all.

Fishermen changing lines on their big game reels will appreciate this tip passed along by veteran Montauk big game skipper, Captain Walter Drobecker.

When reloading a big reel with line—and this applies to either dacron or linen—one-third of the line may be handwound tightly, the rest loosely. When the boat is underway in a clear area of the ocean, the loose line is run out and then reeled back. The line will pack down hard and evenly.

This method of reloading is much less wearing on the hands and arms.

Warning: No fishing should be attempted with loosely wound line. When strain is applied as in fighting a fish, the working line may bury down into the loose line causing a jam and a breakoff.

SALTWATER LURES

Such a vast number of saltwater fishing lures are now available on tackle shelves that it's almost impossible even to catalog them. Still, hundreds of new models are introduced every year.

Some models survive because they are successful—they really attract fish. Others survive be-

Upperman Bucktails: ⅛ oz. to 2 oz.

cause they attract fishermen. But those that attract both fish and fishermen survive the longest and sell the fastest nowadays. In any case, a saltwater angler who sets about buying every lure that will take fish, would probably spend his entire life doing so and would spend all his money.

The truth is that it's possible to stock up on a completely adequate assortment of saltwater lures at relatively small cost. One secret, I think, is to ignore all the "gimmick" designs and flashy colors. Occasionally, some of the unique actions or finishes on plugs or lures are very effective, but on eight or nine days in ten, lures finished in solid white or yellow will be the most effective. The action of a lure or the depth at which it's fished is far more important, I believe, than the color.

The basic saltwater lure as well as the oldest of them all is the jig. This is a simple and inexpensive product that is really nothing more than a lead-headed hook wrapped with feathers, hair, nylon, rubber strips, metal foil or a combination of these. Almost any game fish in saltwater from the tiniest grunt to the heaviest marlin will strike a jig of the proper size fished at the proper depth.

Two things, therefore, influence the selection of jigs: the approximate size of the fish to be caught and the depth of the water to be fished. That means, if you fish the surf one day, the reefs the next day and a bay the following day, you will need a wide selection of jigs both in size and in weight to get along.

For casting with either medium spinning or plug-casting tackle, jigs from ¼ to ⅝ ounce are suitable. For fishing in extremely shallow water as for bonefish, jigs in the ⅛- to ¼-ounce size are best.

When you move out to deep water offshore, perhaps for kingfish and similar species, you'll need more weight. In this case 1- to 2-ounce jigs are best, and occasionally even heavier jigs are necessary. The largest jigs of all are those that are used when trolling for big game fish with heavy tackle.

Another basic type of saltwater lure is the plug that is made from plastic, wood or glass and is designed to imitate a small baitfish. Some plugs are designed for use underwater and others for

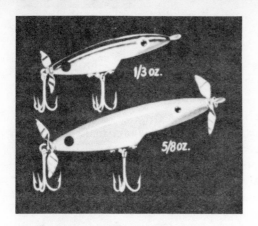

Weber Shadrac

Weber Ball-Fly Jig

use on the surface. There are exceptions to this rule, but generally the plugs without the built-in action are best in saltwater.

Among the surface plugs, some are cup-shaped to pop or bubble loudly on the surface while others are of the darter or silent type. Still a third type of surface plug includes those with whirling metal blades or propellers to increase the surface commotion.

At times when deep-trolling for snook, tarpon, channel bass, kingfish and cobia, a lipped plug with a fast vibrating action is extremely good.

In addition to the jigs and plugs, every saltwater angler's tackle box should include a few spoons of various sizes and weights. Certain fish such as open-water barracudas and bluefish are particularly partial to these slivers of flashing metal.

But to date the new, lifelike plastic lures that have been so successful in freshwater have not been used to any great extent in saltwater. Perhaps this is a field that deserves more pioneering.

Here follows a list of lures now on the market which have been proven successful in various types of saltwater fishing:

Pflueger Mustang: A shallow running, underwater plug with a snappy, wiggling action when retrieved. Comes in 4¼-inch and 5-inch sizes and in ⅝- and 1½-ounce weights. On the 5-inch size are bright metal flashers, top and bottom. It's excellent for surf casting and for trolling in shallow inshore bays. A good snook and cobia bait—the blue mullet finish is extremely effective.

Pflueger Ballerina: A surface minnow imitation in four finishes which weighs ⅝ ounce, measures 4¼ inches long and is an excellent tarpon lure. The silversides shiner and blue mullet finishes are among the best.

Pflueger Record: A metal spoon in six sizes from 3 inches to 7 inches long and in several finishes, has been extremely successful in catching tarpon, kingfish, barracudas and channel bass. It comes in either chrome-plated or blue mullet finishes.

Pflueger Lastword: Was designed as a saltwater spinning lure. It's brightly polished in chrome or blue mullet finish; weighs 1⅜ ounces and has a darting, wobbling motion.

Creek Chub Darter: An excellent surface plug in numerous finishes from ⅛ to ¾ ounce. Great for tarpon, snook, jacks, especially in the silver flash finish.

Upperman Bucktail: Most familiar to Florida fishermen. It's also one of the most deadly and versatile saltwater jigs ever devised. One fisherman, Phil Francis, has taken no less than 113 separate species on Uppermans, which run in size from 1/10 ounce to 2 ounces in size. They're made in a number of colors, but yellow, white and red-white combinations are among the most effective. They're equally good for trolling, surf casting and casting in shallow bays.

Upperman Big Ben: An extra-heavy jig for cast-

Weber Mr. Champ

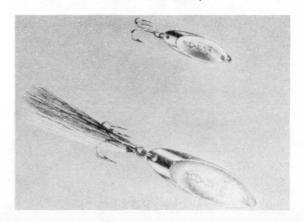

ing or trolling in 2½-ounce size, gets down deep enough to reach big striped bass, bluefish and other tide runners; made in yellow and white colors.

Weber Shadrac: A relatively new surface "jump" bait designed primarily for bass fishing. It comes in ⅜-ounce and ⅝-ounce sizes, but has proven extremely successful in mangrove bay and shallow saltwater fishing.

Weber Ball-Fly Jig: A marabou-dressed jig in ¼ and ½ ounce which is effective on all species of saltwater fish found in Florida and Caribbean waters. Best colors are white and yellow.

Weber Mr. Champ: A darting spoon with a deer-hair-dressed treble hook, is a versatile lure and especially effective for jacks, Spanish mackerel and ladyfish.

Phillips Wiggle Jig: A ¼-ounce jig, 1 inch long with 1/0 hook, a feathered tail and a flat lead body that gives the lure a slight built-in wiggle when retrieved. It comes in six finishes and is an all-around good lure for many saltwater game fish. And in the writer's opinion, at least, it is absolutely the most effective bonefish lure ever offered on the market.

Phillips Baby Wiggle Jig: A ⅛-ounce jig designed for shallow water. It is similar to the ¼-ounce Wiggle Jig. It also is particularly deadly for bonefish.

Phillips Big Boy: A ⅜-ounce, floating, diving lure with a tenite body and saddle-hackle tail is good for casting in tidal rivers and mangrove channels. Will take snook, tarpon, ladyfish, barracudas and other species of saltwater fish.

Phillips Old Joe: A ⅜-ounce surface plug with deer-hair tail and tenite body. It has a noisy surface action and will take tarpon and other saltwater fish.

Phillips Pink Shrimp: A close imitation of shrimp found in United States coastal waters. Tied with a weighted tinsel body on a heavy

hollow point hook. It comes in hook sizes 2, 4 and 6. It is an extremely successful fly for bonefish, permit, spotted weakfish, channel bass, ladyfish.

Phillips Bonefish Bucktail: A small bucktail fly designed for tailing bonefish in shallow water. It comes in five patterns and is tied on a tinned saltwater hook in size 1.

Phillips Big Boy

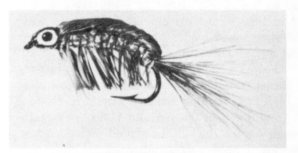

Phillips Pink Shrimp

Phillips Bonefish Bucktail

Phillips Wiggle Jig

Phillips Multi-Wing Streamer

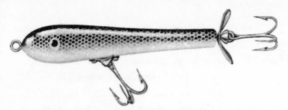

Arbogast Skinny Minny

Arbogast Sputter Bug

Arbogast Scooter

Weber Magnum

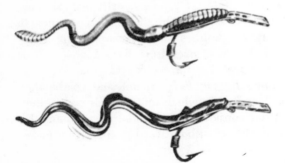

DeLong Axalive Eels

Wallsten Salty Cisco

Horrocks-Ibbotson Nylon Torpedo Jig

Phillips Multi-Wing Streamer: Tied with saddle-hackle wings on a ringed eye hook and finished with a painted, plastic head-type eye. The hook is size 1/0. It comes in six finishes and is effective on a large number of saltwater species.

Arbogast Skinny Minny: A surface lure in four color finishes; yellow, scale, blue mullet and coach dog. Comes in ¼- and ⅝-ounce sizes. Has good potential for tarpon and snook.

Arbogast Scooter: A sinking saltwater lure that can be cast or trolled for such species as weakfish, channel bass or snook. It works best when retrieved slowly and when rod is given a popping action during the retrieve. Made in ⅝-ounce size only.

Arbogast Sputter Bug: A unique plug-behind-a-spinner that comes in sizes from ¼ to ⅝ ounce. Made in numerous finishes and could be effective when a noisy retrieve is required on the surface. The manufacturer suggests it as a good night lure.

Weber Magnum: An extra-heavy gauge, solid brass spoon that comes in sizes from ¼ to ⅞ ounce. It casts well, even into a strong wind, and sinks quickly to fairly deep water. The Magnum could come in handy for many saltwater fishing situations.

DeLong Axalive Eel: A lifelike plastic eel imitation that hasn't been thoroughly tested in saltwater. Since natural eels are so effective on some species, it's possible that this artificial eel has great potential in many situations.

Wallsten Salty Cisco: A plug designed for a variety of saltwater uses. The surface model weighs ¼ ounce and the weighted model weighs ½ ounce, both in twelve finishes. Great for tarpon.

Acme Fiord Spoon: A long thin spoon with an effective action which comes in eleven sizes from ⅛ ounce to 1¾ ounces and in numerous metallic and colored finishes. It's effective on many species of fish such as striped bass, channel bass, bluefish, pollack and barracudas.

L & S Mirrolure: A minnow imitation with

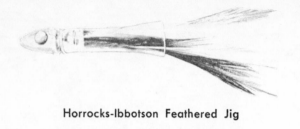

Horrocks-Ibbotson Feathered Jig

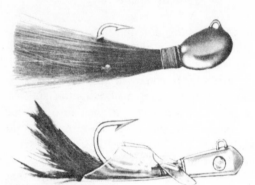

Horrocks-Ibbotson Nylon Special Squid and Bonito Jig

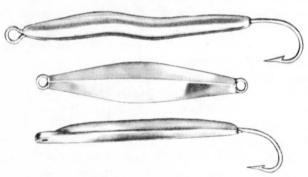

Captain White Squid, Horrocks-Ibbotson Diamond Squid, Horrocks-Ibbotson Bent Sand Eel Squid

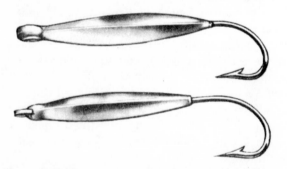

Horrocks-Ibbotson Weakfish and Snapper Jig, Bluefish Squid

Joe's Tasselure

flashy finish to which the angler must apply the action. It is made in five sizes and twelve finishes which are suitable for saltwater. It's made in shallow, medium and deep running models.

Heddon Zara Spook: A modern version of an old tested plug which floats at rest but dives or jumps up when twitched. Comes in six colors, weighs ¾ ounce, and is 4¼ inches long.

Heddon Lucky 13: A chugging surface bait with fair action underwater when retrieved quickly.

Garcia ABU Reflex: A simple spinner that is one of the most versatile baits ever manufactured. In sizes from ⅛ to ¾ ounce. Good on many shallow saltwater species.

Evans Maribou Jig Fly: A quick-sinking jig for bottom fishing. Comes in six colors and weighs ½ ounce.

Evans Hair Jig Fly: A quick-sinking jig for deep fishing in six colors. It weighs ½ ounce.

The Bomber: A deep-running plug made in thirty-three finishes. Bores almost straight down on the retrieve and is suitable for trolling as well as casting. In five sizes from ¼ ounce to ¾ ounce. It's an effective plug for snook.

Bomber Water Dog: An extra-deep-running plug with a fast vibrating action. Comes in twenty-one finishes and is surprisingly snag-proof. In three sizes from ¼ to ⅝ ounce. It is an effective plug for snook and groupers.

DeLong Jigging Eel: An untested combination for deep fishing which imitates eels or lampreys but has considerable potential in saltwater. It's made with or without weed guards. It's 7 inches long and weighs ⅝ ounce.

DeLong Shrimp: A natural imitation of a shrimp with translucent body and fluorescent red eyes. Probably still untested in saltwater but might have great potential.

DeLong Blackjack: A shiny black arrowhead-shaped jig with black nylon tail. Designed for bottom bouncing with a 3/0 hook. Weighs ⅝ ounce.

DeLong Eel: Another untested but soft and wiggly eel imitation that even feels slimy in the water. It's 4¾ inches long and weighs ⅛ ounce. It could be fished with a lead-head jig hook.

Joe's Tasselure (Weber): A curious arrangement of plastic skirts on a bead chain designed by commercial fishermen. It's great at times for surf casting and trolling. Overall length 11¾ inches; 8/0 hook.

Horrocks-Ibbotson Nylon Torpedo Jig: In 3 sizes from ¼ to 1⅛ ounces, has red cut-glass eye, in several finishes.

H-I Feathered Jig: A versatile jig that will take many species, from ⅛ to 4 ounces, with or without stainless steel wire leader.

H-I Bucktail Torpedo Jig: ¼ to 1⅛ ounces in several finishes.

H-I Bonito Jig: In 1/10- to ⅝-ounce sizes. Has transparent skin covering feather tail. Proven fish-taker.

H-I Nylon Special and *Bucktail Special Squid Jig:* From ⅛- to ½-ounce sizes, good for casting or trolling, in three colors.

H-I Diamond Squid: A highly polished diamond-shaped squid. Best for trolling. Three sizes: 1, 2, 3 ounces.

Capt. White Montauk Squid: Keel-shaped from pure block tin, for casting or trolling. Weighs 3 ounces.

H-I Bent Sand Eel Squid: Weighs 2⅝ ounces and is 6 inches long.

Bluefish Squid: Chrome finish body is great for blues, mackerel, other fish. ½ to 4¾ ounces.

H-I Weakfish and Snapper Jig: Weighs ¼ and ⅝ ounce.

H-I Drone Spoon: Extremely versatile and effective lure. Will catch cudas, channel bass, many other species. In sizes 1/0 to 12/0.

H-I Fluke Spoon: A deep-sea trolling rig with double spoons, barrel swivel and glass beads on 30-inch heavy nylon leader tied to 7/0 lock wound hook. Weighs 9¾ ounces.

H-I Spin Fly: A 1/16-ounce jig that is effective in shallow bay fishing. Catches bonefish, too.

H-I Pop Popper and *Spin Popper:* Popping lures for light-tackle spinning or casting.

H-I Spin Queen: Effective spoon, fluted, arrowhead-shaped for bay fishing.

H-I Minno Ette: A weighted spinning lure with propeller and minnow-shaped body.

H-I Game Fishers: A lightweight, wobbler-type spoon for fly rod.

SALTWATER FISHING ACCESSORIES

Although the freshwater fisherman has an extremely wide variety of tackle boxes to choose from, the saltwater angler is not so lucky, because he is limited by saltwater corrosion to the number of materials that can be used. Some wood, of course, will withstand the deterioration of salt breezes for a while, but unfortunately

Horrocks-Ibbotson Drone Spoon

Horrocks-Ibbotson Spin Fly

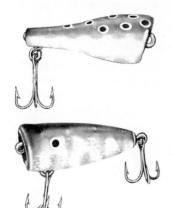

Horrocks-Ibbotson Spin Popper (top), Horrocks-Ibbotson Pop Popper

Horrocks-Ibbotson Spin Queen

Horrocks-Ibbotson Minno Ette

Horrocks-Ibbotson Game Fisher

Weberlite Bait Bucket

only the sturdiest and most expensive wooden boxes hold up very long aboard the pitching, rolling deck of a deep-sea boat.

Perhaps plastic is the best answer to the saltwater angler's tackle box problem, and he's a wise sportsman who selects a roomy box such as those produced by the Plano Molding Company. Their models 4300 and 5200 are especially good. The Gladding Company also has produced a number of suitable saltwater tackle boxes.

Of special interest to bait fishermen are the new Weberlite bait buckets produced by Weber Plastics of Stevens Point, Wisconsin. These are molded of expandable polystyrene, the high-insulation plastic of maximum efficiency. According to Weber, they're compact all-purpose buckets that keep worms, shrimp, minnows and, in fact, any bait alive and fresh for days. They're featherlight and of course float easily, yet they're durable, rugged and will not rot, rust or corrode in saltwater. The larger size has a 4-quart capacity. It weighs 6 ounces and measure 7⅞ inches in diameter by 9⅛ inches high. The 2-quart size weighs 4 ounces and is 6¾ inches in diameter by 7½ inches high. Beyond their use for keeping fishing baits fresh, the buckets are popular as ice savers, lunch boxes, beach tackle kits, food containers, and as any type of compact carrying case.

Similar to the Weberlite bait bucket in construction and in high-insulation plastic material, the Weberlite Go-Koolers are also extremely handy for saltwater fishermen. These, too, can double as bait containers or as coolers that keep drinks and food really cold even during a lengthy fishing trip in hot weather.

The Enterprise Manufacturing Company of Akron, Ohio, better known to the ardent angler as PFLUEGER, has just introduced an entirely new type of electronic Fish-Finder. This Pflueger Fish-Finder will locate a single isolated fish just as easily as a school of fish—anywhere within a radius of 300 to 350 feet. It scans the surface of the water just as well as the bottom—anywhere within this radius.

This new Pflueger Fish-Finder is a portable unit and is also available with a very accurate Depth Meter combined with the Fish Finder.

The New Pflueger Depth Finder works on a principle never before used in the medium of water. It is the Dopler Effect. This principle has been used in airborne radar and in astronomy. Basically the angler using the new Pflueger Fish-Finder listens for the fish. In saltwater, the device is vastly more effective when the water is calm.

The Pflueger Fish-Finder is a transistorized electronic instrument of supreme quality and exceptional durability which enables the user to hear the motion of the fish and to accurately locate and track them wherever they go. If there are moving fish in the vicinity, you hear them. The pitch of the sound heard varies with the speed of the fish and much intelligence with respect to size and type of fish is available to the listener.

Pflueger Fish-Finder in use

Chapter Twenty-two

OFFSHORE FISHING IN SAFETY

Before you head your boat toward deep blue water where big fish live, be sure that you're prepared for any emergency. Remember that beyond the sheltered bays, coves and estuaries are boating problems that differ vastly from those on freshwater lakes and rivers. Some of these problems concern waves and tides, the water's depth and current, violent weather, winds, squalls and storms. No matter whether you're a veteran of saltwater fishing or a beginner planning your first trip, never overlook the ritual of safety which begins before you leave the dock.

Why not make a checklist before every trip? Then mark off the necessary items as they're stowed aboard or as you accomplish them. Keep this list with your charts and maps because it will serve as a good reference on later trips.

Every boat going offshore should include the following: a bilge pump, a strong rope, a reliable compass, binoculars, a searchlight or hand flashlight, a battery-powered portable radio, flares or similar distress signals, proper charts and maps, a life belt for each person aboard, a life ring or cushion, oars, a storm sail, a sea anchor, tools and spare parts for the motor or engine.

Never forget to take a first-aid kit, and the well-stocked kit should contain sterile gauze pads, gauze roller bandages, waterproof adhesive tape, absorbent cotton, adhesive bandages, cotton-tip applicators, a bottle of antiseptic, aromatic spirits of ammonia, burn ointment or cream, suntan lotion, a tourniquet, wood splints, tweezers, scissors, a triangular bandage and a first-aid manual.

Another very obvious necessity and one which is too often overlooked is a large container of fresh water.

Before pointing any boat toward open water, be sure to obtain an official weather report. If you're not sure about the weather, do not go any farther out than where you can reach shore again quickly. Be familiar with flags and lights which are used as storm warnings by the United States Coast Guard and the U. S. Weather Bureau.

If you should be out in the open water and see storm clouds approaching, start for shore immediately. The only way to get out of heavy weather is to be alert at all times for storm signs and to know the quickest, shortest route to shelter.

Such things as clouds, birds and distant smokestacks can keep you posted on what the weather is likely to be.

An early morning dew: high fleecy or scattered clouds: birds not clustering in groups on lighthouses, channel markers and buoys: smoke from chimneys or passing ships rising fairly straight: the chances are good that fair weather is in prospect.

But if there are multiple layers of clouds, some low and moving in different directions: birds clustered: smoke spreading out mushroomlike over nearby land: then it looks like bad weather.

The old saying, "Evening red, morning gray, sends the sailor on his way; evening gray, morning red, sends down showers on his head," really is quite true.

It's a wise fisherman who watches out when clouds begin to gather in layers and winds become variable. These are the forerunners of a front, if on a big scale. On a smaller scale it may be only a local squall, but even this can be quite dangerous. However, a local squall can be avoided if it is sighted in time because it usually passes quickly.

Wind direction and turbulence vary in different geographical locations, of course, but during the summer and in fact, most of the year, the larger fronts move in a westerly to an easterly direction. Hurricanes move in a great circle covering hundreds of miles. If you happen to be in a small boat when a hurricane hits, you are likely to become a statistic before the day is finished.

Next to a gale or hurricane, the most dangerous element to face is fog. It lacks the thrash and impact of the winds, but still it can be deadly because an angler can so easily become lost when he cannot see his way. But by carrying a marine compass and keeping track of your position before the fog moves in and by estimating your speed, you can always reach safety again.

It's easy to pile up on rocks or to run aground on a reef during a fog, so if the morning is foggy, stay ashore until it lifts. If fog begins to form when you're out, aim for shore immediately.

When navigating anywhere, always watch for any unusual disturbance on the water. It can be fish, of course, but it can also indicate the presence of an underwater obstruction, of shallows or crosscurrents.

Rough water even in clear weather is a constant source of trouble to fishermen. To aid in navigating your boat in rough water, remember to cross the waves at right angles or at least to angle into the waves. This is also a good rule for crossing the wakes of other boats. When you're headed upwind, point directly into the waves, but if you're going downwind, run at right angles to the waves.

The time to tack is when your course lies parallel to the waves. To tack means to run a distance into the waves, then reverse your course and run with them, always angling toward your destination in a zigzag fashion. Never run parallel to the waves if they are big enough to upset your boat.

A good way to gain seagoing experience is to watch how veteran boatmen or charter-boat captains manage their boats offshore. Then before you undertake a deep-water fishing trip, make sure you have the proper equipment, that you are in fishing waters you know, that you have good weather, and that the confidence in your ability is well-grounded.

GLOSSARY OF SALTWATER FISHING

Block-Tin Jig—A fish-shaped piece of metal with either a swinging or stationary hook attached to one end. The other end has a hole in which to fasten the leader.

Bucktail—A lure made of hairs taken from the tail of a deer. These hairs are tied over a fish-hook or jig.

Chum—Chum is ground-up fish, mussels, clams or crabs. It's either thrown into the water, a handful at a time, or placed in the water in a bag. It attracts the fish as the natural oils seep from the bag to form a stream or slick. To chum is the act of putting chum into the water.

Drag—A mechanical brake built into a reel. It's applied to slow down the speed of the line as it leaves the reel spool.

Drail—A half-mooned, heavy piece of metal which weighs from ½ to 5 pounds with a swivel at either end. At one end, the long line of a second fishing rod is attached; at the other, a short line of 12 inches. To this short line is fastened a snap clothespin.

Two rods are used when a drail is employed, most often in tuna fishing: the fishing rod proper and the second or drail rod. The purpose of the drail is to hold the lure on the fishing rod at any desired depth. To illustrate: the angler wishes to fish at, say, 20 feet. First 20 feet is measured off on the drail line on the second rod and the line tied to the drail. Then the clothespin is clipped on the fishing line from 5 to 15 inches above the lure. When both lines go into the water, simultaneously, the drail line pays out 20 feet, and stops, holding the lure at that depth. When a fish strikes the lure, the line comes free from the clothespin, thus relieving the angler of the extra weight that served to carry the lure down—something to be considered during a long fight with a big fish.

Feathers—Artificial lure made of the hackle of a fowl tied onto a weighted hook or a jig.

Float—A piece of wood, plastic or cork, which floats on the surface of the water, holding the bait at any desired distance below it.

Free Line—Fishing with line and lure only—no float and no sinker to carry the lure down in the water.

Free Spool—Fishing with a line that has no drag (brake) set on the reel, as the line leaves the reel spool.

Gaff—An oversize hook attached to a handle from 2 to 10 feet long. It is used to land or to lift fish from the water. A flying gaff has a chain or cable handle.

Inshore—Waters relatively close to shore, or just off the shore, as opposed to the open sea.

Jig—A lure of streamlined or fish-shaped metal of from ⅛ to 5 ounces in weight. It has a fishhook attached to one end. Or it is a weighted fishhook partially hidden in feathers. The opposite or heavy end has an eye in which the leader is attached.

Leader—A length of nylon, gut, stainless steel cable, braided wire or piano wire. One end fastens to the lure or the hook; the other end fastens to the line. It protects the line from friction against rocks and rocky ledges, water action, and the abrasion of sand. It also protects against the teeth of many species of fish.

Lure—Any artificial bait.

Metal Squid—A fish-shaped metal lure. It can have a single fixed hook at one end, or a fixed hook and swinging hook. The other end has an eye by which the leader is attached.

Offshore—The open ocean.

Plug—An artificial lure made of plastic, glass or wood which resembles a fish in shape and coloring. It has from 1 to 3 hooks attached to it, generally 1 in the tail and 2 under the belly. Some plugs are one piece; others are jointed.

Ratchet—A mechanism built into reels which, when set, makes a clicking noise when a fish takes the line, signaling a strike. It also slows down the speed of the line as the fish swims away with the baited hook.

Rig—A three-way swivel arrangement. The fishline is attached to one swivel; the sinker to a second and the leader to the third.

Rod Belt—A leather belt that has a pocket appended in front into which the butt of the rod is inserted when reeling or playing a fish.

Rod Tip—The section of the saltwater fishing rod which is inserted into the hole in the metal extension of the rod butt. It is from about 4 feet 6 inches to 6 feet 10 inches in length and is made of bamboo, glass, plastic or metal.

Rod Butt—The heavy section of the saltwater fishing rod which is held in the hand and onto which the reel is fastened.

Sand Spike—A hollow metal tube about 10 to 12 inches long and 2 inches in diameter. It is stuck upright in the sand and the rod butt is inserted in the upper end.

Sinker—A lead weight that is attached to the end of a fishing line, its weight carrying the bait down to the desired depth. Sinkers are either round, oval, bank (long and tapering) or pyramidal in shape.

Spinner—A shiny blade of metal which revolves around a thin metal bar, to one end of which the leader is attached. On the other end is the hook. Used with natural bait.

Spoon—A flat, shiny artificial lure roughly similar in shape to the bowl of the common tablespoon.

Spreader—A piece of stiff, spring wire which terminates in an eye at each end. A leader is attached to either eye. The wire extends horizontally and equidistant from each side of a metal center. The metal center has two eyes, top and bottom. The line is attached to the top eye, the sinker to the bottom eye. The wire spreader serves to keep the leaders and bait apart when in the water.

Streamer—An elongated fly, really a fishhook with feathers attached to it. It is very similar to a bucktail or regular feather lure.

Strike—When a fish hits and/or takes the lure or bait.

Surf Fishing—Fishing in the surf where the swell of the ocean breaks along the shore.

Test Line or Thread Line—Originally based on a linen thread test, each thread that is built into a fishing line will stand a strain of 3 pounds on a direct pull. Thus a line made of 10 threads will stand the strain of a pull of 30 pounds; a line of 70 threads, a strain of 210 pounds, etc., without breaking.

Trolling—Fishing from a constantly moving boat with the fishing line played out beyond the stern.